P9-BYD-502

Timeless Youth Ministry

Timeless Youth Ministry

a handbook for successfully reaching today's youth

Lee Vukich & Steve Vandegriff

MOODY PRESS
CHICAGO

© 2002 by
LEE VUKICH AND STEVE VANDEGRIFF

All rights reserved. No part of this book may be reproduced in any form without permission in writing from the publisher, except in the case of brief quotations embodied in critical articles or reviews.

All Scripture quotations, unless otherwise indicated, are taken from the *New King James Version.* Copyright © 1982 by Thomas Nelson, Inc. Used by permission. All rights reserved.

Scripture quotations marked NIV are taken from the *Holy Bible, New International Version®*. NIV®. Copyright © 1973, 1978, 1984 by International Bible Society. Used by permission of Zondervan Publishing House. All rights reserved.

Scripture quotations marked KJV are taken from the King James Version.

Scripture quotations marked NASB are taken from the *New American Standard Bible®*, © Copyright The Lockman Foundation 1960, 1962, 1963, 1968, 1971, 1972, 1973, 1975, 1977, 1995. Used by permission.

Scripture quotations marked TLB are taken from *The Living Bible* copyright © 1971. Used by permission of Tyndale House Publishers, Inc., Wheaton, Illinois 60189. All rights reserved.

Scripture quotations marked NEB are taken from the *New English Bible* © 1961, 1970 by the Delegates of the Oxford University Press and the Syndics of the Cambridge University Press. Used by permission.

ISBN: 0-8024-2948-3

1 3 5 7 9 10 8 6 4 2

Printed in the United States of America

Contents

Acknowledgments

Dr. Lee Vukich would like to acknowledge:

No book is the product of just its authors; it builds upon the influence and outpouring of those who have gone before us and those who remain. Thus grateful acknowledgment must be given for those who have shaped, in some way, the contents of this book.

First and foremost to my wife, Beth, my partner in life, love, and ministry: Without your support, guidance, and willingness to follow God in this incredible journey, I'd be incomplete. I love you! To my children, Taylor and Parker, thanks for giving me the inspiration to be a man of God. Your laughter and joy of life makes my heart smile. You carry our name well, and I am proud of you both. My prayer is that God will bless whatever you put your hands to.

To Mom and Dad, thanks for "breaking the chain" through your decision to accept Christ. Who would have thought we'd end up here? Thanks.

To my "Paul," Steve Marshall, who invested his life in me and taught me what ministry is and isn't, I am eternally grateful.

To my "Timothy," Dan Ali, whom the Lord has used many ways in my life: Thank you for being a friend and an "adopted" big brother to the kids. We will forever be united together through the bond of Christ.

To Dr. Elmer and Ruth Towns: I praise God for your friendship and influence in the lives of my family. Doc, what can I say?! Thank you for your trust, your example, and your faith. God shines through you.

To Dr. Steve Vandegriff, as I've said a thousand times, "I am glad you're here." I appreciate your vision and hard work, and I am thankful that God has partnered us in this ministry.

To Melanie Beales, my assistant, thanks for your humor in an otherwise crazy environment. Your hard work is very much appreciated.

To all my students at Liberty University: Thank you for challenging, encouraging, and praying for me. Your lives touch me in so many ways. Continue to follow God in all that you do. Remember, "Submit, surrender, and succeed."

Dr. Steve Vandegriff would like to acknowledge:

One's first book is almost like the birth of one's firstborn: exciting, filled with anticipation, and bringing a whole new set of responsibilities, to name a few things. With that firstborn comes the inclusion of both immediate and extended family. This book is no different. I would like to say thank you to Pamela Jo for being patient with me while I thought and typed away. I am thankful that you started praying that prayer of Jabez in Lake Louise, Alberta, while attending the Billy Graham School of Evangelism. Our "borders" definitely started expanding, and this book is a part of that expansion. By the time this book goes to print, you and I will have spent twenty-five crazy years together and still counting. Love you.

To my three kids, Josh, Vanessa, and Jonathan, I know you have seen me reach some of my dreams, and this book is one of them. You know all my stories that I tell in my speaking engagements, and you still laugh. You also know that I talk much about you making your parents proud. Well, all three of you make your mother and me proud. I have to admit that I was a little anxious when each of you hit your adolescent years. Since being the "expert," I was sure hoping that I would do well with you during your adolescence. I can honestly say that your mother and I have enjoyed watching you grow through your adolescence and being a part of it.

I would like to give gratitude to my mom and my late dad (Joe and Sue Vandegriff). Mom, I'm glad you met Dad—the two of you did a great job in raising seven kids. Judges 3:2–3 in the Living Bible says, "For God wanted to *give opportunity* to the youth of Israel to *exercise faith and obedience* in conquering their enemies" (italics added). That is exactly what you and Dad did. You gave each of us the opportunity to experience faith and obedience for ourselves. This is exactly what I challenge my students with, and that is what Pam and I have strived to do with our own kids. You and Dad have always been a source of encouragement to me, and you have always encouraged me to pursue my dreams. Thanks for cheering me on! I love you, Mom.

There are some other "players" in my life who are still amazed that I can read and write. Dr. Frank and Bobbie Schmitt, thanks for keeping me in your home during seminary—and now you have brought me back to teach. Thanks for thinking of me when these ministry opportunities came up. You have been surrogate parents to me. To Dr. Elmer Towns, thanks for giving me the opportunity to teach at Liberty University and for making the presentation of this book idea. This would not have happened if you weren't in the picture. Dr. Gordon Luff, thanks for being a great teacher and mentor to me. Your influence finds its way into my classroom and beyond. Thanks need to be extended to all my colleagues in Youth for Christ (especially to my chairman and good friend, Doug Madill) and our "extended" family of friends at Calvary Community Church in Edmonton, Alberta. You are all special people, and I talk about you often. One doesn't move away from nineteen years of relationships easily. Of course, to Dr. Lee Vukich, thanks for this book idea. You started it! I have appreciated your determination for excellence and your frankness and honesty to me, not only as a colleague but also as a friend.

Finally, thanks to all those kids that God, for whatever reason, entrusted to me during my youth ministry. To my students at Liberty University, you make me laugh, drive me crazy at times, ask hard questions, challenge me. But most important, you make me proud . . . proud that I am your professor and I have the privilege of standing before you each class period. I hope that something we have talked about in class will help shape your ministry to reach kids.

Foreword

I love teenagers and have spent my life teaching them. All too often we ignore teens and what they can do for Christ today, saying, "Teenagers are the future of the church. They are the life of the church of tomorrow." But let's put it in focus: Teens are tomorrow's church, and they are *today's* church. But they have needs that should be met now. We should minister to them today, or there will be no tomorrow for them in the church.

Do you like teens? How do you feel sitting around and talking with three or four young people? Most adults feel uncomfortable in the teen subculture. From this uneasy position adults like to "handle" the teens like children because they are threatening. I hope this book will develop your love for young people and give you some insights in ministry to them.

One of the problems youth workers face is what to call the youth. A number of names could be used. In former generations they were called teens, youth, adolescents, young people, kids, teenagers, students, guys and gals, the gang, etc. Today they are called most of these terms but also by titles labeling their specific generation. Titles can seem impersonal, because they are generic, but we cannot avoid their use when we talk about groups of people.

The purpose of *Timeless Youth Ministry: A Handbook for Successfully Reaching Today's Youth* is to help people in the church minister to teenagers. To do this, we should think in terms of the total needs of young people and the total program of the church. *Total* is a very inclusive term. Not all needs of young people are mentioned in this book—but a *total* overall strategy is suggested. As you implement your strategy, you will want to target the *total* area of the local church.

This book is also written to those doing ministry outside the local church. Many parachurch organizations are working to win young people to Christ and build them up in the faith. These ministries are serving Christ, and any youth worker who forgets them will be weak in understanding what God is doing in the world.

I began teaching a course on youth in 1958 at Midwest Bible College, St. Louis, Missouri, that was titled "The Introduction to Youth Ministry." I had been a youth pastor at New Brighton Community Church in New Brighton, Minnesota, and Southwest Baptist Tabernacle in Dallas, Texas. So I taught my students to do ministry the way I did it; but that's not education, that's mentoring. I didn't have many overall principles, or a strategy for ministering to youth in a church setting. To most youth directors in the 1950s, youth ministry was a weekly program on Sunday night and a yearly camping experience. There was no textbook on youth ministry to use in my Bible college class, only books containing youth programs. So I determined to write one. The first book I wrote was called *Teaching Teens.* It had nine chapters and was eighty-four pages long, published by Baker Book House in 1963. It sold well because it had no competition and it met a need.

As I continued to write further books on the subject, I came to the conclusion the Bible doesn't teach a special or different ministry for youth. The Bible just teaches ministry.

My third book, *Successful Biblical Youth Work,* went through many printings and was used at many colleges as a textbook for college courses on youth work. But because of changes in youth styles, language, and practices with each generation, that book became outdated. As a historical point of reference, you may read it in its entirety at www.elmertowns.com; but you'll laugh at some of the terms and the things that were suggested. I'm now a grandfather—too old to rewrite this book—so I'm glad Lee Vukich and Steve Vandegriff have done it.

Follow the ideas in this book carefully, because these two authors are now suggesting cross-generational ideas. They've "been there and done that" in youth ministry. They've done everything you the reader will be asked to do or will want to do. They've run programs, camps, foreign ministry trips, ScareMare events, plus many other things too numerous to list. They've coordinated and preached to more than five thousand youth at a theme park during an evangelistic outreach planned by the youth department at Liberty University.

These two authors direct one of the most successful youth departments in any college or seminary in America. Their department has more than twenty-five hundred graduates ministering in churches today. Most of the megachurches in the Southern Baptist Convention have Liberty graduates as youth pastors. Why? Because the Youth Department at Liberty involves our youth majors in some of the largest youth ministry projects in America. They learn to minister to youth by ministering to youth, and they have learned to do big things and to do things in a big way by doing them big while learning.

I'm excited about this book. May it accomplish all the authors intend and more.

Sincerely yours in Christ,
Elmer L. Towns, Dean
School of Religion
Liberty University
Lynchburg, Virginia

Introduction

Youth ministry has come of age. We have virtually every kind of programming idea available to us with the click of a mouse. We have the slickest of promotional pieces. We have some of the most adventurous trips imaginable. And when we get there, we have the best speakers and the latest music that can be downloaded. We attend the most inspirational conferences that get us cheering for God and kids again, with new fervor. So what could we possibly write about that is new?

Our society is in a constant state of transition. Technology that was "cutting edge" a few months ago is outdated today. The family unit has gone through cataclysmic changes and continues to be redefined. Not only are our young people juggling new family relationships; they are assuming family-like responsibilities that were never intended for them. As North America moves into the future, one thing is constant . . . the rules of engagement have changed. No place is this more evident than in youth ministry.

Books written fifteen years ago on the subject of youth ministry could be considered relatively current for eight to ten years. Today's works on youth ministry have a shelf life of approximately five years. This relevance factor demands that we examine, research, and share new methods and philosophy for reaching today's young people with the message of hope that is found in Christ (and hopefully will stay in their lives longer than five years).

As former youth pastors and current professors of Youth Ministry, we now have the opportunity to instruct up-and-coming youth workers. It is a humbling experience standing in front of a classroom of wide-eyed students who have a voracious appetite for youth ministry. If you happened to cut some of them, they would "bleed" youth ministry. That is exciting to us. We have the privilege and responsibility to help shape these students' lives for the sake of youth ministry. This position has caused us to do some inner reflection. What do we need to convey? How do we instill a heart for youth ministry that will endure beyond the current youth minister's tenure? From this vantage point in our lives, we have the rare opportunity to see where we have been and evaluate how well we did among the kids and staff who were entrusted to us. We have been in such diverse locales as southern California, east Tennessee, northeast Ohio, and Alberta, Canada. We have been on both sides of the ecclesiastical fence, as youth pastors and as directors of Christian youth organizations (Youth for Christ and the Center for Youth Ministries) as well as on both sides of the U.S./Canada border. We have served in various-sized churches and have had a variety of denominational labels. When we graduated from seminary, we were walking, talking billboards for youth ministry. Now as professors of Youth Ministry in one of the largest

Christian universities, we can honestly say that we still have that freshman-like enthusiasm for youth ministry.

The societal and cultural landscape has changed dramatically. The way things are done has changed dramatically. The only item that has not changed is the eternal message of Christ's love. And that is the message we must get right, or we will lose a generation of young lives. The Enemy's agenda is spelled out in John 10:10a, "The thief does not come except to steal, and to kill, and to destroy." We would dare say that most readers of this book have a personal story that would give illustration to this. The agenda of youth ministry is to give the message of the latter part of that verse to young people, "I have come that they may have life, and that they may have it more abundantly."

This work is not an attempt to "reinvent the wheel," as the principles of youth ministry remain constant through all of time. It is, however, a needed resource to examine afresh what it means to be an adolescent in today's culture and how those who minister to young people can best reach them.

Contemporary Youth Culture

One has to take a good look at culture when discussing youth ministry. And that look has to be especially directed toward contemporary youth culture. It is contemporary youth culture that is not only most relevant to this writing; it can also be the most intriguing, with all its debate and controversy. Hopefully, this discussion will lead the reader to a better understanding of contemporary culture and a balanced response to that culture. "When their generation's culture is honored, more young people feel drawn into the church because they feel more accepted than rejected for their unique expression of spirit."[1]

Culture is a study unto itself. Culture can be good or it can be bad. An unspoken belief has permeated Western Christendom that says if it is cultural, it must be OK.

(Tell that to innocent adolescent rape victims in certain Middle East countries who have been murdered by their own family members because of the "shame" they brought upon their family. These murders are ironically and cruelly called honor crimes.[2]) Maybe we should throw up the white flag of surrender and just leave culture alone. But what if culture is wrong? What if the "crowd" is wrong . . . dead wrong? (I, Steve, should make a point here that the crowd is not always wrong. My father always asked, "If everybody jumped off the bridge, would you jump off the bridge too?" My adolescent answer was always a resounding *yes,* as long as there was water below! My response was based upon the point that the crowd was not always wrong. Obviously, if there were nothing but a freeway below, I would be in the wrong and in traction. Some aspects of "the crowd" are not always wrong; these might include hairstyles and clothing styles.) Should we sit idly by, while culture continues toward an immoral or indifferent conclusion? This dilemma is especially true when talking about adolescents.

Adolescents have a tendency to be different, with little regard for what current mainstream culture is doing. Although it could be argued that culture either follows adolescence or adolescence defines culture, a wise exercise would be to better understand teenagers' reasons behind expressed actions. This would also be wise for the youth worker not only to address these predominant adolescent cultural issues, but also to help adolescents develop the discernment they need to move from being gullible consumers to informed and educated participants.

In any discussion of culture (the moorings, background, ethnicity, traditions, customs, and way of life), the quandary of participation, rejection, or reaction must be addressed. To go with the status quo would not draw nearly as much attention and scrutiny as other responses toward culture. Certainly when it comes to those activities of culture that are amoral, participation could be encouraged. This option encourages involvement and even the enjoyment of cultural activities of young people and adults alike, whether that be enjoying fast food, attending a professional sporting event, or listening to a symphony. A question one would need to ask is, "Does my participation hinder or impede my ability to communicate my faith in Christ?" In summary, are we losing our message? It is one thing to be an active participator in culture, but it becomes a consequence of eternal value when we lose our message because of our participation. It would be safe to say that when our message of hope is jeopardized, we should avoid participation in our contemporary culture. Of course, there is considerable room here for subjectivity when it comes to when or what we should participate in. So because of this, we need to look at our other options.

Rejection is another option we can choose in response to our culture. For the Christian, plenty of activities or thinking in our culture should be rejected. At times, it may be a quiet refusal to participate. At other times, rejection comes in the form of financial sanctions. And at still other times, rejection comes in the form of overt and corporate refusal of participation. It may take the form of a petition or protest. It might even take the form of civil disobedience or an outright blatant refusal to participate in a cultural event or cultural thinking.

A third response to culture is reaction. Reaction is more of an attitude. It is always negative. It is a knee-jerk response that rejects culture simply because it is culture. Reaction takes place before any kind of explanation can be given. Reaction is given without much thought and is based more on emotional preference. Isolation and arrogance usually accompany this reaction. Reaction does not take into consideration that the person reacting just might have it all wrong, a sort of prejudgment. Organizations, churches, and even schools have been started in reaction against culture. This author would be remiss by not saying that these organizations, churches, and schools have further alienated themselves by their very existence, giving their reactionary message less and less credibility. So instead of influencing their culture, they simply are endorsed by those who have reacted the same way, and they appear to be extremely narrow minded and exclusive. It can be almost a form of extremism or fringe thinking. They become their own self-centered and same-thinking subculture. There certainly are times when new subcultures are developed for specific purposes and for all the right reasons. It is at this stage where the subculture moves from reaction to participation (with rejection of the specific problematic elements).

It would be difficult to do taxonomy on the distinctive age levels of contemporary young people. They are characteristically somewhere between the ages of twelve and twenty-four in our American society.[3] The scary part is that the beginning age creeps lower and lower, while on the other end of the timeline, some adults never leave their adolescent behavior. They still have not grown up and embraced their adult responsibilities and characteristics. It can be confusing at the least when young people strive for maturity with a lack of proper models to emulate.

ASPECTS WORTH CONSIDERING IN CONTEMPORARY YOUTH CULTURE

One cannot overlook the impact of the Internet and technology on contemporary youth culture. The wise youth worker overseeing his young people not only knows the state of their hearts but is also state of the art. Young people have mastered technology while many adults still struggle with multitasking. The Internet has given young people access to incredible amounts of information. The Internet and e-mail have removed the element of distance. The Internet has given young people the anonymity and privacy that they value, not to mention a language of code words, passwords, and acrostics (LOL—laughing out loud; LMHO—laughing my head off; etc.) that is only understandable to them.

While we stand amazed at what the Internet has done to define our culture, we are painfully aware of the downside of the Internet. Although it does provide new experiences, information, convenience, and ideas, the Internet has generated technological overkill, dot-com greed, an onslaught of e-mail, and a precipitous continuum of sapping our humanity (not to mention insidious pornographers who seem to be one step ahead of cutting-edge technology for the sole purpose of enticing young and old alike).[4] The Internet has permeated every aspect of society with an almost omnipresent likeness and an omniscient attitude.

When discussing youth culture, we cannot ignore media and music. While the Internet has provided the means, media and music have become the end to that means. From boy bands to shock rock, music cannot be overlooked. Not only is it an integral part of contemporary youth culture; it helps articulate what culture is thinking and saying.

At the same time, music is important to teenagers' identity and helps them define important social and subcultural boundaries. The results of one survey of 2,760 fourteen- to sixteen-year-olds in ten southeastern cities showed that they listened to music an average of forty hours per week. One Swedish study found that adolescents who developed an early interest in rock music were more likely to be influenced by their peers and less influenced by their parents than by older adolescents.[5]

So whether we like it or not, we must, at the very least, pay attention to music. Of course we cannot mention music without including media. Contemporary youth culture is media driven. It is where young people get their "sermons," and shapers of the media know they can "preach" whatever message they want to young people. (One need not look too far to see the blatant messages of reckless and irresponsible sexuality in spite of the physiological and emotional consequences.) The media (its outlets and its personalities and "spin doctors")[6] also know that young people will buy into whatever they say, as long as it is packaged right.

Those interested in contemporary youth culture have to look at a particular attitude that is so characteristic of young people today, "whatever." The attitude goes beyond just using the word. It has become part of the attitudinal landscape. It reflects an "I don't care" attitude. It reflects an "it doesn't matter" attitude. It is a word that summarizes quite succinctly what a contemporary youth culture is thinking and unconsciously practicing. The root of this "whatever" attitude can be found in a contemporary youth culture that is somewhat cynical about the demands and responsibilities of its cultural surroundings. It has become a philosophical way of life.

In discussing contemporary youth culture, one must take a look at the redefining of the family. Hopefully, you come from an intact traditional family[7] (unfortunately I, Steve, do not). But as most contemporary youth workers know, the numbers are pretty much split between young people who come from traditional families and those who do not. This issue raises the bar on complexity in ministering to young people from nontraditional families.

Children who experience parental divorce, compared with children in continuously intact two-parent families, exhibit more conduct problems, more symptoms of psychological maladjustment, lower academic achievement, more social difficulties, and poorer self-concepts. Similarly, adults who experienced parental divorce as children, compared with adults raised in continuously intact two-parent families, score lower on a variety of indicators of psychological, interpersonal, and socioeconomic well-being.[8]

This continental drift in the traditional family also increases the need to minister to parents of nontraditional families. These can be single parents (divorced or never married), remarried parent(s), or part of a blended family, but "once the children in each of these scenarios hit adolescence, many parents begin yearning for a learning curve in the raising of their kids. Whatever his or her family structure, a child has the best opportunity to thrive only when the household provides a loving, nurturing, stable, and protective environment."[9]

THE TENSIONS AND ALTERNATIVES RELATED TO CONTEMPORARY YOUTH CULTURE

In the late 1940s the term "teenager" was invented and the phrase "juvenile delinquent" was coined. The popular press revealed that America was moving toward a youth society. Even as more attention was focused on teens, many magazines predicted that emphasis on young people was a fad. Eventually interest would shift away from the youth society; as one individual was quoted as saying in 1962, there is "little likelihood of American students ever playing a radical role, much less a revolutionary one in our society."[10] Obviously, our contemporary youth culture has not paid much attention to that prediction.

The contemporary youth culture has proven itself more than a "one hit wonder" type of fad. Contemporary youth culture reflects an ideology or way of life based on definite philosophical assumptions. The contemporary youth culture has produced tension between the older generations and young people. This tension was reflected during the sixties with the Vietnam War protests, culminating in a tragic climax with the killing of four Kent State University student protestors. (Living in Akron, Ohio, at the time, I, Steve, personally remember a college friend reaching his father and screaming, "Dad, they're killing us!" The next week I went to the campus and saw the bullet holes in the steel sculptures around the location where the National Guard opened fire.) Then in the summer of 1972 at the National Democratic Convention, there was the ensuing jockeying for political power by many young people who had been previously denied a voice in American politics. That spirit of dissenting continues into this millennium with young people being jailed, injured, or killed when they protest for causes they believe in (consider the protests against the World Trade Organization in Seattle and the G8 Summit in Genoa, Italy).

This tension is also reflected in the American home where teenagers have definite ideas and lifestyles, many times conflicting with their parents. Family tension is not restricted to non-Christians or to a certain segment of the country. It seems to be prevalent in all of society. This should not be construed as a violent tension, even though there have been isolated cases of this. But it is a tension that has family relationships strained.

This tension is also seen in many local churches. Adults yearn for the "good ol' days," while young people want their religion to be on the cutting edge. Tension is manufactured when adults want young people to continue the past lifestyle. Both young people and adults feel deeply about the other's lifestyle. The fact remains that contemporary youth culture is decidedly different from past youth cultures as adults knew it, and it is distinctive from the lifestyle of the older generations in the church today. This tension raises the first major issue in youth work, "What's a youth worker to do in order to keep both sides of the generational 'fence' happy?"

Those who minister to young people have two alternatives. First, they can adapt their principles and techniques to contemporary youth culture, to reach them for Christ, hence becoming relevant.[11] Second, they can hold onto a traditional approach, communicating to teenagers the values of the past, then reinforcing a desired way of behavior, so young people will think and act differently from those around them. We are certainly not against thinking and acting differently (2 Corinthians 5:17 makes it clear that things become different for the believer). What we are against is a coerced, dictated way of life that is void of internal motivation and personal volition but full of external control and personal preferences. Youth for Christ (Campus Life), Campus Crusade for Christ, Young Life, and Word of Life are among the major Christian youth organizations that adapted to contemporary youth culture at their very outset. (Youth for Christ's motto is "Geared to the times. Anchored to the Rock.") These organizations continue to do credible adolescent ministry by incorporating relevance into their ministry. They have used some of the current pop culture's methods with contemporary youth culture, including language, dress, and music. Leaders of these organizations point out that they are still committed to conservative doctrine while their methodology has constantly changed.

The reality of all this is that young people must live in and among their own contemporary youth culture and no church program can completely isolate them from the influence and pressures of the youth world. The Christian must live in the world and not withdraw from it. Therefore, the minister to young people must understand the youth culture, first to reach into that culture and present a message of hope to young people with regards to their relationship with Christ and, second, to equip each Christian young person to be an active participant with a critical and discerning "eye" in that culture as a witness for Jesus Christ.

THE YOUNG PEOPLE OF THIS CONTEMPORARY YOUTH CULTURE

This generation is entertainment oriented. It has been reared on television, movies, computers, and music, all of which has cultivated a new standard of valuing people and things in terms of action and "relevance." It was thought when they were children that their vicarious identification with computers would produce a passive generation. Rather, young people have seen that sex, money, action, and travel can be packaged by the trend-setting media, all for the purpose of providing a new experience to stimulate their senses. Instead of being passive, they want to become part of all they see. Virtual reality has taught them that almost anything is attainable. As a result, young people feel they can do or be anything they desire. But their desires are not tempered. They want it now. Delaying personal gratification simply does not make sense. No longer does the young person want to know what's happening, but wants to *be* what's happening. He does not want to be controlled by his environment but wants to be free to create the setting in which he is to be immersed. The past has little hold upon their lives.

Social psychologist and professor Erik Erickson suggested three reasons that young people are immediate oriented. First, the past grows increasingly distant from the present . . . the past grows progressively more different from the present in fact, and seems more remote and irrelevant psychologically. Second, the future, too, grows more remote and uncertain. Because the future directions of social change are virtually unpredictable, today's young men and women are growing into a world that is more unpredictable than what has been confronted by any previous generation. Third, the present assumes a new significance as the one time in which life is relevant, immediate, and knowable. The past's solutions to life's problems are not necessarily relevant to the here and now. No one can know whether what is decided today will remain valid in tomorrow's world; hence, the present assumes an autonomy unknown in more static societies.[12]

Postmodern Suspicion

Since the past has little influence and the future is remote, this contemporary youth generation would not be inclined to explore historic Christianity for answers to their questions. Inasmuch as the Bible is a Book of history (His story), the church and historic Christianity have little appeal to the contemporary youth culture. But youth have gone one step beyond ignoring Christianity; the young person finds himself in active opposition to tradition.

Two fundamental characteristics of this contemporary youth culture are irreverence and suspicion. Young people do not buy into faith simply because we say so. This irreverence and suspicion has its roots in postmodernity. This way of thinking (or philosophical stance) has been the end result of a historical process of epic proportions. The French philosopher Jean-Francois Lyotard said, "Simplifying to the extreme, I define postmodernism as incredulity toward all metanarratives."[13] In other words, postmodernism sets itself up as disbelieving all other worldviews.[14] The significance here is that for the Christian, his worldview is seen through the lens of biblical instruction and truth. His worldview goes beyond a weekly ritual. His worldview affects his daily life, both personally and externally. In essence, his worldview is voluntarily intrinsic. It is not coerced or legislated. Tony Jones says in his book *Postmodern Youth Ministry,*

> If the 1970s was the decade of "I'm okay, you're okay," then we're entering the era of "My God's okay, your God's okay." You probably already know that students find Christianity's claim of exclusivity the most difficult to swallow. Instead their natural inclination is that all faiths contain elements of truth and any religion is a perfectly good way to express your spirituality.[15]

From the first-century declaration of Constantine making virtually everyone a Christian, to the present-day society that is becoming more secular by the second, postmodern thinking comes from a mental grid that does not have an underlying Christian background or understanding. Dawson McAllister says, "Postmodern culture is a major shift in Western culture, the type of change that happens every several hundred years or so."[16] Yet with the relativity of postmodernism, there are some exceptions to everything being acceptable. First, you must never impose your beliefs on the person beside you or at least not be perceived to be imposing your beliefs on others. It is a "live and let live" attitude. Believe what you believe and don't bother anyone else. If you do try to convince others, you will be accused of preaching. And no one likes to be preached to. This exception has implications on the way we evangelical Christians evangelize. I do not necessarily think it limits our efforts, but it does demand some rethinking and retooling of our methods and verbosity. The other exception is do not mess with "Mother Earth."

Earth Day continues to build momentum. Environmental issues have taken on religious fervor. The creation has been deified while the Creator has been vilified. I would be the first to say that Christians should be environmentally conscious and responsible, but not to the level of radical religious fundamentalists.

Postmodern thinking simply does not have the Christian influence that older generations have had. The Christian linguistics and traditions are not there. In the United States and in Canada, some significant "pockets" of culture (usually referred as the Bible Belt) are still influenced by a Christian way of thinking. The Southern states would certainly have to be included, with parts of the Midwest. In Canada, it would be parts of the provinces of Alberta and Manitoba, with significant pockets in southern British Columbia and Saskatchewan. But you do not have to go far to find states and provinces that are deep in postmodern thinking. Christian influence has been minimized. A prime U.S. example would be the Pacific Northwest, the Northeast, and California. In Canada, prime examples would be many parts of British Columbia, Ontario, Quebec, and some of the east coast provinces.

The Enemy's Strategy

The winner of this epic struggle will capture the minds or the thinking of an entire generation. Never has John 10:10a been so true, "The thief does not come except to steal, and to kill, and to destroy." Once the mind has been "stolen," killing and destroying of lives, both mortally and spiritually, becomes relatively easy. In the classic book *Strategy*, military author B. H. Liddell Hart explains the significance of strategizing. He lists several principles of warfare strategy. One is to choose the line of least expectation. In other words, try to put yourself in the opponent's shoes, and think what course is least probable that he will foresee. Second is to take a line of least resistance. He explains that a good strategist does not attack where the opponent is strong. He always attacks where he is weak. And third, do not renew an attack along the same line (or in the same form) after it has once failed. The reasoning here is that the opponent has had enough time to strengthen himself, and it is even more probable that his success in repulsing you will have strengthened him morally.[17] This strategy seems all too familiar when it comes to adolescents and Satan, our Enemy.

From my perspective, the Enemy has always gone after the young, this being an all too familiar strategy of going after the most vulnerable. From there, it is the mind that is targeted and is most difficult to protect. I am sure there is a significant reason why the apostle Paul admonished the church in Philippi,

> If you do this [give your worries to God] you will experience God's peace, which is far more wonderful than the human mind can understand. His peace will keep your thoughts and your hearts quiet and at rest as you trust in Christ Jesus. And now, brothers, as I close this letter let me say one more thing: Fix your thoughts on what is true and good and right. Think about things that are pure and lovely, and dwell on the fine, good things in others. Think about all you can praise God for and be glad about. (Phil. 4:7–8 TLB)

Whether we like it or not, postmodernism, that irreverent quest for spirituality, is permeating the thought processes of young people. Their thought processes are heavily influenced by the standard fare of the entertainment industry. There is definitely a move away from societal assumptions and more into a subjective and ambiguous way of thinking. The three institutions set up by God—the home, government, and the church—are challenged and sometimes even ignored. Many church young people are caught up in a plethora of feelings, which are reinforced by television, movies, magazines, the Internet, and even public education. Inasmuch as contemporary young people are oblivious to this new way of societal thinking, they are just as much a part of it as those who propagate postmodern doctrine. The youth worker who attempts to minister to young people will have to give substantial reasoning for the obeisance to the commands and demands of historic Christianity. He cannot reach them by simply minimizing their way of thinking for the purpose of favoring Christian norms in thinking. He cannot just undercut the way they think and assume they will now think along Christian norms.

The Impatience with Institutions

Contemporary young people are very impatient with institutions that seem to perpetuate injustice or inequality or are simply unresponsive to human needs. The institution of the church does not escape. Most of us conjure up an image of an edifice or building when asked to formulate in our minds what the church looks like. Along with an architectural image, we add the rules of behavior, regulations, and rituals that have sometimes lost their meaning over the years. Words like *oppressive, irrelevant, irrational,* and *archaic* are used by young people as adjectives to describe the church. Young people see the traditional American church as dead and hypocritical. Many times the church is governed by a board of deacons or elders who may be insensitive to human needs or the needs of adolescents. They tend to hold onto the past rather than following New Testament commands.

Far more often than we would like to admit, young people's antipathy with the traditional American church is valid. Many churches are more known for their religious pomp and social circumstance than their involvement in the betterment of their community, whether it is a social commentary or a concerted effort of evangelism. My own adolescent experience included an intrigue with the fact that Jesus Himself went counterculture with the religious thinkers of His day. His way was revolutionary (the Bible I, Steve, purchased as a teenager was called "Blueprint for Revolution"). Jesus seemed extremely unhappy and disturbed with the religious types of His time. He was a nonconformist in a good way. That nonconformity appeals to adolescents. He was a champion for all that was right, pure, and true. The institution of religion was suspect then, and that way of institutional thinking continues to prevail today.

The Tension with the Adult World

While adults charge youth with being immoral, irresponsible, and irreverent, young people make countercharges against adult hypocrisy. Some of the charges are true. Adolescents look at adults drinking their alcohol while they tell kids not to smoke marijuana. Adults are quick to tell their kids to say no to drugs but are slow in curbing their own uses, or should I say, misuses of prescription medicine to achieve a certain emotional level. (I should note that I personally know of individuals who need prescription drugs in order to achieve an emotional balance. But they are in the minority.) Adults are quick to charge adolescents with being morally bankrupt. Yet if one did an inventory of the purveyors of blatant immoral messages and images or implied or double meaning messages and images, the writers and producers are all adults. Maybe simply stated, we do not have an adolescent problem; we have an adult problem. (Even more simply stated, we have a *cultural* problem that is laced with a tendency for wrongdoing or sin.)

An adult deserves respect, not because he holds a position of authority but because he as an individual has demonstrated his worth as a person and his competence in his position. Perhaps it is more than adult incompetence that has destroyed the teenager's confidence in adults. Perhaps it is adult success in communicating to young people their desires and visions. Adults have long preached excellence and competence to the young people. Now these young people are taking adult advice at its face value and are attempting to fashion an ideal world.

The pursuit of experience is another characteristic of

contemporary young people. The young person seeks experience, first as a thing in itself, and second as a means of learning and growing. Experience entails a heightened attention to the present ongoing movement and far less concern with the past or future. Their experience-oriented life involves a mistrust of belief systems and absolute truth, which young people feel obscures the richness of life. Spontaneity is a highly valued personal trait, as is tolerance. They do what they want to do, when they want to do it, and have tolerance for others to "do their own thing." The idea is to do whatever you want to do, so long as you don't interfere with other people. The average young person is irritated at virtually all restrictions because he sees laws as a limitation of the growth and development of people. Young people passionately demand honesty and are impatient with forms having no content. Youth reject the doctrine that truth is to be found by a ritualistic study of the legacy of the past. Contemporary young people feel that knowledge is not something to be learned and stored up for future use but must serve an immediate end and practical purpose.

Even though there is tension between the generations, young people and adults are similar in many ways. Many studies reveal young people have the same moral values as their parents.[18] They just practice them differently, probably because they are aware of the inconsistencies they have observed.

Religious Interest

The present generation shows a definite and remarkable interest in the study of religion.

> The unsung story of today's teenagers may be how religious or spiritual they are. "We're witnessing a new revival of religion," says Conrad Cherry, director of the Center for Study of Religion and American Culture at Indiana University/Purdue University. Prayer circles and faith-based groups like True Love Waits or

> Fellowship of Christian Athletes have proliferated in high schools and college campuses like so many WWJD bracelets; Christian rock festivals and CDs rival their secular counterparts, bringing the message out of the pulpit and into the mosh pit and tattoo tent.[19]

This interest is a result of a significant amount of personal probing and searching. They want to know themselves, and the religious side of man is unknown. However, most of the religious interest is noninstitutional and, many times, anti-institutional in nature. This is reflected in the growth of interdenominational agencies among evangelicals and is related to the anti-institutional religious search by young people. Well-meaning adults have given young people biblical answers to their questions and told them that a relationship to God can be found outside the local church. Interdenominational agencies claim their ministry is relevant, whereas the church has failed. Contrary to popular opinion, teenage interest in religion is far more serious than casual. Far from being apathetic, they are interested in issues and decisions about the problems that are vital to them.

The new religious search by young people is increasingly secular in nature; they look to the natural world and to this present age for a context and orientation for human life. There has been a collapse of religious beliefs woven into family, community, and national life. Their religious tenets are derived more from culture than from historic Christianity. Yet in spite of the rejection of formal religion on the part of the young people, there remains at this time in life a strong disposition toward the religious. Perhaps it is because young people are searching for their identity by giving themselves to a cause greater than themselves. Hopefully this is a normal growth pattern of adolescents moving from the egocentricity of adolescence to the more mature stages of adulthood.

Today the religious alternatives include cults.

> Cults attract youths experiencing psychological stress, rootlessness, feelings of emptiness and of being disenfranchised, and identity diffusion and confusion. Such youths come from all walks of life and from all classes of society. Cults seem to offer confused and isolated adolescents a moratorium—a period of dropping out, or a "time-out"—as well as a highly structured sense of belonging and a means of escape from being "normless."[20]

You might say that we are experiencing a recovery of religion outside the structures of traditional Christianity.

Moral Choices

Young people go on drugs both as an escape and a search.[21] They are escaping from the reality of this world, and sometimes they are searching for a new thrill or a new experience. For most, drugs are an energizer. Peer pressure is a significant influence on the young person who tries drugs. (I call it a fear of what others are thinking. As a result of this fear, young people tend to do activities they normally would not do, and some of these activities include drug use.) Some of the drugs of choice are more recognized names like marijuana and cocaine, but newer and more chic drugs like ecstasy have been almost championed by adolescents. Yet in spite of the popularity of drugs, the physical dangers remain, both short term and long term.[22] Other significant factors associated with drug usage are permissive child-rearing practices and a rebellion against restrictive parental controls or rules. Young people, by and large, are convinced that it is no more harmful to smoke marijuana than it is to drink alcohol.

The music of adolescents is clearly more direct in its sensuality, anger, and chagrin than the music of young people in the immediate past. Music videos leave little to the imagination. Their music boldly depicts the confusion of the contemporary scene. The major emphasis is to lay aside preoccupations with boundaries, moderation, and the postponements of personal gratification for the sake of free expression and artistic creativity. Another theme is that of a stranger moving through an alien environment, searching for meaningful values and a new world appropriate for the modern spirit. Many who believe the music is an accurate expression of adolescent attitude and emotions do not deny that much of the music itself is suggestive and sexually arousing.

There is a shift in adolescent morality taking place from somewhat traditional values to a more liberal, and sometimes debasing, ethic, based on the behavioral sciences. Moral practices tend to be immediate, gratifying solutions rather than principles of self-control that are basic for all young people. Many young people are openly rejecting traditional morality. "They see sex as mechanical, about body parts, our cultural portrayal of sex," says Deborah Roffman, a leading U.S. human sexuality educator based in Baltimore. The best way to teach kids about sex is to talk about intimacy, to put sex in the context of a relationship. The precocious sexual activities of today's teens are a wake-up call, Roffman says. "They're screaming at us because they need context and values."[23]

Society's perception is that public education is the main source for adolescent information on sexuality. For many years, the focus of sex education has been on the mechanics of sex. Public education seems to have felt the need to explain these mechanics and encouraged their experimentation for the purpose of determining sexual compatibility between two people and for the two to gain sexual experience. Of course we cannot forget the "noble" concern of public education in the encouragement of safe sex practices.

One exaggeration about adolescents is that they are all having sex. This belief arises from the media portrayal and stereotyping of teenagers. Media play a large role in how society views adolescent sexuality. Almost every teenager in television, movies, and print media is characterized as a "typical" teenager who is always having sex and is not the least concerned about the consequences. In fact, in most situations, the possible consequences are not even mentioned. The adult community views these programs and quickly draws false conclusions about adolescents.

Another reason for this exaggeration about adolescent sexuality is stereotyping. Adults tend to observe a small group of teenagers who may act or be a certain way and apply those attributes to every teen. It is as if promiscuous sexual behavior is a biological part of a teenager's composition and the very fact of being an adolescent predisposes a kid to irresponsible behavior.

This then is today's contemporary young person. He lives in a world created by a clan of influential adults that most adults now repudiate, a world the young person doesn't want to surrender. It is a culture that places him at the center, feeds his desires, and allows him to develop according to an internal pattern, called "individual differences" by psychologists, but titled "selfish egotism" by church leaders. The adolescent world is logged on to relevance, and the password to enter its sanctuary is "now." Inside the youth culture, we see young people searching for a purpose that they have never sought before. Contemporary youth culture has created the kind of young person who has never existed before. The young are searching for self-identity. Identity crisis is a product of the several previous decades that continues into this millennium. It has roots in cultural blending, pervasive relativity, and an irreverent religiosity.

WHERE DO WE GO FROM HERE?

The question remains to be explored, "Are young people searching for something that doesn't exist?" They are trying to find purpose, but perhaps purpose is not something to be found but something to be developed or discovered. Young people are skeptical of adult authority, attempting to live coequal with adults, while at the same time they don't have the facilities to do so. We think of adolescents as children in adult bodies. They are neither child nor adult. They are young people, teenagers, adolescents. They are, for the most part, the most spiritually open in their lives to consider faith in Christ.

Are we to fashion a ministry to youth based on cultural sensitivity, attempting to make life meaningful and relevant? Are we to design our programs on an experience-based curriculum, because contemporary youth culture has produced young people who guide their life through experience? Are we to accept postmodernity as the foundation for our philosophy of youth work, because this is "where they are"? Are we to construct a noninstitutional religious program because of the erosion of respect for anything that resembles the institutional hierarchy of the church? Is ethnocentricity our answer to their search for identity? Do we rule out traditional Christianity because young people are irreverent to established traditions? The answer: sometimes yes, sometimes no.

Young people need an objective answer to their needs, and the Word of God is the only source for an ultimate answer. Our ministry should be grounded on the Scripture because it is the Word of God that produces changed lives. Regeneration (1 Peter 1:23) causes contemporary young people to grow (1 Peter 2:2); it keeps young people from sin (Ps. 119:9, 11); and it meets their need (Phil. 4:19). The Bible is an absolute that will satisfy the desires of young people who live in an unsure and unstable world. This book takes the position that both the *message* to communicate to young people and the *methods* used in the youth program should be based on the Scriptures.

Perhaps one of the reasons for the decline of Christian influence among contemporary youth culture is the lack of allegiance Christians give to the church. Christ founded the church: "I will build My church" (Matt. 16:18), and it is next to His heart. "Christ . . . loved the church, and gave himself for it" (Eph. 5:25b KJV). The New Testament gives priority to the gathering of believers, and the local assembly was the only basis for ministry in the pages of Scripture.

The closer you come in the ministry to the model of the New Testament church, the more you will experience the blessings of God. A church is a group of baptized believers, in whom Christ dwells, under the discipline of the Word of God, organized for evangelism, education, worship, fellowship, and the administration of the ordinances. An interdenominational agency or a Christian youth organization can have a ministry on a significant level. But the farther it departs from the local church, the less likely it has the full blessing or favor of God (more will be said about Christian youth organizations or parachurch organizations in a later chapter).

Experience must be based on the Word of God. Young people are correct in their sensitivity to people and their desire to help their fellow man. Man is the highest created being, made in the image of God, and every human has such great value that God gave His Son for him. We should understand the teenager and his culture, along with the basis of our ministry being the Word of God.

What Do Our Young People Need from Us?

There is a devilish attack on the institutions of the home, the government, and the church. Those who believe in the inspiration of Scripture must place themselves under its absolute authority and recognize the place of the home, the government, and the church. A Christian teenager should be under authority: (1) to his father and mother, because God placed him in that family, (2) to his local government, because God constituted municipal authority, and (3) to his local church, because a lost world needs disciplined witnesses (disciples) and the Christian young person needs a place to grow.

When a young person accepts Christ, the first thing he must do is to be baptized, then be instructed in "all things that I have commanded you" (Matt. 28:19–20). Then the young person should get involved in the church's program of evangelism, worship, and fellowship. Strong New Testament churches produce strong Christians, not vice versa. However, you cannot have a strong church without strong Christians. Contemporary young people need the church more than any other generation has. It is within the church that young people find community, relationships, support, and natural accountability.

Other young people are fed up with the bureaucracy of some churches or politics found in other ecclesiastical groups. True, many churches are bogged down with institutionalism and are more concerned with the *form* of a church than fulfilling the *function* of a church (evangelism, education, worship, and fellowship). These pseudochurches are not the groups that deserve the loyalty of dedicated young people. We need to return to the basic New Testament church practices. Young people need such a church.

Finally, there needs to be an emphasis on leadership. The current emphasis on small groups and dialogue is an extension of the youth culture's need for relationships and irreverence for traditionalism. Young people feel they have equal stature with adults, so they hesitate to give allegiance to traditional authority persons. The young person is an individual and should be accepted on an equal basis with adults. However, the Scriptures teach that certain men are "called" to be leaders (prophets, pastors, teachers), and these men are given abilities to carry out their God-given tasks. Therefore, a biblical youth ministry will be built on biblical leadership. (See chapter 10 on the youth pastor as a shepherd-leader.)

How Can We Meet the Challenge?

If you are going to work with young people, expect problems. There is no easy place to serve Christ, and this is especially true in youth work. But with every problem is a challenge. Don't view your young people as a headache but as a challenge. Place every gift and capacity in the work, and trust God for results. There are certain ways in which you can meet the challenge of modern youth. These basic principles will leave their imprint over and over again in this book:

1. *By venturing into the real but sometimes hidden world of adolescents.*

You must understand the Bible before you can teach it. And you must understand an adolescent before you can teach him. Adolescence is one of the hardest areas of life to understand. Many people think that they understand the teenage period of life just because they were teenagers once. This is not so. The person who went through adolescence five years ago is five years outdated. Times are changing, and if we are going to minister to young people, we must change, even though the Gospel never changes. You must understand why teenagers feel as they do, how they think, and who they are. Only by understanding adolescents can you help them. The purpose of this book is to take you on a trip through the world of adolescents. Be prepared to study, think, observe, and reflect.

2. *By learning the coordinates of your destination.*

Aims—goals—procedures—methods—philosophy: these are important to help you help young people. Many youth workers want to work with young people, but they have no basic direction. The youth worker who knows where he is going goes someplace. First, you must have a road map. Your road map may be a philosophy for working with young people or basic opinions on how youth work should be carried out. Second, your road map must be accurate. This book will be like a road map, pointing you in the right direction and giving you principles of operation. This book will not be a read-only handbook of programs. This book is intended to be like a manual of timeless principles. Every church, youth group, and community will have a variety of distinctives, but the principles of working with young people are the same.

3. *By using current methods and materials.*

Never before in the history of the church have there been so many materials and methods with which to work. You have helps, books, kits, and resources not available to the leaders of a generation ago. Today large churches are not the only ones that have their youth workers on salaries. Generally speaking, volunteers are well trained. Most denominations furnish curriculum and resources for their youth workers. Christian education materials and curricula are on sale in any bookstore. At many youth ministry conventions you will find techniques and programs of long-range strategy for reaching and keeping young people. Also you find at your disposal short-term plans and techniques for capturing the attention of youth. Teacher-training classes and workshops are available. Avail yourself of all these advantages in youth work. These up-to-date materials will not compensate for the working of the Holy Spirit in your young people. However, God does not delight in ignorance. The Spirit works most effectually through organized, well-prepared biblical content that is interesting and meets the needs of young people. Try using some of the latest materials and methods in your youth group. The latest up-to-date method may accomplish an old-fashioned result.

4. *By merging the Bible and life.*

The Bible was written, among a number of significant reasons, to meet the needs of people, including teenagers. Remember, we work with people, not programs, with lives, not lines. Only when we become "people-centered" in our interest and application do we truly become basically "Bible-centered." Some youth leaders become "completely Bible-centered." They become so "Bible-centered" that the young people are forgotten; the youth are manipulated and treated as objects rather than people. The young people's worker who does this is neither Bible-centered nor Christ-centered. The youth leader who is Bible-centered and Christ-centered will be youth-centered.

This text is unashamed in acceptance of the Word of God as the final authority for belief and practice. The thrust of this book will be "Get teens into the Bible and the Bible into teens." Young people seek answers to life, and these are found only in God's inspired revelation, the Bible. The Word of God will be appealed to as the final authority and directive for working with young people.

Contemporary youth culture can be summed up in one word: fickle. Just when we think we've identified particular trends and characteristics, they change. And even if we get some right, adolescents would never admit it (it's that independence thing). So as adults, we cannot be intellectually arrogant when it comes to this type of pertinent information. It is privileged information, so to speak. It is information that adolescents reluctantly yield, except to those adults they trust. So let's take what we do know about contemporary youth culture and begin to use it to our advantage . . . a spiritual advantage. The young people of this contemporary youth culture are depending on us, whether they know it or not.

NOTES

1. Aaron Kipnis, *Angry Young Men* (San Francisco: Jossey-Bass, 1999), 202.
2. For a better description of these heinous crimes, I went to www.hanania.com/columns and clicked the February 14, 2000, article, "'Honor Killings' Exposed as Real Crimes in Cinemax Documentary," written by Arab author Ray Hanania (accessed August 2001).
3. Based upon charts presented in Kenda Creasy Dean, Chap Clark, and Dave Rahn, eds., *Starting Right* (Grand Rapids: Zondervan, 2001), 18.

4. A study by NetValue, an international Internet measuring company in Paris, found that if given the freedom, kids would indeed go to porn sites. The facts they found:
   - 27.5% of teens younger than 17 had visited adult sites in a recent month.
   - 21% of teens accessing porn were 14 or younger.
   - 40% of porn visitors were girls.
   - Once on porn sites, kids spent 65% more time there than on game sites.

   Source: Janet Kornblum, "Challenge Promised over Library Filters," *USA Today*, 19 December 2000.
5. Marjorie Hoga and Miriam Bar-on, "Impact of Music Lyrics and Music Videos on Children and Youth," *Pediatrics* 98, no. 6 (December 1996): part 1, 1219.
6. The term is applied to those who take the least bit of information and turn it into an exaggerated headline, or one who can pull out the most minuscule fact and fabricate an entire story around it. In either case, the "spin doctor's" primary goal is to make something that wasn't actually there or to interpret something so the facts would actually favor their position more than go against it.
7. The traditional family is one that has, intact, its original set of married parents, with their own biological and/or adopted children.
8. Dr. Paul Amato, "Life-Span Adjustment of Children to Their Parents' Divorce," *The Future of Children*, 4 No. 1-Spring 1994.
9. Richard E. Behrman and Linda Sandham Quinn, "Children and Divorce: Overview and Analysis," *The Future of Children* 4, no. 1 (spring 1994).
10. Robert J. Bartel, "Campus Tensions and Evangelical Response," *Christianity Today* XIII (6 June 1969): 12.
11. *Relevant* is defined as that which is pertinent, related, applicable, and appropriate.
12. Erik Erikson, *Youth, Change and Challenge* (New York: Basic Books, 1962), 168.
13. Robert O. Piehl, "Narrative Therapy and the Christian Counselor," *Christian Counseling Today* 9, no. 3 (2001): 25.
14. A worldview answers such questions as: Where am I? Who's in control? What's right or wrong about the world? How do I know right from wrong? What is the remedy? It is the grid we "look" through when we look at life and our world.
15. Tony Jones, *Postmodern Youth Ministry* (Grand Rapids: Zondervan, 2001), 33.
16. Dawson McAllister, *Saving the Millennial Generation* (Nashville: Nelson, 1999), 16.
17. B. H. Liddell Hart, *Strategy*, 2d rev. ed. (New York: Praeger, 1967), 335–36.
18. For a further look at this subject, see Jim Hancock, *Raising Adults* (Colorado Springs: Pinon Press, 1999), 38.
19. John Leland, "Searching for a Holy Spirit," *Newsweek* (8 May 2000): 60.
20. Hunter Eagon, "Adolescent Attraction to Cults," *Adolescence*, 33, no. 131 (fall 1998): 709.
21.
   - Steroid use among 10th graders increased from 1.7% to 2.2%.
   - Marijuana is still widely used with 16% of 8th graders using it; 32% of 10th graders; and 37% of 12th graders.
   - Alcohol use is remaining stable with 43% of 8th graders, 65% of 10th graders, and 73% of 12th graders trying it.

   Source: "Teen Drug Survey: Heroin, Ecstasy Use Up; Smoking Down," *Chicago Tribune*, December, 2000.
22. Between August 2–7, 2001, eighteen people died because of cocaine or heroin. For the full story, see http://www.cnn.com/2001/US/08/14/houston.drug.deaths
23. Sandy Naiman, "Never Too Late to Talk to Teens," *The Toronto Sun*, 25 February 2001.

What the Future Holds in Youth Ministry

Anyone involved in youth ministry needs to be as relevant as possible. Youth workers are relatively good at identifying the latest youth trends. Why? Because they know kids, they watch kids, they talk to kids, and they do things with kids. Staying up with the latest youth trends can help effective ministry programming and outreach. Figuring out the next trend this is a multibillion-dollar question (just ask the marketers). The problem with trends is that what is chic today may be archaic and irrelevant tomorrow.

Now that a new century and new millennium is here, the questions of what the future holds in youth ministry will need to be answered. The answer cannot be absolutely certain. Yet based on projections, specific trends, and changes, some forecasts can be determined that are directly related to the executing of a youth program and the effectiveness of ministering to young people. Someone has said that God did man a favor by putting a veil over what will take place tomorrow. There is a tremendous amount of truth there. Forecasting the future can be similar to forecasting the weather. Man does not always get it right. But there are some occasions when all the elements and conditions are in place for a relatively accurate forecast, give or take a few degrees. That is the intention here.

A HISTORICAL BACKGROUND OF YOUTH MINISTRY

Some historicity needs to be mentioned in order to track where youth ministry has been and hopefully where it is going.

> 1950 shows American religion for what it has been since colonial times and probably will be for a good while to come: diverse, pluralistic, frustrating in its inability to find a common voice or any significant unity—yet for that very reason an indispensable protector of individual freedom and nurturer of civil rights. For unless American religion were itself quieted and forced into conformity, all freedoms could not be lost. The seeds of fresh dissent, capable of taking root and crumbling the foundation of any state church or totalitarian superimposition will always be present, awaiting water and sun.[1]

It was out of this 1950s era that youth ministry began to come of age: "After the war, this mood (evangelicalism) was continued or created anew by the Youth for Christ organization, and above all by Billy Graham, the greatest evangelist of the postwar who had earlier worked for Youth for Christ."[2]

In the 1960s, rebellion and rising unrest against the norms and values of society were rampant among young people. During this time fundamental churches and their youth groups seemed to flourish. Dr. Elmer Towns has been quoted for saying in the sixties, "The largest churches in America are unashamedly fundamentalist in doctrine. Youth groups in fundamental churches appear to be large and vibrant. Fundamentalist churches have the capacity for the fastest numerical growth and the largest youth groups."[3]

In the 1970s, parachurch ministries plateaued and the era of entrepreneurial youth ministry began. In the 1980s, Carnegie Council on Adolescent Development called the decade an era of "massive cuts" in denominational support for youth ministry. The 1990s saw a return to the seriousness of youth ministry, not only as a ministry but also as a profession. Now, as we begin the twenty-first century, we are seeing seminaries and Christian colleges begin to integrate youth ministry into their academic curricula.[4]

TRENDS IN TEEN SOCIETY

The tracking of trends can be a highly sophisticated skill. Businesses are constantly trying to crack the tastes, preferences, and styles of elusive and fickle young people. In youth ministry, this trend tracking can mean the difference between being relevant and archaic.

> Trend. Such a small word for all the power behind it. A word, a label that often identifies a movement . . . trends can affect our lifestyle and our purchasing decisions, and eventually give us a new outlook. The visible manifestations of trends—the ones you can spot easily on the streets—often start with the youth culture.[5]

In 1980, I made some observations and predictions about society and the impact on future trends in youth ministry.[6] They included the godless direction of society, the negative downturn of the economy, energy concerns with an emphasis on the costs of fuel, the influence of the media, and the cooperation of churches and Christian youth organizations. The economy and energy are trends that come and go. One trend that will continue into the next decade is the godless direction of society. Eric Harris and Dylan Klebold's images have been seared into the conscience of society because of a cold-blooded act of anger at Columbine High School. Many young people can get guns from the arsenals their parents keep. They can fill their minds with violence and ill-advised sexuality via television and movies. They can download all the pornography imaginable to feed depraved minds. Young people continue to be blamed for a lot of social ills, but the harsh reality is that much of this misbehavior has been conjured and marketed by adults to teenagers. Example after example can be cited that reflect the godlessness of society.

One of the most challenging problems facing society today is the use and abuse of chemical substances by teenagers. The number one drug problem, without a doubt, is alcoholism. Alcohol is clearly the substance with which adolescents have the most experience. Statistics vary, but the best estimates indicate that there could be more than 4 million American alcoholics under the age of eighteen.[7]

Suicide is a raging epidemic in America. Each year the national statistics on suicide climb—especially for adolescents. Suicide is the third leading cause of death for ten- to twenty-year-olds, after car accidents and homicide. However, because many suicides are disguised as accidents, it may be the number one cause of teenage death. Between 1962 and 1996, the teenage suicide rate increased 155 percent.[8]

Not only will social ills continue to increase at a rapid rate, but also the morals of young people will continue to degrade. The following statements reflect this:

> It is estimated that 2.5 million teens are infected with STDs (Sexually Transmitted Diseases) each year. That means that every thirteen seconds a teen in the U.S. contracts a sexually transmitted disease. . . . The risk of infection with STDs increases enormously in relation to the number of different people with whom they have had sexual contact.[9]

The generation coming to maturity in this decade will be a hurt generation. This is primarily due to the breakup of the family. The breakdown of the family unit is considered the most significant factor that has negatively changed the sociological landscape in our culture. Divorce has forced young people to choose between parents.

Even with the divorce rate leveling off, about one million U.S. marriages are going to be breaking up each year. That prospect has led to calculations that up to 40 percent of all today's children and youth will live in a single parent family at some time before they reach the age of eighteen.[10] About 40 percent of children will experience a parental divorce prior to the age of sixteen.[11]

The Sheer Numbers

According to *NBC Nightly News* on August 16, 1999, more than 53 million children enrolled for school in the fall of 1999—the greatest number in U.S. history. Several states, including California, are scrambling for teachers, enticing them with "fast-track" teaching degrees, higher pay, and signing bonuses. Even investment firms are using television advertisements showing how investors can retire from their present jobs with supplemental income from their investments and then take on teaching positions. School systems are trying to find funds to build more schools and improve the existing ones. The U.S. government is planning on putting more money into education for the express purpose of hiring one hundred thousand more schoolteachers (1999).

> The teen population is expected to grow at twice the rate of the rest of the population during the next decade, peaking in 2010 with approximately 30.8 million teenagers. This is 900,000 more teens than ever before. In fact, it's 4.1 million more than in 1969—when Woodstock woke up mainstream America to youth culture's existence.[12]

The Disappearance of Adolescence

Besides the volume of adolescents, another phenomenon has been subtly taking place. Adolescence is disappearing.

> In the 1800s, social historians tell us, the average girl began to menstruate at 15; now the average age is 12. . . . The next distinction to vanish will be social. One thing that used to make teenagers teenagers was the postponement of family responsibilities, but these days even 30- and 40-year-olds are postponing family responsibilities, often permanently. . . . Teenagerhood as preparation for life makes no sense when the life being prepared for resembles the one you've been living all along. . . . What will a world without teenagers look like? Like the adult world does now. Adolescents will feel the same pressures as their parents do: to succeed financially, to maintain their health, to stay on society's good side. What's more, adolescents will field these pressures using their elders' traditional techniques: spending money, taking medication, contracting for professional advice.[13]

Sociology teaches us that each successive generation is more mature intellectually and socially than the previous one. Everything is better, faster, and easier. But as the rate of maturity increases, the time kids have time to be kids also dramatically decreases.

> The question for the new century is, How much longer will teenagers exist, at least in the form that James Dean made famous? Twenty years, tops, is my guess. Teenagers, as classically defined, are already dying out, or at least changing into something different. The buffer zone they once inhabited is being squeezed out of existence for two reasons: children are growing up faster than ever before, and adults are growing up more slowly.[14]

What has exacerbated the problem is the disappearance of markers in teens' lives. A marker is a sign that indicates the direction a person is going on this highway we call life. When these markers are approached or reached, societal fanfare indicates this individual is prepared for the next wave of privileges, responsibilities, and freedoms (e.g., getting a driver's license). Some of these disappearing markers that used to distinguish adolescence from childhood would include something as simple as clothing styles. Case in point: Have you been to a GAP Kids store lately? How about doing some demographics of the crowd at the latest boy band concert? The distinction between childhood and adolescence has blurred. Some activities, including organized sports, used to be reserved for adolescents. Yet overzealous parents continue to push their elementary-aged child into organized sports, complete with uniforms, referees, and the occasional parental fisticuffs. Is it any wonder that interest and involvement in traditional team sports is on the decline among adolescents?

Even religious markers have disappeared. I would argue that the ordinances, the Lord's Supper and baptism, have been blurred as markers. The specifics of baptism vary so widely among denominations: (1) Some baptize infants. (2) Some baptize believers as long as they are adults. (3) Some baptize believers, generally adolescent and up, but have no set age and thus often baptize children. My, Steve's, own personal opinion is that participation in the ordinances be considered for those who can grasp the magnitude of them, more specifically adolescents. (I would certainly not minimize childhood decisions. But one should reaffirm those childhood decisions or reconsider their cognitive nature at such early ages. I would be included in those who made childhood decisions, but I would have to honestly say that my recollection of the significance of that decision faded until my adolescent years. I would also admit that at an early age, I might have mistaken the leading of the Holy Spirit for the pleasing of my Christian parents.)

There is even a more looming disappearing marker. It is the marker of innocence. For some unknown reason this present society has opened the floodgates of information to the youngest. (Educators and intellectuals would argue that we can never get too much information.) Many act as though it does not matter how crude, depraved, or explicit that information is—the better we are informed, the better off we will be. Much of this information is being disseminated to individuals regardless of their age. There seems to be a societal propensity to expose anyone to anything. This marker needs to be identifiable for those who can handle such information responsibly, particularly older adolescents. Public education has championed sex education, for the most part, with an emphasis on the mechanics of sexuality. Somewhere along the way, the mystery and surprises of sexuality have been exposed. It would seem to me that attitudes and values in this area, along with responsibility, would be the focus, not merely mechanics. A married couple has a lifetime to figure out the mechanics of sexuality. Yet society continues to expose or, at the very least, insinuate, the how-to to younger and younger age groups.

Lifelong commitment; fidelity; mutual intimate love, protection, and provision within a marriage relationship; and the natural progression of bringing life into the world are mere appendixes to the discussion. What better place to learn the mechanics of sexuality than with a lifelong marriage partner, knowing that you have a lifetime to get the mechanics right! The bottom line message for adolescents is that sex is worth waiting for.[15]

The whole matter of life's markers has biblical evidence. Luke chapter 2 describes the story of a twelve-year-old Jesus. On this particular annual trip to Jerusalem, Jesus finally reached some significant markers in His life. Not only was He left on His own for three days (partly due to parental negligence or at least that of someone who was supposed to be watching the "kids"); He made His way to the right place (the temple) and was "hanging out" with the right kind of people (older and more mature religious types). The Scripture makes it clear that in spite of the misunderstanding Jesus' parents (mother and stepfather) had, He was "obedient to them." Luke 2:52 identifies the markers that Jesus reached, "And Jesus grew in wisdom and stature, and in favor with God and men" (NIV). First Corinthians 13:11 gives us another indication of markers. "When I was a child, I talked like a child, I thought like a child, I reasoned like a child. When I became a man, I put childish ways behind me" (NIV).

There should be concern as to the disappearance of these markers. Markers are meant for the protection of adolescents. They protect teenagers from unnecessary stress and lessen the impact of stress they will inevitably encounter. Markers provide rules of behavior, limit certain activities, and prohibit teenagers from making age-inappropriate decisions. They give new responsibilities and privileges as young people are ready for them. When markers continue to disappear, teenagers will be left alone to decide on matters that will have consequences that are lifelong and irreversible, or at the very least, they will be confined to inexperienced advice and counsel from their peers.

WORSHIP THAT IS FRIENDLY TO THE YOUNG

Because of the increase in peer pressure, youth ministries will have to address the "crowd." Youth ministries will have to be more service oriented with their Christian young people. Christian service will give young people the practical abilities they will need in coping with societal pressures. Too often, youth ministries deal with religious abstracts (being theoretical, as opposed to practical) that have nothing to do with living in today's world.

Entertainment has replaced the instruction of scriptural principles for daily living in many youth ministries. This has been and is producing a group of young people who are observers and not participants. They sit back in their comfortable world and let the few people up front do all the Christian activity. As a result of this entertainment-style program, the young people in these churches are becoming spiritually callused. Because of their numbness, they cannot and would not know how to minister to someone who had a need or problem. "When youth ministry focuses on playing into the entertainment culture, it encourages passivity and reduces it to just another consumer item," says Greg Jones, minister of discipleship at Arbutus United Methodist Church in Baltimore.

To remedy this problem, the youth minister has to develop a program that involves the young people's participation. "Don't overlook the fact that there is a treasure in your young people. Each one has something significant to say. Youth leaders who don't equip young people to do ministry are missing the joy of seeing what's inside of them, not to mention cutting off some of the effectiveness they can bring to a group."[16]

Remedy would include student participation in Sunday morning instruction. Instead of a single instructor, teaching sessions should facilitate student response. Student response would encourage young people to conceptualize scriptural principles and help to relate them to everyday life. There has to be more student involvement, even if it means that it may not attain adult-oriented expectations. Young people need to be encouraged to identify their spiritual gifts. When those gifts are not as obvious, young people need to be taught to "stir up the gift" that is within them. This would take the form of working or ministering with these gifts in mind. By the simple act of practicing spiritual gifts, young people might discover one gift and learn more about another.

Youth ministry has a growing focus on praise and worship, along with young seeker-friendly worship. This has been a point of contention as far as worship styles go. "True worship can indeed lead to controversy. The first murder in human history seems to have taken place between brothers in a disagreement over worship."[17] Some have encouraged non-Christian young people to participate in worship. Some might wonder whether worship is really taking place within a non-Christian young person. I would argue that millions of people around the world participate in some form of worship each Sunday without having a personal relationship with the One they worship. I would also argue that the worship experience for seeking young people might be a large step in their progress toward a personal relationship with Christ. I still believe in single-date salvation, but I also believe in a salvation experience that is at the conclusion of a process of searching. At the end of that process begins another process, the process of discipleship.

This step in seeker-friendly worship has been misinterpreted as the next step in entertainment-based worship. What these trends reflect is a move away from a centralized professional ministry to empowered young laity. Praise and worship allow students to begin taking ownership, and seeker-sensitive services allow young people to minister where they feel called, no matter what it looks like, even if it is a bit unconventional. It is not the role of a ministry to help young people adjust to their programs. It is the role of a youth minister to help adjust the programs to fit the young people. It is a necessity that we move the focus off of our professional selves and onto the work of the Holy Spirit. We can only do this if we truly believe in the priesthood of every believer, even if they happen to be a bit young.

Involving the Youth as Partners

Service projects will need to increase to provide an opportunity for young people to give application to their spiritual instruction. "At every level of schooling, youth participation in service is at an all-time high. Distrustful of politicians and adversarial politics, young people are the vanguard of a new politics of participation and voluntary service. Fueled largely by renewed interest in national service and citizenship, the service-learning movement demands nothing less than reconceptualizing the role of young people . . ."[18] The idea of Christian service is a necessity. In fact, we need to introduce service projects and ministry experiences at the earliest stages of adolescent ministry. One of the predominant challenges of effective ministry is to see students more as vessels of ministry than objects of ministry. The church today must move away from ministry aimed at students and focus on ministry with students.

"Authenticity is job one in youth ministry. That's why ministry trips and service projects offer such a powerful ministry punch—they involve kids in real-life experiences in which their actions and beliefs make a real-life difference."[19]

We must see them as partners in the Gospel ministry and not solely the products of our ministry. This type of focus forces a "fleshing out of the Gospel" that creates a grounded personal theology built upon guided personal discovery. Young people need fewer lectures and more ministry experience. They need to get "dirty" for Christ's sake if they are to develop lives of personal holiness.

With the possibilities of new mission fields opening, youth ministers will need to encourage their young people to become involved in mission work. Instead of just preaching challenging messages about mission fields, the youth pastor needs to give his young people specific opportunities and means of being practically involved. Once that missionary door opens, there have to be prepared missionaries to take on this global task.

English as a Second Language (ESL) may be one method of opportunity for young people of this decade to use. As visas for vocational missionaries become more difficult to procure, young people will have to offer more services to foreign countries besides the Gospel. With the explosion of the Internet and the shrinking world through modern technology, it is both practical and necessary to cross international boundaries, just as it was necessary years ago to cross state lines. The International Mission Board (IMB) of the Southern Baptist Convention has set and broken recruiting records for its journeyman program for the last several years. Through this program, college students are volunteering for two- to three-year experiences overseas for little or no money. They are volunteering en masse because they seek a real, viable faith. This same attitude is found among middle schoolers and high schoolers. It would be hard to imagine an effective youth ministry without an active international mission component to it.

Reaching the Public School Campus

A major function of a relevant youth ministry is developing a contemporary program that reaches public school campuses. Wayne Rice and Chap Clark make the following point about the opportunity of ministry in public schools.

> There's no shortage of complaints about public schools in America. Test scores are slipping. New schools are expensive. Teachers don't seem to be able to care the way they did back in the good old days. This list goes on, and Christians often add a few more items to the list. Schools don't encourage prayer or Bible study. They teach evolution as fact. Drugs, sex, and rock 'n' roll have overrun middle and high school campuses and turned them into cesspools of sin.
>
> However, the public school remains one of the finest ideas God ever put into the hearts of people. Why? Because every school day, schools are packed with *students*.[20]

There needs to be an attraction that catches the secular mind and holds his attention long enough to present the Gospel to him. If you want to see an active "mission field," simply walk the halls of any middle or high school public campus. If youth ministry is to have any significant impact among an adolescent community, it must be actively involved in some aspect of campus ministry and outreach. One's attitude must not and cannot be one of antagonism and arrogance toward a public school. Instead, there must be an attitude of service and cooperation. Strategy would involve becoming a part of the school through such avenues as coaching, substitute teaching, helping with a campus club, chaperoning, etc., in addition to training the kids themselves to be missionaries to their peers.

BEING CONTEMPORARY

There has been much debate on what *contemporary* really is. Instead of arguing over what others say it is, a look at our perfect example, Jesus Christ, will provide some answers. When Christ walked upon this earth, He used illustrations taken from the culture of that day. This included fig trees, grapes, vines, seeds, fish, sheep, and the like, which permeated His illustrations. Much of His time was spent with tax collectors and the sexually immoral, trying to reach them. Ironically, local churches have attempted to take the Gospel around the world with different languages, dialects, and cultures. Yet when it has come to reaching the youth of America, many churches have remained traditional.

My question is: Why the hang-up when we begin conversation about contemporary programs and music or programming to youth? The argument is always, "We don't have to resort to their music and ideas to win them to Christ." However, we use ideas of interest to women to attract ladies, and Christian sports personalities to attract the sports enthusiast. Why not use the contemporary to attract those who can identify the most with the contemporary—the youth?[21]

With all the social ills and their effects, what will happen to attendance in youth ministry? There are mixed opinions. Some believe that there will be an upcoming revival in the church. If a strong movement does not take place, we can truly consider ourselves in a post-Christian era.

On the other end of the opinion spectrum is a youth pastor in southern California who believes that local church youth groups will decrease in size but will grow in spiritual depth. This is the result of lowering societal norms. These norms will inevitably result in Christian young people becoming more and more persecuted. This persecution, whether it be an actual physical harm or a type of social discrimination, will cause many to separate themselves from Christian circles. Shooting tragedies in the United States and Canada have glaringly revealed that Christian young people have been singled out. Adolescent rebellion that is somewhat expected has been tragically redefined. Regardless of whose opinion he follows, the youth pastor needs to make the necessary preparation and adjustments.

The sheer numbers of adolescents are going to have significant ministry implications. With a somewhat faceless adolescence because of growing up digital, the simple gesture of acknowledging and recognizing a teenager will have impact. In his book *The Circle of Innovation,* business guru Tom Peters recalls an experience he has noticed in Ritz-Carlton Hotels. Each time he has stayed at a hotel in the chain, Peters has noticed that every employee, from doorman to bellhop, gives him a few seconds, eye to eye, and asks how everything is going and if there is anything he can do to make Peters's stay more pleasant. Peters has dubbed this "the Ritz Pause." That pause makes him feel recognized and important. The ministry application is obvious: Someone needs to acknowledge that those teenagers who grace our ministry exist and that someone has noticed. In a sea of teenagers trudging along in public school hallways, the simple fact that someone knows his first name will go a long way toward helping a kid feel connected. Whether it be the professional youth minister or a concerned adult leader does not matter. What does matter is that someone has personally connected with this teenager.

The sheer numbers of teenagers will bring cries from civic and community leaders about what is to be done with all these teenagers. Churches and Christian youth organizations have an opportunity to address this issue with creative means of ministry.

Hosting a Youth Center

The youth center will become more of an accepted ministry model. The challenge here will be to design programs and activities that make the large crowd seem small. The connectedness with a concerned adult leader is critical. Community and relationships need to be of utmost priority. Another challenge will be the method or plan in which the message of Christ's life-changing love will be presented, whether subtly or overtly. Great care and planning need to go into this. If not, the youth center will become no more than a communal hangout, with no spiritual distinctives.[22]

Hiring New Vocational Youth Workers

The sheer numbers will also bring about a renewed emphasis on youth ministry. Congregations will put more money into the youth budget, enabling multiple youth staff and interns. A side benefit of this would be the number of youth ministers needed to fill these positions. Many churches are beginning to see the value and wisdom of mature older youth ministers being on staff. Energy and enthusiasm are giving way to experience and steadiness.

Having Safe Zones

Adolescents will always find some behavior or activity that distances them from other age groups. Striving for independence does that in a teenager. The ministry implication for youth ministers will be to develop and build "safe zones" for teenagers.

These safe zones may take the shape of a regular youth activity or an identifiable location. Whatever the shape or ministry model, this safe zone must take on a minimum of three characteristics. First, the teenager is safe from bodily harm. There must be zero tolerance for anything or anyone who would want to hurt someone else. This kind of policy will add assurance to parents who may be a bit wary of your "religious" youth group, if they know that the youth minister will look after the physical well-being of their teenagers. Our society continues to debate violence, guns, and freedom of expression. Within the walls of our churches, the physical safety of teenagers is not something that can be taken for granted. There must be conscious effort to ensure that young people are protected.

Another related area of safety would be the issue of sexual harassment. The family of God is the perfect context in which the proper treatment of the opposite sex can be taught. The teaching and modeling of respect, responsibility, proper behavior, and the protection of members of the opposite sex is paramount. Many adolescent females face a daily barrage of sexual innuendoes and, many times, blatant comments or advances at school. The place of youth ministry must discourage it. It cannot tolerate it. It must deal with it with the same vigor and seriousness of any other type of abuse.

Second, a safe zone is a place where teenagers are safe from being emotionally or socially abused. When I (Steve) was in junior high school, I could not wait to get home after school. Junior high students can be cruel in the best of times, but cruelty increases exponentially when you are a new kid in class. Home was a safe place for me because I knew I was accepted, loved, and embraced. My parents did not hurl harsh words at me. With the fragmenting of the family, the home will become less and less of a safe place for teenagers. Many teenagers will be going from one unsafe zone (school) to another unsafe zone (home). For many teenagers, the ridicule, harsh words, and social outcasting do not let up, even at home. Others will experience domestic hazing (demeaning and belittling behavior). Some teenagers are good at masking unpleasant experiences or circumstances they are enduring. But for the most part, constantly belittled teens are easily recognizable. Their body language alone gives them away, with a "beaten down" look that accompanies discouraged and withdrawn behavior.

The youth ministry must be a place where every teenager is accepted, imperfections included. Anything that even resembles sibling or peer rivalry must be dealt with immediately and firmly. Any teenager walking into a youth program of any type must be assured that no one will berate him and neither will he berate anyone. Loving instruction in this area will give the necessary social skills adolescents need in order to be well-adjusted individuals who get along well with others.

A safe zone's third characteristic must be that it is a place where a teenager can be a teenager, having behavior that is typical of adolescent behavior. Teenagers are in those awkward years of development. Energy levels go from World Wrestling Federation to that of a sluggish tortoise. They have outbursts of emotions and behavior. They say one thing and do another. But the two main areas of differences between adolescents and adults are age and experience. The safe youth ministry model will accept adolescents with all their peculiarities and idiosyncrasies. In fact, the safe youth ministry model will find delight and joy in watching these adolescents grow, develop, mature, make mistakes, and eventually make the right choices about life. Safe youth ministries will still be present and supportive when their adolescents make these mistakes. They are not surprised by the shortcomings of adolescents. They recognize them as necessary steps along the way toward maturity and assimilation into the adult world. It is the role of the youth minister to be a part of this process so as to prevent teenagers from making decisions that will be damaging and irreversible.

Many young people will always be skeptical of the future because of the failure of their parents to remain together. The youth pastor will need to minister to these young people by helping them to heal the emotional wounds they have suffered. They will have to be taught how to forgive and how to establish meaningful relationships. Most of all, they will need to be taught and shown an example of God's ideal for a marriage relationship. Even the social skills of parenting, whether it be raising children or raising parents, will need to be taught and modeled. Some young people have had to endure the prolonged onset of adolescence with their own parent(s). There will be parents who have yet to grow up and accept their adulthood, with all its uniquenesses and responsibilities. In the meantime, their own teenagers gaze in disbelief, confused as to what their adulthood should look like. In mid-1997 about 19 million children (one in four) under the age of eighteen lived with only one parent.[23] Youth ministry programming needs to include activities that encourage inclusiveness of families, especially parents and their teenagers.

> Luckily the majority of kids cope successfully with these stresses, and they owe that in large part to the adults in their lives. A recent National Institute of Health study found that kids who feel connected to home, family, and school are better protected from violence, suicide, sexual activity, and substance abuse. Adolescents also fare better if their parents are home at key times of the day—in the morning, after school, at dinner, and at bedtime.[24]

Parental involvement in lay leadership or volunteering also needs to be encouraged. (Obviously some discretion and qualification would be needed here. I personally inquire with the related teenager if having their parent[s] involved meets with their approval. You would not want any obvious family discord being displayed.)

The ministry implications of the Internet are simple as well as profound. Youth ministry cannot deny the use of the Internet. Youth ministry has always been at the forefront of embracing technological advances, mainly because the young people we are trying to reach are embracing these technological advances. Youth ministry will have to remain at the forefront of any future technological waves. E-mail, chatrooms, Web pages, videoconferencing, and the like will be a mainstay of youth ministry. These will provide the convenience of informing and staying informed. The Internet will continue to provide instant communication and response, something even parents of teenagers appreciate.

Another ministry implication of this digital generation would be the challenge of youth ministry to enhance, build, develop, and nurture relationships. Even though interaction takes place on the Internet in real time, it is faceless and emotionless. It may mean that youth ministry takes the initiative of getting back to basics: listening, talking, reacting, waiting. Youth ministry must get back to personal contact, face-to-face meetings, hanging out (with purpose), and simply getting together. Society is beginning to react against all of this technology, and even businesses are getting the message that people want to deal with people. Youth ministry must take the lead here. It may take the initiative of challenging teenagers to simply "turn it off." With all the peripheral sights and sounds teenagers input into their lives, it becomes more of a challenge to "hear" the voice of God. The discipline of silence, combined with a new form of fasting, fasting from technology, will bring a new appreciation to seeking God and His "still small voice."

> I don't believe ancient disciplines and comtemplative practices of the church will ever be as widespread and popular as game nights, ski retreats, and those models of ministry that imitate the surrounding culture. But in the next 10 to 20 years, more youth workers will recognize that, in this period in the life of the church, it is silence that proclaims good news, stillness that brings justice, fasting that feeds the hungry, and prayer that trains the heart to hear the quiet beckoning of the living Christ.[25]

There simply is more to give up for God's sake today. Teenagers will meet this challenge. Technology will remain commonplace in their lives, but with a Spirit-led challenge to keep it in its proper place, teenagers will master technology and not vice versa. There will be a renewed commitment to friends and youth workers when adolescents begin to decide for themselves what really is important. With proper guidance, they will see that God places His highest priority on people and relationships. Youth ministry must develop and introduce those ministry models that enhance the relationships between teenagers, their parents, and other adults.

Developing Cooperative Ministries

This decade will see a cooperation between youth ministries and youth-oriented organizations or Christian youth organizations. Youth pastors will begin to realize that other ministries and organizations do have something to offer. This could involve help with special programs, communication techniques, ideas for activities, or just knowing that each ministry is a part of a greater ministry that involves other people and organizations. Attempting to be exclusive and isolated will no longer be advantageous. It is clear that the Gospel can be taken to more young people when there is a coordinated, cooperative effort. Small youth ministries should be uniting with other local youth ministries in order to execute youth programs that can attract a large crowd. This kind of cooperative effort will be needed when it comes to securing a facility for exclusive use and being able to produce a special program. It would be expensive and impractical for the smaller youth ministries to attempt certain activities alone (i.e., renting an entire skateboard park, ice skating rink, etc.).

Local church youth ministries will see the value of youth organizations such as Campus Life (Youth for Christ), Word of Life, Campus Crusade for Christ, and the like. Christian youth organizations are a part of the overall church family.[26] Youth ministries need to be aware that these organizations do extensive research in finding methods that can market their programs to young people. This research reveals, for the most part, what young people are attracted to. If they were not in tune with the adolescent mind, these organizations would not be able to propagate their programs. The youth pastor, too, needs to know what the adolescent mind is in tune with.

The youth minister can learn from these organizations and use whatever methods or programs he thinks will aid his ministry. These Christian youth organizations will see the value of working with local churches. The relationship between Christian youth organizations and local congregations will be nurtured and developed. Instead of avoiding them, these organizations will realize that the perpetuation of their programs can be increased significantly with cooperation among local churches. Both local church youth ministries and youth organizations will exhibit a genuine cooperation.

From the perspective of what Christian youth organizations can learn, Pete Ward, author of *God at the Mall,* says,

> Parachurch youth ministries need to start to consider how they can bridge the gap between church and the young people with whom they have significant contact. All of this inevitably means that some kind of understanding needs to be reached with local church leaders, church communities, and denominations. How this is done will depend on local church relationships and politics.[27]

Facing Postmodernity

Postmodernity has several ministry implications. First, these young people need to be heard. Our ministry models need to move from a "talking head" or monologue to more dialogue. Young people have a lot to say, and at times it might be profound. Whether it is or not is almost irrelevant. Their story must be heard. It will, for the most part, be more complex and consequential than that of previous generations. Part of this "hearing" will help youth leaders and adults identify what is the problem or the issue. Youth ministry has been quick to say that "Jesus is the answer," but we need to know, at the very least, what is the question.

Second, young people will need to be "engaged." Being engaged or endeared by youth ministry will require involvement. Ministry models must be participatory, even if it means taking a few risks with adolescent inexperience. I have previously mentioned the importance of nurturing and developing relationships. But this can be taken a step further. A large number of adolescents are disconnected and disenfranchised with the church as a whole. That group of teenagers will need aggressive effort in building relationships. More and more teenagers will fall into a category of being socially disadvantaged, whether it is due to cultural stereotyping, church irrelevance, their own behavior, or the behavior of significant others in their lives (siblings or parents). The ingredients of these relationships, if they are to work, must include honesty, transparency, listening skills, respect, time, and permanence.

Because the millennial generation is media driven and streetwise, a third ministry implication would be to practice discernment in our selectivity of popular culture. Media is an amoral means. It is the content that makes the difference. Young people consume the content without giving a thought to the values being propagated. Whether it is sexuality, violence, profane linguistics, or substance abuse, adolescents are like young children who learn by putting everything into their mouths. Sometimes it is all right. But often it leaves a bad taste, and at its most damaging, it could choke the life out of them. Even more disturbing is when something is in their mouths that should not be there, and they do not have the wisdom to spit it out.

In a somewhat similar vein, when my own children were off to a public school after eight years of private Christian school education, I explained to them that there would be a number of "manure piles" in public education. The difference between them and other kids in school would be the fact that when they stepped into a "manure pile," they would at least know they had stepped into one and know what to do next. The tragedy would be that many of their classmates would step in them and not even know it.

Youth ministry will need to help young people make sophisticated choices about the content to which they subject themselves. Youth ministers will have to be able to stealthily maneuver among venues of popular culture, gleaning what they can and identifying the values that are contrary to scriptural truth or even contrary to common sense. Plenty of messages are being presented, both subliminal and blatant. (Spend an hour watching MTV or scan the CD covers at your local music store.) Youth ministry will have to use a tightly woven filter, looking beyond the entertainment value in its selectivity of popular culture usage. Music and movies are here to stay. If one argues style, he will lose every time. But one can always dialogue about content and the values being propagated. Once there is open and honest dialogue, the defining lines of right and wrong will materialize. The wise youth minister will have to develop a listening ear as to the messages or cries of youth that come through popular culture. This will lend itself to the relevance of faith in Christ among this generation.

A fourth ministry implication will involve the importance of spirituality among this generation. Birthed by generation X as an irreverent search, this search for a personal spirituality will continue with the next generation as postmodernity continues its demagogue-like progression.

> In spite of many common cultural experiences, there is no singular expression of GenX religion. In a broad stroke, there are individuals with a generic interest in spirituality, but who find it a bit confining to attend a church. . . . Then there are the religious dabblers, who appropriate various elements from this religion and that one, and may even get serious for short periods of time as they do yoga, practice mediation, or revert, like good romantics, for a short dip back into the religion of their heritage. From the dabblers, we get many interesting hybrids of new religious combinations, but authority is vested in the individual, not in any particular tradition.[28]

Spirituality will have to be taught and experienced with clarity and straight talk. Worship will be something that is participatory in nature, involving the arts and the artists (i.e., writings, poetry, artistic designs, etc.) to communicate to the senses of this visual generation. A modest lifestyle, with a Christian sense of time, not the "normal" frenetic overcommitment that so many adults find themselves into, will have to be modeled and exemplified. (Keep in mind that relationships are paramount. So there must be a sense that a particular teenager is not bothering us or infringing upon our time.) Faith in Christ will have to present itself as an easy, thoughtful decision to make but a difficult and unique lifestyle to follow. The benefits as well as the responsibilities (service) and consequences (suffering) of faith in Christ must be presented. Young people must know and understand what they are getting into. To know even better what young people want to get into, *Group* magazine asked ten thousand Christian teenagers attending its work camp program to fill out a "Cool Church Survey." The survey asked them to check which of ten factors they found important in influencing their commitment to church. They are as follows:

1. A welcoming atmosphere where you can be yourself—73%
2. Quality relationships with teenagers—70%
3. A senior pastor who understands and loves teenagers—59%
4. Interesting preaching that tackles key questions—53%
5. Spiritual growth experiences that actively involve you—51%
6. Fun activities—51%
7. Engaging music and worship—50%
8. Quality relationships with adults—36%

9. Multiple opportunities to lead, teach, and serve—35%
10. A fast-paced, high-tech, entertaining ministry approach —21%[29]

Youth ministers need to take notice if they are to be successful in this profession called youth ministry.

CONCLUSION

Regardless of the changes, both seen and unseen, and the adjustments that will face youth ministries to come, a prepared youth minister will have to be able to cope and adjust to them. Culture will change, sometimes for the better, usually for the worse. Methodologies come and go. Ideas are born and produced. They are intended for certain times and places, and they will eventually run their course and their usefulness. There is nothing sacred about them. It is the message of hope to this generation that will never change. Youth ministry is in an enviable position to change with the times with an unchangeable message.

NOTES

1. Robert S. Ellwood, *1950: Crossroads of American Religious Life* (Louisville.: Westminster, 2000), 225.
2. Ibid., 191.
3. Elmer Towns, *Successful Biblical Youth Work* (Nashville: Impact Books, 1973), 28, 30.
4. Information based upon a historical graph in *Starting Right,* edited by Kenda Creasy Dean, Chap Clark, and Dave Rahn (Grand Rapids: Zondervan, 2001), 84.
5. Janine Lopiano-Misdom and Joanna De Luca, *Street Trends* (New York: HarperBusiness, 1998), 3.
6. Steve Vandegriff, "Factors for Successful Adolescent Ministry in the Local Church Today" (doctoral thesis, California graduate School of theology, 1980), chapter 10.
7. Les Parrott III, *Helping the Struggling Adolescent* (Grand Rapids: Zondervan, 2000), 124.
8. Ibid., 430.
9. Ibid., 349.
10. Jim Reapsome, ed., "Children and Youth Face Severe Trauma Because of Divorce," *Youthletter* (December 1978).
11. L. Bumpass, "Children and Marital Disruption: A Replication and Update," *Demography* 21(1984):71–82.

12. http://www.youthspecialties.com/ywj/articles/culture/seven.html.
13. Walter Kirn, "Will Teenagers Disappear?" *Time* 155, no. 7 (21 February 2000): 60.
14. Ibid.
15. For more information on the benefits of waiting, log on to www.truelovewaits.com.
16. Wayne Rice and Chap Clark, *New Directions for Youth Ministry* (Loveland, Colo.: Group, 1998), 111.
17. Elmer Towns and Warren Bird, *Into the Future* (Grand Rapids: Revell, 2000), 134.
18. *Phi Delta Kappan,* 81, no. 9 (May 2000): 652.
19. Rick Lawrence, *Trendwatch* (Loveland, Colo.: Group, 2000), 22.
20. Rice and Clark, *New Directions for Youth Ministry,* 117.
21. Roger Van Loan, "What Is Contemporary?" *Religious Broadcasting Sourcebook,* ed. Ben Armstrong, rev. ed. (Morristown, N.J.: National Religious Broadcasters, 1978), G-9.
22. On a personal visit to Tipp City, Ohio, a small rural community of six thousand people, I toured Ginghamsburg United Methodist Church. This church has more than three thousand people attending five services on a weekend. More than 45 percent of their present congregation would be considered community-reached people. They have an obvious need to build a larger facility to house their congregation. This church opted to do something for the youth of the community. They built a thirty-five thousand square foot youth center, complete with staging, basketball, weight room, game room, coffee shop, etc. Their youth center has become the place to be for hundreds of teenagers in the community. The church readily admits that they are struggling with ways to present the Gospel to the many teenagers who enter their building. Ministry is happening but is not as organized and structured as they would like. This is a good example of a church using its resources to make a youth center happen.
23. U.S. Census Bureau, *Vital Statistics Report as of October 1998* and *US Census Bureau Brief,* CENBR/97-1, September 1997.
24. Angie Cannon and Carolyn Kleiner, "Teens Get Real," *U.S. News & World Report,* 17 April 2000.
25. Mark Yaconelli, "Seven Trends to Watch in the Next Decade," *Youth Worker Magazine* (January/February 2000): 29.
26. Being a former executive director of a Youth for Christ ministry for thirteen years, I know the strong mandate we had as a Christian youth organization. Our mandate was simple: Youth for Christ existed to reach teenagers with the Gospel of Christ. What made Youth for Christ "unique" was the fact that we could be as creative as we wanted, provided we could demonstrate ministry effectiveness and financial responsibility. Our staff and board of directors were all focused on our mandate. As a Christian youth organization, we could move quickly and change directions quickly if it would enhance our mission. Bureaucracy was kept at a minimum. Many churches and youth groups looked to Youth for Christ, and organizations like us, for leadership, ministry initiatives, and creative ideas.
27. Pete Ward, *God at the Mall* (Peabody, Mass.: Hendrickson, 1999), 138.
28. Richard W. Flory and Donald E. Miller, eds., *GenX Religion* (New York: Routledge, 2000), 9.
29. Rick Lawrence, "The Cool Church," *Group Magazine* (6 May 2001): 37.

An Analysis of Different Types of Youth Work

Youth ministry takes a variety of shapes. It can be considered a consumer's approach to ministry. If an adolescent doesn't like the "product" in one place, he can check out the "product" in another and see if he wants to go there. There are clear and explicit differences when it comes to youth ministry. In Dr. Elmer Towns's book *Putting an End to Worship Wars,* he identifies six types of churches: the evangelistic church, which focuses on winning the lost; the Bible expositional church, which emphasizes teaching of the Word of God; the renewal church, which focuses on excitement, revival, and touching God; the body life church, which focuses on fellowship, relationships, and small groups; the liturgical church, which centers on serving and glorifying God through worship; and the congregational church, which has a balanced approach to worship, expressed by the laypeople.[1] There is no question that the accompanying youth ministry in each of these church models would more or less take on the same model.

CONGREGATIONAL MODELS

Dr. Doug Randlett did his doctoral thesis on the study of youth ministry models in evangelical churches.[2] In that study, Dr. Randlett lists characteristics of each model.

Bible Expositional Model Characteristics

1. The goal as viewed in Ephesians 4:11–12 points to the pastor's role of equipping the saints as foundational and primary.
2. Bible teaching is central, produced through expositional methodology with additional emphasis upon application.
3. Bible teaching is often accompanied with the use of teaching aids, such as outlines, notes, and PowerPoint presentations.
4. The Christian should know, understand, and minister spiritual gifts within the church. Their use is essential for spiritual maturity to take place within the body.
5. A strong emphasis is placed upon community penetration with the Gospel as believers are equipped through preaching and teaching.
6. The establishment of discipleship is another key principle for church growth in this model.
7. The use of the laity in doing the work of the ministry is an inevitable outcome of the biblical goal in Ephesians 4:11–12.

Body Life Model Characteristics

1. The focus is to enhance the quality of fellowship among believers. This fellowship emphasizes the idea of sharing in common as partners, resulting in a oneness.
2. The goal for the Christian is to develop a shared intimacy with one another and Christ.
3. Programmatic keys are the cells, defined as the clustering of Christians together for shared intimacy, and the celebration, a large group service for the collective cells.
4. The groups perform hospitality evangelism. This involves the inviting of friends, relatives, and neighbors to the cell meetings.
5. The effectiveness of the cell depends upon commitment, openness, reliance/accountability, and enlargement.
6. A cell is characterized by an environment of honesty and transparency.
7. An effective cell group provides spiritual follow-up, social relations, opportunity for participation, and assimilation into the larger church family.
8. The body of Christ ministers to the body of Christ. Emphasis is placed upon the ministry of the cell members.
9. The pulpit ministry is often not as dominant in this model as in others.
10. Because of the important function of the cell members, the church often establishes a plurality of elders.
11. The church services are primarily for believers. Evangelism takes place outside the church building.

12. Keeping statistics is usually minimized.
13. Emphasis is placed upon the understanding and use of spiritual gifts.
14. Celebration services are usually informal in style.

Congregational Model Characteristics

1. The goal is a people-led church expressed with deacons, church boards, and church committees.
2. The primary role of the pastor is to organize the ministry.
3. The church program is reflected in a balance between worship, Christian education, fellowship, and evangelism.
4. A high percentage of involvement by the laypeople is seen in the programs of the church.
5. People are more responsible for the ministry of the church than is the pastor. Ministry belongs to the people.
6. Sunday school enrollment and attendance is emphasized.
7. The visitation program of the church is important and is emphasized as a ministry for lay involvement.
8. The congregational church is often a single-cell church, resulting in mostly smaller churches. A church of 250–300 is viewed as a larger congregation.

Evangelistic Model Characteristics

1. Matthew 28:19–20 serves as the goal for this model. Win the lost, baptize them to identify with Christ and the local church, and teach them obedience to the Scriptures.

2. This is an action-oriented ministry, as opposed to meditative or instructive.
3. Outreach evangelism is a priority.
4. A strong pastoral leadership has the spiritual gift of evangelism.
5. The pastor leads the entire flock; the sheep do not lead the shepherd/pastor.
6. Persuasive evangelistic preaching has as its goal to get people saved.
7. This model has a simple organization of church programs and policies. There is caution against overorganization.
8. A paid pastoral or educational staff is often evident.
9. It emphasizes the use of laity in outreach programs.
10. It is growth oriented and numbers oriented. The church must grow in attendance, conversions, and baptisms.
11. It is platform oriented. The platform is used primarily for preaching and special music.
12. Sunday school has large classes with a high teacher-pupil ratio.
13. The Bible is central in all preaching and teaching.
14. Preaching is usually evangelistic or prophetic in nature.
15. The style of ministry may take various appearances. Some may be seeker sensitive with contemporary music and an up-to-date environment. Others may resemble an evangelistic crusade but held on Sunday morning.
16. The pastor motivates the laity to "soul winning." A goal is to produce a church noted for "soul winners."

Renewal Model Characteristics

1. Worshiping God is a priority in purpose and practice. A reverence of God is emphasized.
2. Reviving the worshiper is an objective of the worship experience.
3. Music is the key element in the worship experience. Newer praise choruses are at the heart of this experience.
4. A strong worship leader is necessary. This person most often is the pastor.
5. A strong emphasis is placed upon the role and ministry of the Holy Spirit in the life of the worshiper.
6. A worship celebration service is programmed each week.
7. The celebration service is a planned, yet informal service.
8. Active participation by the people is encouraged in all services.
9. The worshiper is encouraged to have freedom of expression toward God in worshiping.
10. Evangelism is seen as important; however, it is planned to take place outside the church service in the community.
11. The Word of God is a priority and is provided by an exhorter pastor with emphasis upon practical application.
12. Other elements of worship, besides preaching and music, are encouraged.

Liturgical Model Characteristics

1. The primary goal is to glorify and serve God through worship.

2. The style of worship is described as "atmospheric"—that is, quiet and meditative.
3. The focus of this model is upon God the Father.
4. A priority is to honor the worship traditions of the historical church.
5. The worship service is structured in a formal, traditional style.
6. The model can be described as nonfeeling and nonexpressive.
7. The emphasis for the church member is upon the expression of faith through practical action.
8. Meeting felt needs in the community is a priority. Social and charitable projects are evident.
9. This is a gift colony for those with the gift of helps and serving.

Four Ministry Models

The book *Four Views of Youth Ministry and the Church* synthesizes the models of youth ministry to four, and the book describes exactly what its title suggests.[3] The four views are:

1. The Inclusive Congregational Approach—integrates young people into congregational life. It is characterized by friendly relations between young people, children, and adults. This approach sees young people as full partners in every aspect of God's faith community.
2. The Missional Approach—views youth ministry as a mission. Using responsible evangelism to disciple young people into established churches, young people and youth pastors are considered to be missionaries. By functioning semi-autonomously as church, school,

or community based, their responsibility is to communicate the Gospel to their generation.

3. The Preparatory Approach—a specialized ministry to adolescents that prepares them to participate in the life of existing churches as leaders, disciples, or evangelists. Students are viewed as disciples-in-training with opportunities for service, both in the present and future. Developmental dynamics suggest the youth ministry be viewed as a laboratory in which disciples are permitted to grow in a culture guided by spiritual coaches.
4. The Strategic Approach—prepares the youth group to become a new church. Using continuity in discipleship between the youth minister and teens, potential leaders are nurtured to assume responsibility for roles in evangelism and fellowship. The youth pastor then becomes the pastor, and a new church is formed with the blessing of the mother church.

YOUTH MINISTRY MODELS

For some time youth pastors and their ministries have had emphases on two major aspects. These two major aspects are program- and individual-centered ministries. It does not take long for an observer to detect what type of ministry a youth pastor is following. Each has its own distinctive characteristics.

Characteristics of a Program-Centered Ministry

The program-centered ministry does activities on a regular basis. Being on a regular basis would be interpreted as traditional (for example, going to the same summer camp every year, an annual banquet, or a seasonal activity such as an all-night New Year's Eve party that takes place each year at the same place). These activities are done not because there is a real interest but because it has been done that way for years.

Frequency

Activities on a regular basis also means frequency. A program-centered activity will have activities a certain number of times a month. The young people can almost predict when an activity is scheduled. Once there is a slacking period in activities, the young people and their parents get the sense that the youth ministry is not doing its job. Program-centered ministries are constantly in search of new activities (as youth become bored with always doing the same thing) that will draw young people to the ministry. The youth pastor will try almost anything that is new and innovative. Most often, the activities that are put on have been borrowed from another youth pastor who saw some results with it. These results could include a well-attended event, new kids coming to the ministry, and salvation decisions. The problem here is that these programs are attractive to the "new youth," while those who have been attending see them as the same old thing.

Media

Being program centered, the youth ministry makes a futile attempt to compete with the media. Obviously, there is no way to compete with the major networks. The youth minister can occasionally bring in a celebrity or noted personality, but to maintain a consistent program that surpasses anything Hollywood soundstages can produce is not possible. Not only is it impossible, but it is impractical, financially unreasonable, and improbable.

Attendance

The program-centered ministry is preoccupied with attendance. Unless a large number are in attendance, the activity has not been a success. Usually the youth pastor encourages his young people to bring as many of their friends as possible. If youth do not come, the youth pastor makes them aware of it via guilt from messages he gives publicly. Sooner or later, the young people will quit trying to fill up an empty room for the sake of numbers.

Philosophy

The philosophy of a program-centered ministry is simple: The social aspect of a young person's life is almost equally important to his spiritual life. This philosophy believes that the local church is providing for the needs of young people by supplying activities for them. This ministry holds to the belief that Christians can have as much fun and amusement as the secular adolescent population. Many times any kind of devotional thought or evangelistic appeal somewhere in the format at an activity is avoided.

Entertainment

After a steady diet of "fun and games" given to the Christian teenager, his life will still have a spiritual void. In an attempt to fill the vacuum in his life, the teenager will be faced by some decisions. One decision is to leave the youth group for more involvement in worldly pleasures and amusements. The youth program can entertain and amuse to a certain point. Once it reaches its maximum capabilities, if the young person wants bigger and more extravagant entertainment, he will move on to what the secular world has to offer. This decision usually leaves the Christian young person's spiritual life ineffective. The teenager becomes disillusioned with church in general. The local church is no longer a lighthouse in a spiritually dark world. It has become nothing more than a social institution—no different from a rotary club, sorority or fraternity house, or a dating service. Often this teenager becomes embittered toward church and will have no part of it. His excuse for not going back to church is because of the hypocrisy in it, but the young person, unaware of it, has become a part of the problem.

Another decision that the Christian young person may make is that of going where he can be spiritually fed. The major danger in this is susceptibility toward false teaching and doctrine. His spiritual hunger needs to be filled, but many times, the young person is led unaware by false teachers and preachers. An extreme of this falling into false religions is the Jonestown Massacre, the Branch Davidian cult in Waco, Texas, and an apparent increased interest in Wicca.[4] Even with the danger of cults deceiving some of these program-centered young people, most of them who decide to be spiritually fed will find a church that meets their need. The main characteristic of the youth ministry they will choose is that it teaches the Bible. It may have a program that is lackluster, but the simple fact that they can be taught the Bible will usually keep them there.

Other teens may stay in the unsatisfactory church and "graduate" into the adult congregation. Another situation is that the youth leaders will resign and the youth group will collapse, because such a youth group has built around the leaders rather than building youth into the church.

Drawing a Crowd

The youth ministry that is program-centered will draw a crowd—temporarily. The inquisitive youth pastor who is looking for success in his ministry may observe large numbers of teenagers flocking to a program-centered youth ministry. In the youth minister's desire to be a success, he may reproduce the techniques of the program-centered ministry. He, too, may experience temporary success. But when the program is over, the young people will be gone. The ones who do remain will be spiritually shallow young people. Without a solid foundation, they will experience a crumbling away of their life's foundation when they are faced with adversity or worldly pressures to go against scriptural principles.

Week after week youth workers are constantly trying to cater to their students' whims and nothing is happening. This shouldn't be your position. This is the first thing wrong with a program-centered approach. You shouldn't try to meet their wants; you should be trying to meet their needs.

There are two types of needs: real and felt. A *real need* is something we need, but we may not realize it. A *felt need* is when we come to realize this is what we really need or even merely something we feel we need. For instance, you can say to someone, "You need to come to the youth group." But unless that student *feels* the need himself he will never understand his *real* need to attend. It is only when he's having problems in his relationships with others or in his relationship with himself that he realizes God could possibly be a solution. It is then that he decides that his attendance might be a good thing.[5]

Characteristics of an Individual-Centered Ministry

On one end of the philosophical scale, there is the program-centered ministry. On the other end is the individual-centered ministry. Instead of programs getting all the energies of the youth pastor, the young people do.

Discipleship

The individual-centered program puts much emphasis on personal discipleship. The youth pastor usually disciples a handful of young people. They in turn get a handful of Christian teenagers to disciple, and so on. The main drawback for this activity is it usually produces a group of disciples of their own leader. The drawback comes when the youth leader leads "his disciples" in unscriptural ways. His negative characteristics can be copied as well as his positive. Discipleship hinges on the personal walk of the youth leader.

Bible Study

Individual-centered youth ministries involve their young people in much Bible study. The study of Scripture is in every aspect of the ministry. Youth Sunday school centers around studies from Scripture. Topical studies are discussed more by accident than on purpose. When they are discussed, it is because of Scripture's obvious reference to them. One of the highlights of the youth program is a weeknight Bible study. The central purpose is to glean from the Scriptures. This is done via verse-by-verse exegesis. Usually there is one main leader who has properly prepared for the study and whose responsibility is to guide the study. The students are encouraged to express their thoughts and feelings about certain Bible verses.

Quality

An emphasis on numbers of young people is not a priority of the individual-centered ministry. The youth ministry does not make any special drives or programs to attract masses of young people. Instead it depends on the attractive life that the Christian young person portrays. With this attraction, non-Christian young people will be drawn because of curiosity, friendships with Christian teenagers, or personal desire for spiritual fulfillment. The numerical growth of this type of ministry does not tend to be rapid. Instead, it tends to be a slow but steady growth. At times, this kind of ministry can be exclusive, in a sense that the members have no desire to grow numerically. The young people are preoccupied with learning factual information about the Bible. To the extent that they become disinterested in taking the responsibility of reaching other young people with the Gospel, their growth rate is almost nil.

The negative aspect of this type of ministry is that the young people are often satisfied with their exclusive group. There is no real concern to expand numerically. The main thrust is to expand their biblical knowledge. The danger in talking about "Christian practices" is that we might delude ourselves into thinking that our salvation has more to do with human initiative and goodness than God's initiative and goodness towards us.[6]

Spiritual Pride

Becoming spiritually proud is a negative trait of the individual-centered ministry. Knowing various types of doctrine or knowing some stray fact about a phrase in the Scriptures can result in prideful knowledge. This kind of knowledge says, "I know something that you don't know." These kinds of young people are able to intelligently discuss or debate with other believers and nonbelievers. Usually this debating leads to nothing more than argument supported with memorized Bible verses. These quoted Bible verses are sometimes canned replies to statements they have already memorized. These young people may be sadly neglectful of an individual's personal or spiritual needs. They are more interested in displaying their biblical knowledge and being mentally superior to their acquaintances.

THE BEST MODEL

After knowing the characteristics of these two extremes, the youth pastor will ask, "Which one should be followed?" The answer is, "Both of them." Each extreme has its positive points along with its negative points. An intelligent youth minister should take the positive aspects of both and activate them in his ministry. Some youth ministers know how to draw a crowd but do not know what to do with young people spiritually after they get them. Other youth ministers know how to develop a teenager spiritually but would not know what to do if a crowd came to one of their infrequent activities.

Evangelism

By incorporating program-centered characteristics into his ministry, the youth pastor should be planning programs that attract Christian and non-Christian young people. A youth leader should have a program to reach dozens of kids in his community (e.g., concerts), the purpose being an opportunity to present the Gospel in a simple manner to young people who normally would not enter the doors of a religious institution. This provides an evangelistic opportunity for the Christian young people to invite their non-Christian friends.

Obviously, there are innumerable other areas of outreach. All of them are simply methods of putting into action concern for the unsaved and a desire to explain the Gospel. Not only will the quality of the youth program improve through an outreach ministry and through the young people expressing an active witness to the unsaved, but after the outreach, training provides a resource for future youth group leaders and officers. Young people have more fun and feel more purposeful in an outreach ministry that fulfills the Great Commission than they do in merely meeting together for a social once a month.[7]

Attendance

The youth pastor should put a priority on the youth program and church attendance among his young people. To make it attractive to attend, the youth pastor should make his program an exciting place to be. The large group time, whether it be Sunday morning, Wednesday night, or Monday night, should be one that is alive with music, activity, and fellowship. To have any kind of spiritual development, the young person must be physically and mentally awake. An atmosphere that wakes up the teenager in this manner would be spiritually advantageous.

After using program-centered methodology, the youth minister should begin using individual-centered methods. Once the crowds have come and the Gospel has been presented, those who have made decisions should be contacted for further spiritual growth. Assisting a young person to be born again is a small step in relation to the many steps he will have to take throughout his spiritual maturity. If there has been a weakness in youth ministries, it has been the spiritual follow-up of new teenage believers.

Follow-Up

The problem with following up on new adolescent believers is not with methods. There are canned follow-up programs to satisfy the spiritual qualifications of any youth pastor. The real problem has been with the attitude of follow-up. Follow-up is not a method; it is a lifelong process. Instead of its being a series of booklets to read and fill out, it is a daily process of growth and development. Of course there are principles that must be learned, such as confession of sin, forgiving others, witnessing, consecration, etc. Yet just as an infant has to learn how to walk, eat with a fork, and drink out of a cup over a period of time, so the newborn Christian must learn principles of growth over a long period of time.

Spiritual Growth

Just as a baby needs adult assistance in learning, so the new Christian will need the assistance of spiritually more mature Christians. This task falls into the hands of the youth pastor. Of course, he cannot do this vital task by himself, and he should train others to assist him. Follow-up should consist of letters that encourage the new believer; phone calls and personal visits are also important. Yet it should not stop here. It is equally important to show that the Christian life is an everyday experience, not just for Sunday morning. The youth pastor and leaders should set an example that portrays Christian maturity in every aspect of life, including family, school, occupation, recreation, and spiritual life. This maturity should also be evident in relationships, decision making, and reactions to problems. The Christian life should be portrayed to the effect that if it is sufficient for dying, it is sufficient for living. The psychological makeup of an adolescent is preoccupied with living in the present tense. A life that exemplifies the abundance that only *Christ* can give would do much to reinforce the adolescent's new life in Christ.

It is important to remember that they are babes in Christ and have *much* to learn. Some of the adults in our church fail to realize that the youth's ideas, standards, and convictions may be completely different than the adults' own. We should not judge, criticize, or condemn less mature young people but rather accept, love, and pray for them. Rather than telling them to have devotions, it would be better for us to show them how. For the first few days, we could supervise their reading and study the Bible with them. We should help them establish a prayer life. Study some of the prayer passages together and discuss the mechanics of prayer. Guide them into formulating a prayer list, and then spend time praying with them. They will learn much from our example. Maybe it would be possible to take the individuals with us when we do visitation and let them see how witnessing can be done.[8]

Effective follow-up of young people also involves building friendships. Too often youth ministers and youth leaders are quick to provide spiritual guidance, yet at the same time they are neglectful of personal needs and problems that seem to have no connections with spirituality. The youth pastor should not be afraid to develop friendships with those he helps to grow spiritually. He should be involved and interested in other areas of an adolescent's life. Through these friendships, the youth pastor can teach balanced Christian lifestyles via his example. A young Christian will always have peer pressure. He will need the instruction and encouragement of his youth pastor and youth leaders to strengthen a life that is lived by scriptural principles.

The key word that would unite the program-centered ministry and the individual-centered ministry is *balance*. Balance is also needed in the area of holiness. Christian young people should not only be known for what they do not do. Instead they should be known for what they do for the Lord and for their love for others. A second key word would be *purpose*. "By revealing a purpose statement, you'll take away the mystery of your ministry. A clear purpose statement will help you make sense of your programs, utilize your volunteers more effectively, and provide direction for your students' spiritual maturity."[9] For a youth program to be well rounded, accomplishing its stated purpose, there must be some kind of programming that meets the needs of students at various levels of commitment. This would include those who are not into religion at all and those who need to be motivated to move forward in their faith.

CHRISTIAN YOUTH ORGANIZATIONS

When it comes to different types of youth work, one cannot neglect the differences between the local church and the Christian youth organization (or parachurch). These two entities have taught each other a lot. In fact, they need each other. It is an uneasy relationship. Having been on both sides of the ecclesiastical "fence," I, Steve, have seen these distinctives, both positive and negative. (My experiences have taken me to local church youth ministries in southern California; Tennessee; and Edmonton, Alberta, Canada, both as a youth pastor in the local church and as the executive director with Youth for Christ.)

In each of my experiences, I embraced the freedoms and limitations of each, without any malice or bitterness to the opposite side of the "fence." I was immersed in whatever form of ministry I was involved.

I have personally never cared for the term *parachurch*. It carries a negative connotation as other prefixed words, like para-psychology, paranormal, etc. In other words, parachurch organizations are outside the norm and may appear a bit odd and out of the ordinary, even to the extreme of something to be feared and avoided. For the most part, Christian youth organizations are not of the mainstream but are not abnormal. Of course, there are some who feel the opposite is true.

Views of the Parachurch

In Jerry White's book *The Church and the Parachurch: An Uneasy Marriage,* he describes six theological perspectives regarding the "parachurch."[10]

1. Local church only. The view judges any structure outside the local congregation as illegitimate. All mission sending or other efforts must be under the direct authority of a local congregation.
2. Temporary legitimacy. This view believes that the local church is God's primary agency for ministry in the world. However, para-local church structures have been raised up for a temporary corrective influence on the local church. When the church begins meeting the need as it should, para-local church structures should disappear.
3. Two structures. The local church and the mobile church are two distinct biblical structures in God's plan. The local congregation meets the growth needs of a body of believers. The mobile function is the mission outreach of evangelizing and discipling in the world.
4. Church planting. This position gives legitimacy to para-local

church societies as long as their goal is church planting. It is insufficient to simply perform a part of the function of a church, such as evangelism, if a direct result is not integration into an existing congregation or planting a new one.

5. Dual legitimacy. Dual legitimacy indicates that both the local congregation and para-local church are legitimate expressions of God working in the body of Christ. It permits varied kinds of structures both in missions and local expressions. Since all are part of the broader body of Christ, individual believers, though part of a local congregation, express their ministry to the world in a variety of semi-autonomous structures. This differs from the two-structures view in that it does not require the two-structures analysis and would allow for nonmobile paralocal church agencies (a rescue mission, a local businessmen's outreach, a seminary) and nonmissionary specialists.
6. Anti-institutional. This view looks upon the church in its institutions, organizations, and buildings as ineffective and unnecessary. It seeks nearly total freedom in individual expression with resistance to authority from either a local or para-local church.

The defining characteristic of a Christian youth organization is that it stands outside of the organizational structure of well-established religious bodies. The autonomy of the Christian youth organization from established religious bodies allows a much greater degree of flexibility for innovation than is possible within an established organizational hierarchy. Christian youth organizations are often the creation of an entrepreneur or a small group of motivated people who seek to achieve specific ministry goals.

The Place of Christian Youth Organizations

The Christian youth organization is effectively a new form of religious organization that dates from the early nineteenth century. In the first quarter of the nineteenth century, Christian organizations were abundant in many forms—Bible tract societies, independent educational organizations (Bible colleges and schools), independent missionary groups, and moral reform organizations. The Christian organization model is the most significant organizational form in urban revivalism from the early nineteenth century. In the twentieth century, major religious broadcasters could be characterized as Christian organizations. Although Christian organizations are organizationally autonomous, they typically function with a considerable degree of interdependence with established religious organizations.

In an article written by Randal Matheny, he suggests three qualifications of Christian organizations.[11] "First, the mission of any Christian ministry must be the mission of Christ, to seek and save the lost" (Mark 10:45; Luke 19:10). Some Christian youth organizations "may especially fall prey to substituting good works and relief to hurting young people for preaching the good news of salvation." The ultimate goal is to present the Gospel to lost young people. Strategies must be in place to ensure that this most important goal is reached. Second, Christian youth organizations must be composed of Christians. We might think that this idea is a given, but it is not. Christian youth organizations that include people who do not hold convictions about the Gospel will inevitably compromise our message to the lost. So how in the world can they "hear" if they don't have a messenger? The critical point would be a clear distinction between *Christian* and *religious*. They are as different as night and day to the believer, but to the nonbeliever, they are not. We must make that distinction. The third and final qualification is that Christian youth organizations must not replace the local church.

> At any point where a ministry begins to obscure the local church in its work, it loses its reason for existence. Most ministries purport to "assist" [or "come alongside"] the local church to fulfill its mission, but many actually invade its territory to form an artificial organization foreign to the New Testament plan.

Preston Graham Jr. says,

> We therefore recognize the possible role and prudential value of various parachurch organizations in so far as they complement, and not compete with, the church. We believe that the parachurch, by self-definition in its use of the word "para," logically presupposes the church as an essential element of the gospel. Therefore, a "parachurch" organization seeks to complement and assist the church rather than to compete with the church for the church's spiritual jurisdiction. We believe that the parachurch can have a legitimate and powerful function until it functions to usurp the divinely sanctioned ministry of the church. At the same time, the church must recognize her limited mission and her purely spiritual jurisdiction; in those matters beyond her pale, she must yield to other organizations.
>
> Although we will not require participation in a parachurch organization as essential to Biblical discipleship, we may allow it, and at times even encourage such participation up until the point that it compromises the church's responsibility for spiritual oversight. There are many ways in which a person's needs can be uniquely met, and their ministry specially enhanced, through involvement with a parachurch organization. We recognize and encourage these potential benefits as long as the relationship does not undermine the authority of the church. We believe that a person who desires to place his/her life under the care and oversight of a local church is doing the proper thing so as to satisfy the Great Commission. This ought never to be considered as hindering or competing with the parachurch whose mission by definition is to assist the church. Since the mission of the church and parachurch ought to be complementary and not competing, so should an individual's involvement be coordinated so as to assist each in their proper mission.[12]

Others are not so kind or edifying toward Christian youth organizations. Stephen E. Mays asks the question,

What is a para-church organization? Any organization attempting to minister in the name of Jesus Christ that is not under the authority of a local church and the God given authority in that church, the pastor, is a para-church organization. This would include any Christian radio station, any mission agency, any Christian college or university, any organization whose goal is to minister to or evangelize a particular group, or any newspaper or other publication that is not based in a local church. . . . The Word of God has no promises of any kind for the para-church organization. In fact the para-church organization has no basis in Scripture at all. The only body directed to carry out the work of the ministry is the local churches. Any other organization taking upon itself the authority or responsibility given to the churches is not only non-biblical, but as I believe I can demonstrate, is anti-church as well.[13]

One conservative magazine says this about Christian youth organizations,

The responsibility of fulfilling the Great Commission, therefore, lies with local churches, and not with para-church organizations, nor with individuals. Today, there are many individuals who, out of misguided zeal, set themselves to the task of fulfilling the Great Commission. They are not committed to the life of any local church, and they attend church only at their convenience. They look upon the evangelisation of the lost as their chief service to the Lord. We are not saying that this is wrong in itself. They are wrong, however, in doing it out of the context of the local church. They are answerable to no one but themselves. Since the Great Commission has been wrested out of the proper context of the church, they are able only to fulfil it partially.[14]

Those who say that Christian youth organizations are outside the perimeters of the local church have not experienced the dependency on the local church that Christian youth organizations have. This dependency does not validate organizations' existence, but it certainly confirms the community aspect of a local congregation and Christian youth organizations. Numerous times when I, Steve, worked with Youth for Christ we relied on our local congregation of people to assist us, whether it was personally or for the sake of our ministry. We were involved in a loving community of people who were genuinely concerned about the well-being of our ministry as well as our personal well-being.[15] The community aspect of our relationship was paramount. Our local congregation provided a loving and involved relationship that made my Christian youth organization involvement and my local congregation involvement an engaged one. Accountability was another aspect of the relationship we had with our Christian youth organization and our local congregation. People who knew us would inquire as to how we were doing as well as how the ministry was functioning. It is refreshing to be able to answer honestly to people who have your best interest at heart.

Being within a local congregation does not necessarily mean being under the authority of a local congregation. Most Christian youth organizations have bylaws and articles of operation that include the overseeing of a group of mature Christian individuals.

> It is important that para-church organizations have good and complete doctrinal and hermeneutical statements, and for their leaders to make sure their "body members" understand them. Also, their "elders," leaders, and those in the various ministries, must exemplify submission in their roles. The New Testament does not teach a "church body" is to be governed by a single authoritarian.[16]

Their responsibilities usually include seeing their mandate of specific aspects of the Great Commission accomplished. For most Christian youth organizations, that would be one or a combination of particulars of the Great Commission as found in Matthew 28:18–20 (go everywhere—make disciples—baptize them—teach them). When a Christian youth organization exists for the purpose of self-preservation, it has moved from a living and vibrant part of the church into a self-determined institution, which is not part of the church's commission. There is no question that some Christian youth organizations have slid into a self-preservation mode and should take serious ministerial inventory as to the validity of their prolonged existence.[17]

> Because Christian organizations are under the mandate to be Christian, not only to have members who are Christians, the organization itself can and must experience the impact of the Word of God and the Holy Spirit. Because Christian organizations also experience Christian community in their organizational life and function, they must exhibit the ethical mandate of demonstrating love in relationships as well as in mission. Because Christian organizations are under the mandate of theological reflection, an understanding of Biblical teachings and principles is essential to each component of the organization's life and practice.[18]

The Christian youth organization carries the Gospel beyond the gathered church in all its form and community. It is doing something that perhaps a gathered group would not have the wherewithal or the know-how to do.

Second Corinthians 5:18 says, "All things are of God, who has reconciled us to Himself through Jesus Christ, and has given us the ministry of reconciliation." Here is the ministry that God has given to all of us. It is the ministry of reconciliation. When we hear the term *reconcile,* it is usually in the context of a divorced couple. When this couple decides to get back together, it is called being reconciled. It is the coming together of two parties who were formerly estranged or alienated from each other. This coming together is a closing of the distance between the two estranged parties. So in the biblical sense, this ministry of reconciliation is given to all of us so we may close the distance between two estranged parties, namely, God and man. It is this ministry that motivates the vast majority of Christian youth organizations, because they are ever conscious of the fact that so much of what they do is closing the distance between lost young people and a loving God.

> We acknowledge that the local church is presented in scripture as the sending organization (Acts 13), but we believe God has raised up para-church agencies—denominational institutions, mission agencies, etc.—to be servant facilitators and partners in the global task. This is going to require a new respect by para-church agencies for the primacy of the local church in God's global plan. We do not believe local churches are going to have a proper partnership with para-church agencies unless para-church agencies adopt the partner paradigm and see themselves as servant facilitators of local churches, servants who are dedicated to empowering local churches to reach the world more effectively than ever.[19]

In other words, Christian youth organizations are just as much a part of the local church as the members within the local congregation. Each entity can learn from the other, and each can complement and encourage each other in carrying out the specific elements of the Great Commission.

CONCLUSION

Youth ministry takes a variety of shapes and models, complete with a blending, mixing, and matching of desirable characteristics. Just when we think we've identified a certain model, it is morphed into something that is active, spiritual, and connecting with young people. For some youth pastors, their church body defines their model. Others have the opportunity, with spiritual guidance, to shape their ministry, taking into consideration geographical and cultural adaptations, into a model that is best for their young people.

NOTES

1. Elmer Towns, *Putting an End to Worship Wars* (Nashville: Broadman & Holman, 1997), 13.
2. Doug Randlett, "A Descriptive Study of Youth Ministry Models in Evangelical Churches" (doctoral thesis, Liberty Baptist Theological Seminary, March 2000).
3. Mark H. Senter III, gen. ed., *Four Views of Youth Ministry and the Church* (Grand Rapids: Zondervan, 2001), xv.
4. Wicca is a type of witchcraft that has captured the attention of many young people, with its spells, beliefs, and a misperceived "nice" image.
5. Pat Hurley, *Penetrating the Magic Bubble* (Wheaton: Scripture Press, 1978), 13.
6. Kenda Creasy Dean, Chap Clark, and Dave Rahn, eds., *Starting Right* (Grand Rapids: Zondervan, 2001), 84.
7. Jim Klubnik, "Outreach Ministry of the Local Church," *Leaders' Resource Book* 2, ed. Fern Robertson (Wheaton: Scripture Press, 1971), 74.
8. Elmer Towns, "Evangelism and Teens," *Leader's Guide of the Local Church Youth Ministry* (Lynchburg, Va.: Thomas Road Baptist Church, 1975), 10.
9. Ginny Olson, Diane Elliot, and Mike Work, *Youth Ministry Management Tools* (Grand Rapids: Zondervan, 2001), 71.
10. Jerry White, *The Church and the Parachurch: An Uneasy Marriage* (Portland, Oreg.: Multnomah, 1983), 67–68.
11. Randal Matheny, "Are Christian Ministries Christian?" http://www.churchofchrist.pair.com/projeto/bzeal/artminis.html (accessed September 2001).
12. Preston Graham Jr., "The Church in Relation to the Parachurch." http://www.christpresnewhaven.org/sts/pamphlets/parachurch.html. (accessed September 2001).
13. Stephen E. Mays, "So, What About Para-Church Organizations?" http://www.faithbaptisttrumpet.org/trumpet/septtrumpet/para.html (accessed September 2001).
14. "Studies on the Great Commission: No 3., A Command to Local Churches," *Gospel Highway* 1 (1998), http://www.rbcm.net/gh/articles/gh98-1/a_command_to_local_churches.html (accessed September 2001).
15. You can find this church in Edmonton, Alberta, Canada. Its name is Calvary Community Church, and we were active members for nineteen years.
16. Dan Kazarian, "Parachurch Organizations," http://home1.gte.net/kazarian/ (accessed September 2001).
17. I personally witnessed the closure of a Christian youth organization. The board members had the courage and fortitude to conclude that their mandate had been fulfilled and there was no other choice but to dissolve and distribute their assets to other Christian organizations who are still in the process of fulfilling their mandate.
18. Ray S. Anderson, *Minding God's Business* (Grand Rapids: Eerdmans, 1986), 39.
19. Larry Reesor, "What Kind of Church Will It Take?" http://www.missionfrontiers.org/2000/05/reesor.htm (accessed September 2001).

4

Adolescence—A Description

Adolescence has been called a variety of things from a disease to a miracle. People look back on the years from twelve to eighteen (or somewhat earlier and later) as some of the happiest of their life—and also the most distressing. G. Stanley Hall, the father of the scientific study of adolescence, calls it a time of storm and stress. In other words, adolescence is a time of turbulence, charged with conflict and mood swings. Hall was also convinced both that adolescence was controlled by genetically determined physiological factors but also that the environment accounts for more change in development than we would like to admit. Adolescence is the age of revelation, awakening emotions, and newly discovered capabilities. It is the age of revolution against adult control and adult direction.

Adolescence is the age of anxiety and moodiness. Altogether it is the joy and pain of growing up.

This transition from childhood to adulthood brings changing attitudes and behavior that begin to show as the youngster approaches puberty. He suddenly becomes oversensitive about many things and hypercritical about his family, home, school, and church. These years are important to the junior high/middle and senior high school student. You can probably recall with ease what your last year of high school was like, but maybe you are rather hazy in the memories of your junior high school experience. (This has been called selective memory since adults tend to erase the turbulence of adolescence from their memory banks.) A great many changes take place within the adolescent male or female between junior high/middle school and graduation from high school.

WHO IS THE TEENAGER?

Actually the teenager is three persons wrapped in one. You must unwrap the coverings to get at the core of the real person in addition to who he is becoming.

THE TEENAGER'S SELF-CONCEPT

The teenager is the person he thinks he is. The teenager's self-estimation determines the approach and attitude of the youth worker. What the teenager is may or may not correspond to real life. Even though what the teenager thinks himself to be may not be the real person, his attitude will have to be understood. This will help the youth worker to determine an approach in meeting his needs.

OTHERS' CONCEPT OF THE TEENAGER

The teenager, as others see him, becomes very important to how he views himself. The opinions of his friends, teachers, parents, siblings, and youth workers are very important in determining his personality and outlook on life. Their opinions may not be accurate, but they will help the youth worker determine what the teenager really is. The teenager necessarily reacts to their evaluation of him as a person. What others think of us determines to a large extent the way we live.

The Real Teenager

The real teenager often is hidden and never brought to the surface. The real teenager is the person the youth worker is trying to reach. The true person on the inside may not be what the teenager thinks of as himself, and he may not correspond to what others think him to be. The many veneers of life must be peeled off to help the teenager understand himself as he really is. Socrates said, "Know thyself." A true self-appraisal is the first step to adjustment. Adjustment leads to happiness, confidence, and purpose in life. A false concept of one's self may lead to maladjustment and problems in life. The youth worker must remind himself that God knows the individual as he really exists. Thus the worker depends on the leadership of the Holy Spirit and the principles of God's Word to know the teenager better.

FOUR TYPES OF TEENAGERS

One of the great habits of human nature is the tendency to categorize human nature. Most new studies in physiology attempt to do this; but environment, social demands, and personality are so complex that human nature resists any attempt at stereotyping its makeup. The world has prejudged the teenager and come up with broad categories. These categories may influence business or church leaders, but they should not influence the Christian youth leader. There are four false broad categories of teenagers:

The Historical Teenager

This teenager has his existence in the minds of many adults. "Well, when I was your age, we used to . . ." is often heard from adults today. Adults remember the past when they were teenagers and try to understand teenagers today in light of their own actions. Even though adults think their images of the past are accurate, they are subject to error. With time one tends to glorify the past and, generally speaking, remember only the good things.

Teenagers do not change in their basic nature or development. The growth patterns, desires, drives, and psychological makeup remain the same. But the expression of drives and growth changes.

The historical teenager is a "springboard" used by adults to attempt to understand modern youth. The historical teenager cannot always help the adult understand youth because outer expression and inner makeup have been confused. The historical teenager is not a real teenager and exists only in the minds of adults recalling the past.

The Statistical Teenager

The statistical teenager is one who affects much of life today; however, this teenager does not exist. Many business firms receive substantial income for interviewing teenagers, conducting polls, and arriving at opinions on how the average teenager lives, thinks, and reacts. Statistics are used to sell products and encourage fads, movements, and commercial enterprises. The statistical teenager does not exist—he has his existence only on paper. Statistics do tell a story, but statistics can be manipulated. What is more significant is that teenagers will almost always strive to be anything but what statistics say they should be.

THE COMMERCIAL TEENAGER

The modern media of communication present a vivid picture of teenagers. Movies, television, and music present the teenager today on one hand as nearing physiological perfection and on the other extreme as a promiscuous juvenile delinquent. The commercial teenage boy is very typical in his appearance. He looks like the latest TV commercial or an ad for a sports magazine. The commercial teenager does not have a real existence. He exists in the minds of the modern media-oriented audience.

THE IDEAL TEENAGER

Much is written, portrayed, and discussed concerning the ideal teenager. The ideal is supposed to be a median between the extremes of terrible and wonderful. He is better than "average"; he is desired. Much is said concerning the "ideal" teenager today. Scholars and psychologists try to understand him. Teenagers try to imitate him. However, the ideal teenager does not exist.

So who are teenagers? They are the ones who venture into our ministries because someone showed them some attention. Or maybe they cross our programming path because our activity was designed with teenagers in mind. They are the ones who may annoy us because they fool around when we are trying to get their attention. They are the ones who man most fast-food chains and serve us when we are in a hurry. They are the ones who step out in front of our cars when we happen to be passing through a school zone. They fill our malls, cruise our streets, jam our stadiums, and stay up really late at night. Teenagers are your children or your neighbor's children. They are individuals who need to hear the message of hope in Christ.

THE AVERAGE TEENAGER

Today's teenagers need to be understood, and they need to be helped. You must have a clear picture of them before you can help in their developmental process. You must understand adolescent needs, characteristics, desires, and interests.

Most people feel that teenagers are unstable. Instability may or may not be true of teenagers. However, how can we expect them to be stable in today's shaken world? The effects of world wars, destructive and violent behavior, the daily talk of world terrorism, and the unprecedented number of broken homes have all taken their toll on the lives of teenagers. When we talk about instability of our teenagers, we need also to take a look at ourselves. Are we stable? We tend to think that we were more stable as teenagers than we actually were. Perhaps we are bewildered by the behavior of our teenagers because we have forgotten our own youthful behavior and/or misbehavior.

Teenagers must be accepted for what they are rather than for what we expect them to be. Our expectations are usually called "normal" or "average." If we are not careful, this "normal" or "average" becomes the standard set for all teenagers. The average teenager will fall short of the normal or average standard at some point. Usually the church is very negative and condemnatory, and the teenager who falls short (which includes all teenagers in at least one point) is frustrated. Church leaders sometimes cause more frustrations for teenagers than they imagine.

In his book *All Grown Up and No Place to Go,* Dr. David Elkind describes teenagers in a simple yet profound way.[1] First, teenagers are beginning to think. This can be unnerving for parents and adults alike, who might be surprised at this fact. Instead of asking "What?" teenagers are asking "Why?" The "why" question can be intimidating. But we should not be unnerved. Instead, we should do our best to answer their "why" questions and have the courage to say "I don't know" when we don't know. Youth ministry should not shy away from this question. Young people are learning to define their tastes, values, and preferences. They are learning what they like and dislike. Youth ministry is an exciting opportunity to help define what goes on inside the mind of an adolescent. Not only will youth ministry aid in their apologetics, but youth ministry will take young people through experiences and activities that they will carry with them well into their adult years.[2]

Young people need to be challenged to think for themselves. They need to be challenged to do their own thinking and not the thinking of media moguls or even the thinking of the group. This kind of thinking takes time and energy and sometimes personal research and investigation. Thinking can be hard work. Paul said, "Finally, brethren, whatever is true, whatever is honorable, whatever is right, whatever is pure, whatever is lovely, whatever is of good repute . . . dwell on these things" (Phil. 4:8 NASB). Peter said, "Therefore, prepare your minds for action" (1 Peter 1:13 NASB).

I, Steve, have had parents complain to me, "My teenager argues for the sake of arguing!" Precisely! Because they are becoming cognitively aware, they want to argue. Teenagers are argumentative. They need help in distinguishing between arguing as an exercise in thinking or an exercise in trying to persuade. Parents/adults are threatened when teens begin to question and argue. This mental exercise disguised as arguing can be an engaging experience. Many times the argument, unfortunately, escalates to a point where the parents'/adults' voices are raised, the veins in their necks are protruding, and blood pressure numbers are dangerously high. As adults, we should attempt to defuse emotionally charged subjects (music styles, clothing styles, etc.), while giving them opportunity to argue. First Peter 3:15 admonishes us to always be "ready to make a defense to everyone who asks you to give an account for the hope that is in you, yet with gentleness and reverence" (NASB).

Teenagers tend to be self-centered. They feel that everything that happens to them is unique and original. They can be overheard proclaiming, "It can't happen to me," or "No one has it as bad as me." What can adults do? Adults can help by pointing out how other people are unique too. We can learn from other people's experiences.

Teenagers have difficulty making decisions. Yet when teens are forced to make decisions, they often come up with choices that seem misinformed and unusual. This is the main reason that they like fast-food joints. The choices are easy.

The critical difference between adults and teenagers in decision making is experience. Guidance will need to be given in the decision-making process.[3]

Teenagers appear to be hypocritical. They are vocal about their ideals but often fail in carrying out actions that go along with them. Young people need to engage in meaningful work, the application of their faith. Adolescent ministry can be the bridge that moves adolescent ideals into useful and practical application. James 1:22 makes it clear that our obedience to Scripture has two key elements: "Do not merely listen to the word, and so deceive yourselves. Do what it says" (NIV).

Teenagers can also be religious or spiritual. They are moving from an institutional religion to a private faith. It is critical during adolescence that young people move from their parental faith (the faith that they have grown up with or inherited) to a personal faith. Only when their faith becomes personal does it become meaningful and real. This is an important responsibility of youth workers to move young people to faith that is their own. Young people value their privacy. The idea of a personal God seems like a great idea, because God keeps confidences!

Chapter 3 raised the issue of markers and their significance in an adolescent's life. Markers cannot be overlooked or minimized. Even the Scriptures indicate markers in the apostle Paul's life and in the life of Christ. First Corinthians 13:11 says, "It's like this: when I was a child I spoke and thought and reasoned as a child does. But when I became a man my thoughts grew far beyond those of my childhood, and now I have put away the childish things" (TLB). Luke 2:42–52 describes what Jesus' parents found when they could not find Jesus. In verse 47, Jesus was respectfully interacting with the elders in the temple. He was listening and asking questions, and His answers were amazing those present. Verse 52 says, "So Jesus grew both tall and wise, and was loved by God and man" (TLB). Jesus' markers included His physiology, His mental capabilities, His relationship with people, and His relationship with God. It would do the youth worker good if he or she recognized and celebrated these markers in an attempt to bring back a milestone in an adolescent's life that would otherwise be overlooked or ignored.

NOTES

1. David Elkind, *All Grown Up and No Place to Go: Teenagers in Crisis,* rev. ed. (Reading, Mass.: Addison-Wesley, 1998).
2. Even though a maturing faith is what we strive for in youth ministry, the very nature of youth ministry includes activities that young people will want to pursue and develop for years to come. It may come in the form of winter sports, water sports, extreme sports, team and individual sports, music, outdoor activities (including backpacking, white-water rafting, rock climbing or bouldering, rappelling, spelunking, Tyrolean traversing, and mountain biking at Frontier Lodge in Nordegg, Alberta), amusement parks, just to name a few.
3. The following is a suggested grid of questions to be used in the decision-making process:
   - Is there any conflict or admonition from the Scriptures?
   - What are other people saying, especially your parents or, at the very minimum, spiritual friends who have your best interest at heart?
   - Are there any promptings from the Holy Spirit?
   - What would be the most spiritually advantageous decision?
   - Do circumstances line up with the previous questions?
   - Are there any negative or harmful irreversible consequences?
   - Once you've made the decision, can you make it work?

Age Characteristics of Teenagers

Teenagers are developing in several areas at the same time.[1] They are growing in their physical, mental, emotional, social, and spiritual development.

Personality theorists, notably Erik Erikson and his followers, feel that the most important psychological task of the adolescent is to integrate the various aspects of their rapidly changing selves into a coherent identity. If they are unable to successfully accomplish this integration they risk becoming fragmented and confused about who they are and how they should behave at any given time.[2] The intent of this chapter is to divide the teen life into four areas and examine each area separately. The four areas in order are: physical, mental, emotional, and social. Spiritual development is related to all four and integrated into the total growth pattern.

PHYSICAL DEVELOPMENT OF TEENAGERS

Teenagers think of themselves primarily as physical, even though other factors enter into their life. For them, the body is the main factor they bring into adolescence. The body develops and changes, but still it is the same body. To this body are added the factors of mental, emotional, and social development. All of these go to make up the personality of the teenager. The personality may be radically transformed during the teenage years. The development of the inner life is important. However, the teenagers consider their bodies the most important factor in development—whether they are or not.

The physical changes, which revolutionize the body during adolescence, have a very significant effect on the other phases of life. In general, there are three stages of physical growth through which teens pass: early, middle, and late.

THE EARLY PERIOD

During the early period, covering ages ten through fourteen, young people experience the effects of puberty. Puberty is a time when the adolescent matures sexually—the earliest age at which a person is capable of procreating offspring. Young people experience a rapid and uneven rate of growth during puberty. A boy will find himself buying a size larger shoe every time he visits a shoe store, and a girl will find herself three inches taller within seven months. As a result of these staggering rates of growth, this early teenage group experiences lack of coordination. Before adolescence the youngster takes all of these changes in stride, but not so in the adolescent period. His acute sensitivity has made any changes in his body a small crisis.

Teenagers are self-conscious. Now that teenagers can think

about thinking, they can think about what goes on not only in their head, but also in the heads of others. They assume that everyone around them is concerned about the same thing they are concerned about . . . namely, themselves! This is called an "imaginary audience." It is also referred to as adolescent egocentrism. The heightened self-consciousness of adolescents is reflected in their belief that others are as interested in them as they themselves are.[3] Teens feel that they are always on stage and everyone is concerned about their appearance and behavior.

What can adults do with self-conscious adolescents? Adults can help by avoiding public criticism and ridicule. Be more sensitive about public exposure. Don't ever point out physiological features (you don't have to remind a teenager that she has a complexion problem or that his feet are huge or his ears protrude; teens are well aware of their physical shortcomings). This kind of public scrutiny at the expense of a teenager does nothing but damage, both internally as well as relationally. Fortunately, as young people grow older, their concern with the imaginary audience diminishes.

Adults can make adolescents even more self-conscious by labels! We have all types of labels: temperament labels (choleric, melancholy, phlegmatic, sanguine); doctrinal/denominational labels (dispensationalist, pretribulationist, Calvinist, fundamentalist, neoevangelist); negative ethnic stereotypical labels; negative social stereotypical labels; even name-calling. The problem with labels is that they can be wrong, and young people tend to live up (or down) to those labels. Proverbs 12:17–23 encourages us to be careful in our selection of words, along with their benefits and consequences:

> A truthful witness gives honest testimony, but a false witness tells lies. Reckless words pierce like a sword, but the tongue of the wise brings healing. Truthful lips endure forever, but a lying tongue lasts only a moment. There is deceit in the hearts of those who plot evil, but joy for those who promote peace. No harm befalls the righteous, but the wicked have their fill of trouble. The

LORD detests lying lips, but he delights in men who are truthful. A prudent man keeps his knowledge to himself, but the heart of fools blurts out folly. (NIV)

Youth workers must have real patience in working with teenagers who are growing into adolescence. Physiological changes sometimes trigger psychological problems. The early teenager's concern for his physical appearance is so complete that it overshadows all else. He must learn to accept himself as he is. He must learn to accept his body as given by God.

Since fluctuations of mood and energy are characteristic of the teenage period of life, it does little good to lecture teenagers. The youth counselor who plays down the lethargy of the teenager and capitalizes on his bursts of energy will accomplish the most. The teenager is extremely serious about himself and wants to be taken seriously. Fear of ridicule concerning his appearance can shut the teenager off to any and all outside help. The teenager desires his leader to have a sense of humor, but this sense of humor must never be turned upon the physique of the teenager.

Teenagers must be prepared to travel this path to adulthood. Build a solid foundation for their growth. During the early stage of physical development, young people are experiencing the breakdown of many old habits; they are left wide open to acquiring new habits—we hope they are better habits. Make sure that teenagers are well prepared to meet this change in life. Furnish them with good information and personal counsel so they may meet this rapid growth intelligently. Physical adjustment and maturity constitute the first and important step toward spiritual adjustment and maturity.

THE MIDDLE PERIOD

During the middle period, ages fifteen through eighteen, the growth rate levels off and decreases. The body has almost assumed its adult proportion. The girl reaches her optimum size physically at age seventeen, while the guy reaches his physical peak at age twenty-two. As a result the teen feels more confident and life is tackled with a greater degree of daring and independence.

The Late Period

In the late stage, covering ages nineteen through twenty-four, the guys catch up with the girls in maturity, never to lag behind again except in individual cases. This age group is characterized by physical maturity, the assumption of adult responsibilities, and the realization of adult proportions. The personality is becoming fully developed, and the young person is off on new and exciting paths leading to adulthood.

During the late stage of growth, habits are fairly well formed, physical patterns are established, and lives are evidencing the foundations and impressions gained through previous years.

Guiding Principles for Dealing with Physical Development

1. *Create acceptance of physical makeup.*

The body is given to the teenager from God. To a certain extent he is small, tall, fat, or an invalid because God has given him his body. The youth leader must lead the teenager not only to accept his body but to realize God gave it to him for a reason. The attractive girl must not glory in her beauty, nor must the obese teen with acne and unattractive features be bitter or disappointed at God. You, as the youth worker, must never make fun of a guy who is awkward, nor must you praise too highly the attractive girl. Adjustment and maturity come in acceptance of one's self.

2. *Develop scriptural attitudes toward the body.*

The teenager must be taught that the "body is the temple of the Holy Spirit" (1 Cor. 6:19). His body is not to be abused, nor is it to be used in violation of scriptural principles. The Bible teaches that the body is not to be used as a vehicle for sinful purposes. Avoid any action or conversation that degenerates character, destroys inhibitions or modesty, or makes fun of morals. There should be restraint in the area of grossness. Simply because it will get a laugh due to the shock value should never be justification for its use. The teenager considers his body important. He dresses it to extremes, develops it, magnifies sexual attributes, and stuffs his stomach with hamburgers and pizza. The youth worker must get the youth to view his body as God does.

3. *See the body as a vehicle for worship and service.*

God desires the teenager to bring his body under control of the inner man. This is called discipline. When most of society teaches uninhibited freedom, the Bible calls for self-control. "If anyone desires to come after Me, let him deny himself, and take up his cross daily, and follow Me" (Luke 9:23). The body is to be controlled and used as an instrument to serve and glorify God. This is not a negative attitude. Paul said, "I discipline my body and bring it into subjection" (1 Cor. 9:27). By this he meant the body should not be a hindrance to service but should become a means of service. The teenager must see his body as a vehicle given to serve and glorify the God who gave it to him.

MENTAL DEVELOPMENT OF TEENAGERS

"I cannot understand teenagers," most people will argue. What makes our teenagers think the way they think? Where do they get their wild styles? Have you ever noticed how interested they are in trivial things?

Often adults try to put teenagers into an "adult mold" and try to understand them. The teenager vehemently insists that he is an adult when he isn't. The teenager doesn't think as an adult but as a teenager.

The Early Teen

First, let's look at the early teen—the junior high school student. These young people love to daydream. Why? This mental preoccupation involves thought and will lay the basis for forming character and opinions as the years pass on. Daydreams can be healthy in building the aspirations of teenagers. Daydreams, at the same time, can be harmful. The teenager may set ideals for himself that are way out of proportion to his personality, physical build, and ability. Daydreaming could develop into lusting for sexual pleasures, material possessions, and adulation of others.

At this stage of life, present Christ—the most valid Hero of all. If teenagers pattern their lives after Christ, they will have a successful and fruitful development to Christian maturity. Can your teenagers see Christ in you? Shouldn't they?

How can they find out about Christ? What influences them daily? Literature is a constant part of their lives; make sure that they are supplied with good literature.

In the early teenage years their memories are keen, so supply them with memory work that will build good foundations. In order to stimulate good memory work, give them reasons that you are asking them to memorize. Teenagers won't memorize to obtain a prize—if they are typical teenagers. But they will memorize toward the end that their lives will be more like the Christ with whom they seek to identify.

Don't fill teenage heads with knowledge that is too deep or lofty. Treat and teach them as adults, but give them facts that are simple and concrete. We will build a solid spiritual life if we give them simple but understandable truths that meet their needs at their age level.

Teenagers love to laugh. But underneath the thin veneer of frivolity is a serious, searching mind. Teenagers are cruel in their humor and you may become the butt of their joke. If they laugh at you to your face—good—but if they laugh behind your back—beware. Even Christian teenagers test people through humor. Their first impressions of you will determine your effectiveness with them. Be able to laugh with them, even if their humor turns against you.

Quick judgment is characteristic of adolescence. Teenagers do not think through a problem, and their discrimination is not always best. They are capable of much serious thinking, but since they haven't had a lot of experience with thinking, they may stop at first impressions. You must "stretch" the minds of your young people. When you lead a group discussion, have your material together. Be prepared with information and facts. You may have to challenge a young person who is not thinking deeply or logically.

Teenagers follow the leader, especially in mental suggestibility. You should get next to the group leader and influence the group through him. Not only can you better influence the group, but this leader may enlighten you as to the needs of your youth group. He holds the key to the others' affection and respect.

The young junior high/middle school students are in the midst of puberty. They are inquisitive about religious matters, but they are determined that you not know about it. Inwardly they are searching for answers, but outwardly they may be obstinate in rejecting yours. As they experiment with their new reasoning processes, they are filled with doubts and uncertainties. One day they may seek and need your advice; the next day they will ignore you completely.

Unpredictable? Yes! At this confusing time of life, present to your boys and girls an image of stable and consistent spiritual maturity. Their ego receives a shock when they find they can't count on themselves. May they learn to count and depend on you.

THE HIGH SCHOOL STUDENT

Take a look in the high school age group. Note one outstanding characteristic: These teenagers are extremely critical. Why? They have just come through puberty, and their greatest developmental task is answering the question, "Who am I?" Before puberty, the young person thought of himself primarily as a physical body. The young person is seeking to find out who he is, even though he can't verbalize his search. Adolescence could be called "a search for self."

Teens' Idealism

Teenagers are idealistic. They are idealistic about a world of peace, the church, and their family. Unfortunately their idealism has been let down. Parents aren't perfect. Families have all kinds of shortcomings. The world has proven to be a deadly place, with peace becoming ever so scarce and so costly. Even our churches have not measured up to adolescent idealism. As a result of this, young people have become very critical. They have the mentality "The grass is greener on the other side of the fence." Their criticisms should not be taken too seriously, but they should not go unanswered. We should do our best to demonstrate that just because someone or something is imperfect, it should not necessarily be ignored or discarded. Although perfection is something that will happen only in our heavenly afterlife, we can always be part of a solution, instead of part of the problem.

When it comes to people, no one is infallible. We should show respect without worshiping. We should be objective rather than cynical when people fail us. The Scriptures seem to encourage investigation without arrogance, and honesty tempered with responsibility and commitment. In Acts 17:11, the believers were "examining the Scriptures daily to see whether these things were so" (NASB). First Corinthians 3:7 says, "So then neither the one who plants nor the one who waters is anything, but

God who causes the growth" (NASB). Proverbs 27:5–6 (NASB) says, "Better is open rebuke than love that is concealed. Faithful are the wounds of a friend, but deceitful are the kisses of an enemy" (the key word being *friend*).

Teenagers expect the *best, ultimate,* or *optimum* of everybody and everything. Anybody who doesn't live up to their standards is criticized—even you. They criticize mother, father, sister, and pastor. These teenagers haven't lived long enough to recognize their own limitations. They will criticize parents for not producing, but they themselves can't produce by their own standards.

Teenagers constantly test others by their own standards. No matter how hard an adult attempts to please the teenager, it is not good enough. At the same time youth are not always free in expressing their opinions unless they have a high opinion of you. If the kids sit around and complain about the youth program, they probably criticize you behind your back. When they make you the target for criticism—face-to-face—be of good cheer; they love you. Open discussion can be a means of their spiritual growth.

When you plan your youth programs, keep the young people's criticism in mind. Allow opportunities for them to express their judgments. Let them know that you will not accept mediocrity, so why should they? Give opportunities for group evaluation. When they criticize without a basis, call them on it. Analyze their faulty reasoning and show them where they are off on a tangent. Cultivate an attitude in your youth group that we all learn through our mistakes.

Critical thinking can lead to creative thinking. Give opportunity for creativity in the high school department. The important thing is that we guide teenagers through this period of critical analysis. When the teen has learned to become "person-centered," thinking of others as well as self, he is on the road to maturity. So you should learn to understand the needs of teenagers at each level and seek to meet them accordingly.

Do you give advice to the teenagers? Be cautious! If you offer advice, remember they are very critical. They believe they are experts in most fields. Provide good Christian literature for them. Christian fiction, biographies, and devotional books will help.

Teens' Guidance

Don't judge your teenagers by the standards you had when you were in adolescence. The Word of God is our eternal standard. Styles of clothes and music change. We must seek to understand the subculture of the teenage life. They live in a stress-filled society. Still, teenagers are very susceptible to suggestion—especially if they think they decided it for themselves. As a youth leader, use diplomacy and tact, but above all be understanding and tolerant.

Christian teenagers should be diligent in choosing "the path of life." As a youth director, provide them with biographical studies of men and women of God who have achieved their own goals in life. These biographies help them know *how* to go about achieving their own goals. Provide them with good reasons for scriptural study and Bible memorization. These teenagers demand to know what the Bible will help them achieve in life. Emphasize "how-to" programs.

These late adolescents have a budding cultural life. Their tastes and appreciation are growing and developing. Show them the beauty of a personality when Christ has control of the life, again demonstrating the practical results of a Christ-centered life.

In the field of humor, it is still important that you be able to take a joke—one aimed at you as well as at others. The humor of teenagers at this stage of life has become more subtle—more personal. They like to match wits with one another and enjoy laughing at themselves when the joke is on them. You must be willing and able to join in too. Because the youth in the upper teens has increasing ability to think along constructive lines, allow opportunities for him to use his abilities and ideas. Be ready to advise and counsel when needed. The youth should be permitted and encouraged to plan and promote a special program. Their specialized interest and vitality can do much for your youth program.

Discipline problems are greatly lessened in the later teens. Rational thinking can be the appeal for good conduct. Serious discussion about behavior can yield much fruit. They will measure your influence by the life you live before them. They can spot a "phony" more quickly than the younger teen. If you don't really desire to spend time with them—don't. They will sense your true attitude and then your words will really have no effect.

Teens' Decisions

"What am I going to be?" Often the first major choice with far-reaching implications the teenager must make is between a college preparation course and a general high school program. What he is going to be after he graduates from high school is usually begun by his high school course program.

High schools of today are increasingly pushing teenagers to decide their vocational future. The vocational choice is one of the major developmental tasks the adolescent must make—before he is equipped or ready to make such a decision.

The factors surrounding a sound vocational choice are complex. The adolescent probably does not know enough about work to choose a vocation that will continue to be satisfying to him after high school. Families sometimes pressure a teenager into a field for which he has little aptitude or interest. Sometimes the choice of a job boils down to the social status or amount of money a young person wants. There are many other factors to be considered. Will the job offer hours and wages that are acceptable? What about security? Does the young person want to work with people or things, with his mind or with his hands? Does he want to be dependent or independent? Does he want to work for himself or for others? Can he take orders? What kind of job or profession will make him happy? The amount of vocational guidance given to teenagers in school is gradually increasing. Much more effective guidance needs to be given by the churches.

A common opinion today is that any teenager can do anything after he graduates from high school. The world is lying at the doorstep of every graduate—only to be conquered. Any teenager can go from a log cabin to the White House. This may be the common reaction and outlook on job opportunities today—but this is not the scriptural attitude, and it doesn't fit with experience.

The Scriptures teach that there is a gift (a capacity for service) given by God to every young person. The teaching of spiritual gifts (Romans 12; 1 Corinthians 12; Ephesians 4) is a needed subject for teenagers today. The Bible teaches that every person is given a capacity for service both in and out of the church. Therefore, every young person should find the will of God for his life and the call of God for His service.

Some feel that only young people entering full-time service receive a call from God and have a place in the will of God. This is not true. Every young person has a call of God (see chapter 10 for a more detailed discussion of the call of God) and a capacity of service given by God—whether this is to be a homemaker, a public school teacher, a nurse, or a vocational minister.

Adolescence is an impressionable stage of life. Use every opportunity to demonstrate a positive relationship of the Christian Gospel. You may have to treat the teenagers as adults and yet understand that they are young and unsure of themselves. They need positive and consistent counsel, even though they will adamantly insist on independence. "We don't need your help" is the cry of teenagers, and they reject our advice. But underneath, they appreciate guidance and example. They will accept, mimic, and produce your life in theirs if you are worthy. Your best avenue to worthiness: Produce Christ's life in yours.

The College Student

The college student is beginning to worry about his life and how he is going to achieve. Wages, vocational goals, marriage, and personal abilities are foremost in his thinking. Young people need to face the seriousness of decision making and then live with the results. Give them guidelines to direct their lives, make decisions, and face problems of adult life.

Constructive thinking is characteristic of late adolescents. They are becoming more consistent in guiding their own personality and career advancement. As they arrive at a better understanding of themselves, they narrow down their interests to specialized areas that fit more suitably with their personality. When Laura has to choose a college major, she is forced to consider her own desires in life and her abilities to carry out those desires. John has to choose a profession, so he gives it serious consideration.

Guiding Principles for Mental Development

The youth leader will want to apply the following principles in guiding the mental development of teenagers to full maturity in Jesus Christ.

1. *Never laugh at their problems.*

The youth leader will have to accept the mental struggles of youth. If you tend to belittle the teenager and laugh at his problems, you can never minister to him. Also, beware of easy "cure-all" answers to problems. The youth needs empathy and understanding when he is struggling with a problem.

2. *Recognize religious and spiritual doubts.*

Some youth workers are disturbed when their youth have doubts. They should be concerned for teenagers who have no doubts. Growth comes through stress and pressure. Mental growth results from mental stresses. The youth faces opinions that contradict childhood beliefs. As the youth struggles to synthesize all information coming to him into a consistent belief, he will have doubts. This is when the youth leader is needed. The youth must be guided through doubts to spiritual reality.

3. *Provide leadership built on an intelligent interpretation of the Bible.*

Youth demand answers to the doubts that face them. The Word of God has the answer to the mental problems of young people. Their answers are not found in rationalism, logic, or science. However, the Bible when correctly interpreted will be viewed rationally, logically, and scientifically. The Bible will then speak to the problems of youth in an intelligent manner. When the Bible is thus approached by a literal, inductive interpretation, the results will be embraced by the teen looking for intelligent answers to intellectual problems.

4. *Never be ashamed to admit "I don't know."*

Too many church leaders have an answer to every problem. Some of these answers are, like the modern cake mix, "ready mixed." Problems are complex. Times are demanding. Personalities are multiphased, and conditions are multilateral. Therefore, beware of superficial answers, and be careful of trying to answer when you don't know. As one wise man said, "Be careful of speaking to the edge of your knowledge; you might fall off."

5. *Provide information before asking for convictions.*

Many teens have convictions that are "second generation." They believe their parents' convictions without having any personal understanding. We don't want to produce hypocrites. Empty convictions are useless. At the other extreme are teens who rebel against their parents and believe the first alternative presented. You, as a youth leader, should not be guilty of fostering such ideas. One weakness of adolescents is that they believe the first opinion presented and stubbornly hold to that opinion in light of contrary facts. This is probably because of self-esteem and rebellion against adult control of their thinking. Therefore, make sure the beliefs of your teenagers are well grounded on facts.

6. *Teach youth the difference between criticism and evaluation.*

Show them the difference between destructive and constructive criticism. Constructive criticism is evaluation. We want teenagers to think for themselves. This thinking involves an analysis of weakness in present projects and a possibility for improvement. Why? How? Where? These should always be in the teens' minds. The youth are critical. They want progress and advancement. They are not bound by tradition, and they can view objectively. Therefore they will be critical. Their criticism may be rebellion against adult authority. They may criticize their father, their mother, and you. However, the young person should be taught to criticize with love and empathy.

7. *Reach and teach youth through their interests.*

The teen is interested in life—cars, dating, eating, sports, media, and traveling. Young people are interested in themselves. Their personalities are awakening and their bodies are developing. The high school student is interested in achievement. All youth can be reached through their interests. You will have to be interested in their interests if you are to reach and teach youth.

EMOTIONAL DEVELOPMENT OF TEENAGERS

A roller coaster would best characterize the emotions of the junior high/middle school student. They go from mountain peak to valley as quickly as they will later change gears on a car. Their physical and mental development affects their emotional stability.

The emotions of these early teenagers may be controlled by appealing to positive peer pressure. Don't use these techniques only; build strong inner discipline. The inner forces may not be sufficiently present in the teen, so build their "self-acceptance."

The high school student *enjoys* his emotions. He looks for opportunities to experiment with them and stimulate them. Recognize emotions—crying, laughter, peace, hate, arguments, bereavement, frustrations. However, don't let emotions just be feelings. Emotions can be a "mirror" to reflect the personality within. Use emotions as a launching pad for teaching.

In the college-age student, emotions have reached a point of "controlled rationality." The late teens understand themselves. Also, the older youth is not so chaotic in expressing emotions. Time is needed for him to come out of the valley of despair and climb the hill of peace. College-age young people delight to conform to adult emotional patterns. May they see a needed example in you. The following is a checklist of questions for teenagers to ask themselves.

CHECKLIST FOR EMOTIONAL GROWTH

1. Do I often feel guilty about the things I have done?
2. Am I troubled over my lack of self-confidence?
3. Can I take disappointment in stride?
4. Do surprises sometimes cause me to panic?
5. Can I laugh at myself?
6. Do I have a tendency to feel gloomy and depressed?

7. Is my sleep frequently disturbed? Do I have difficulty getting to sleep?
8. Do I often feel nervous and tense inwardly?
9. Are my problems usually inside myself rather than outside?
10. Do I often seem to say and do the wrong thing?
11. Do I feel crushed by failure?
12. Do I often push myself to do more than I can do comfortably?
13. Does it bother me that I can't live up to my high standards?
14. Do I have trouble getting realistic goals for myself?
15. Do I find it hard to make decisions and abide by them?
16. Am I usually able to discern the will of God in large and small matters?
17. Do I keep putting off the things that I don't like to do?
18. Does it seem as if I am often getting a bad break?
19. Do I feel tired and weary a great deal?
20. Do I feel insecure about the future?
21. Do I steer clear of situations in which risks are involved?
22. Am I able to accept the responsibilities that come my way?
23. Am I more attracted than threatened by new experiences and new ideas?
24. Am I able to put myself heartily into what I do?
25. Do I enjoy being alone as well as being with other people?
26. Do I feel an integral part when in a group?

27. Do I express myself freely and naturally in a group?
28. Are my feelings sensitive and easily hurt?
29. Do I resent people in authority and people with status?
30. Do I tend to blame others when things go wrong?
31. Do I tend to dislike people who disagree with me?
32. Do I respect the many differences that I find in people?
33. Is it difficult to find people who really understand me?
34. Do I limit my friends to just a few?
35. Do I resent people who have to correct or criticize me?
36. Do I find it difficult to refuse anyone a request, though it may be unreasonable?
37. Does it disturb me that I like and dislike a person at the same time?
38. Do I have personal relationships that are satisfying and lasting?
39. Do I enjoy being both conventional and unconventional?
40. Do I get satisfaction from simple, everyday pleasures?

Sex is no joke to the adolescent, even though he may joke about it. Physically he has reached sexual maturity; emotionally he has not reached the maturity of judgment concerning sexual self-control and understanding. Spiritually he is groping for values in life—adult values. As the sex organs mature, there is increased capacity for sexual arousal. Lead the teenager to accept himself for what he is.

Sexuality is not dirty. It is the most wonderful gift that God can give to any teenager, but it must be kept within the limitations that God has decreed. Morality and self-control constitute the greatest problem with the deepest implications for the adolescent. The problem is confused by a multiplicity of standards of conduct. The home has one standard, the school has one standard, and the church has a different standard. The teenager must see the standard of the Word of God for every area of his sex life.

The natural rebelliousness of some teenagers will often result in revolt against the more rigid moral ideals set down for youth by the adults of society. Youth leaders must understand this rebellion by teenagers, but never forget that the young person is an insecure person searching for the answer to the sex problem. Lead the teenager to the standards of the Word of God.

The adolescent's quest for values is not limited to sex alone. The teenager has a great desire to find an adequate pattern of behavior, ranging all the way from etiquette to a broad concept of integrality. The teenager wants to be at peace with himself and to be accepted by his peers—yet he is idealistic enough to want to be acceptable to society.

"I wish you would tell me what to do" is a frequent plea of the adolescent to the youth leader. He needs controls and limitations, for in restrictions there is security. He also needs to feel grown-up and mature. This will cause him to resist and defy controls, but given no restrictions he is likely to lose his sense of values. Without the youth worker to help draw the line of desirable behavior, he may have a feeling that no one cares what he does. He may react to this feeling by unrestrained behavior. You are not narrow-minded to limit teenagers to the Word of God. The nature of adolescence and common sense dictate that the teenager must be given a standard of behavior that is authoritative and directive.

Guiding Principles for Emotional Development

1. *Judge emotional response at its age level.*

At each phase of life's development we have different expressions of emotion. You can't judge the thirteen-year-old and the college senior in the same way. The young teenager has extremes in emotional feeling and has not learned to control himself. He can move from joy to depression more quickly than the older teen. His emotions are fleeting. The older a teenager becomes, the more he can control his emotions by rational means. Each emotion and each teen will have to be judged in light of his own age characteristics and his level of maturity.

2. *Don't expect youth to respond as you do.*

Devotion and convictions are shown in different ways. The quiet guy will express religious love through a quiet, controlled personality. The girl with an outgoing personality will resonate with life as she testifies of Christ. Both may have the same deep emotional love, yet show it in different manners. Both may be different from you, so don't expect teens to respond emotionally as you do.

3. *Present an image of emotional stability.*

We are constituted toward extremes in our emotional life. We enjoy extreme laughter when happy, and extreme crying satisfies us when we are sad. We must be emotionally qualified to help teenagers.

(a) We must be unchangeable. This is emotional stability. The adolescent is very unstable and demands stability in his leader.
(b) We must be emotionally balanced. Here we are to provide the "image" to the teenager that will cause him to have confidence in us.

SOCIAL DEVELOPMENT OF TEENAGERS

Teenagers love to be in a group. Giving, receiving, sharing—all are part of the thrill and risk of growing up. Social development is the most important, yet least understood, developmental task of adolescents.

In the junior high/middle school years, teenagers enjoy physical activity and games in which they can make a name for themselves. Spectator sports are not very appealing here. The teenager wants to be at the center of things and share in the action. As a youth worker, you must be willing to actively take part in these activities with them, or else you will have very little influence.

In planning for their recreation, use group games. Try not to single out one teenager to represent the team. If he fails, he is ostracized by the group. A group of junior high/middle school students would rather participate than have someone participate for them.

You will have to prove that you are worthy of their respect. Their powers of judgment and reason are beginning to take form. They consider themselves to be authorities on many matters. Therefore, you must be their "proven authority," or you will merit little respect and confidence. Of course their desires are very idealistic. Present Christ to these junior high/middle school students as the only perfect One who will meet their standards. Some might say we must lower our standards. No! Who are we to destroy the dreams of youth?

In the middle teenage years (senior high), sports activities are used to gain individual attention and excellence. Spectator sports among high school students are still popular today, but mainly because of the social aspect of being with the group. Individual or extreme sports are gaining considerable interest of this age group. Use these interests to establish rapport with your young people. Attend their high school group sports events when possible. You can demonstrate your interest and concern for them not only by attending the games in which they are involved, but also by letting them show you their abilities or skills in individual sports. Even better would be enabling them to participate. If they know you give time to their interests, they will be willing to give time to your interests—the work of Christ.

The average high school student is about as large physically as the average adult. But in their social development, high school students are growing kids. They are not at home in the presence of many adults; for this reason they distrust themselves socially in the presence of adults. This distrust makes them critical and cynical. You must prove yourself in their sight before they will accept your leadership. Give them a solid example to believe in—someone they can trust. Teenagers are searching desperately for worthy beliefs and social standards. Don't fail them now.

The high school student is probably aware of his own social shortcomings. Perhaps he has risked himself in a social situation and experienced defeat. You can best provide teenagers with helpful answers now. Show them the relevance of Jesus Christ in their everyday social needs. Most teenagers want a good reputation with their particular group—not necessarily with the adult world. Show them why and how Christ fits into their lives, giving them the only reputation that is everlastingly satisfying. Make sure the church is providing social outlets for the desires and needs of your teenagers. If the church will not meet the social needs of the teenagers, they will go elsewhere.

High school students are beginning to recognize and accept social authority. Be sure you live up to your position as youth *counselor.* Also, the teen leaders must develop and present Christian standards based on God's Word. Here we will find willingness on the part of teenagers to seek help and counsel of church leaders. They will accept guidance from respected leaders. This is an opportunity that depends on you; don't miss it.

Since sex has become the catalyst of modern society, you can't ignore the subject. If you never treat the problem of morality and sex, the teenager will conclude the Bible is out-of-date and your ministry does not meet his needs. At the same time you can go into an expanded program of sex education. Too much knowledge, too early in life, will cause problems. Curiosity, desire to experiment, and frustration are the result of an overexpanded program of sex education.

The necessary facts of sex should be explained in the light of the Word of God. Sexual distinction, functions, and enjoyment are from God. They are a gift of God, to be used in accordance with the will of God, and ultimately for the glory of God.

In late adolescence, social ideals are becoming more realistic and practical. The post–high school student wants to know what can be done to solve his real life problems and how he can build a future. In this later period of development, the young people are interested more in quieter skill games. Use games where mental alertness is needed and social interaction is encouraged.

Self-criticism has become more realistic. You'll discover that the young people at this age are earnestly trying to improve themselves objectively. As the teenager is able to see himself in a more honest light, his attitude will mature. He will need encouragement at this point. Most of all, teenagers should be shown the ultimate goal of their self-improvement: the glory of God.

The Drive for Social Acceptance

Teenagers have a great need to belong. This need shows up in the fads of the day—the way the guys and girls dress, the way they wear their hair, the slang expressions, the places they go and their hangouts. The group usually sets the pace and the rest must follow.

The Clique

The need to belong finds expression in several relationships. First are small intimate groups or *cliques*. To be a part of a popular clique in school carries high prestige. Cliques are usually made up of teenagers from the same socioeconomic background or same interest. Members of the clique agree on whom to include or to exclude from membership. This group usually constitutes the greatest source of suggestibility to the teens.

Cliques are relatively stable and furnish "belonging" to the young person who joins.

The Group

The group is a large amalgamation of youth. The membership is usually fluid. This group is usually informal, and membership relatively accessible. Teenagers who join a group usually come from different socioeconomic backgrounds. The group usually congregates at a favored hangout or stretch of road. Here the members can show off before an appreciative audience. The group furnishes a place to meet new people, and the teenager feels he belongs. Teenagers enjoy a crowd.

TEENAGE DATING

As guys and girls approach adolescence, they have an increasing interest in each other. As they mature physically, interest for the opposite sex deepens and becomes all-important. There is an intense need to be attractive to the other sex. Standards of attractiveness, particularly in early adolescence, are modeled after the current movie or music icon. You can do some directive counseling to show them the scriptural standard of love, courtship, and marriage. The teenager who has not made a mature adjustment to the social demands of culture often makes real progress now because of the strong need of acceptance by the other sex.

The first attempts at socialization are made through informal mixing. There is security in numbers. Next comes dating in groups and then pairing off. Going with a steady has become a custom for many of the high school population as a form of guaranteed dating. Nobody wants to be left out.

Social adjustment in the early teens does not run smoothly because girls mature a little earlier than boys. They want the boys' interest before the boys are ready to give it to them. Sometimes a girl who fails to attract boys at this age becomes afraid that boys don't like her. She may react by chasing the boys or using too much makeup and overdressing in the attempt to make herself more attractive. This type of girl needs your direction. Sympathy from one who understands will help her to understand herself.

The teenager has mixed feelings about affection. He wants to demonstrate what he feels inside when he is with people he likes. But his oversensitivity makes him uneasy about gestures of affection. The church has not given good direction to young people and teenagers as to how to show affection. There are pure and positive standards based on the teachings of the Word of God for the young people. But we have not helped them. At the same time the youngsters are bound by the fear of being rebuffed or rejected by the opposite sex. These feelings make them hide their true approach to the opposite sex.

Dating, going with a steady, being part of the group are all steps toward becoming an adult among adults. Learning to get along with the same sex and the opposite sex, to look upon girls as women and boys as men, to become ready for marriage, family life, and church life—all are parts of becoming a member of the adult society. Adolescence is the opportune time for young people to establish a proper relationship with the opposite sex. If this task is not accomplished successfully during these years, it may never come naturally again. Close guy-girl relations and a sense of belonging to a group helps the teenager's self-confidence and diminishes his insecurity. You must recognize that good relationships are essential to adjustment.

Group pressure becomes a vital factor in adjustment at this period of life. The teenager's friends are eager to give him tips on the things to do and the things to say. Comparing notes, they profit from each other's mistakes and successes. Conventional behavior of his age group has become the standard. Some parents may forbid going steady; others may even forbid dating, with the result that the boy or girl is driven farther away from parents' suggestion and direction. Of course, submission to parents always supersedes the desire to date, even if dating is discounted or not allowed. Youth leaders need to respect kids and parents from such homes.

The church youth group is a natural place for young people to find companionship. It often provides the greatest opportunity for guys and girls to widen their circle of acquaintance. Young people who date Christian young people will hopefully marry Christian young people. The adolescent who dates outside the church will marry outside the church. Help keep adolescent friendships on a wholesome level. Provide activities that will encourage opportunity to meet others and to see the opposite sex in a variety of settings and situations.

Guiding Principles for Social Development

1. *Provide leadership that is indirect, tactful, yet firm.*

Teenagers are idealistic, and everything is black or white. They set ideals and standards for adulthood that they expect to attain. They have not had the experience as adults to discover that they may not be able to attain these ideals and standards.

Teenagers respond to proven and respected authority. Often they rebel against domineering authority, because it causes an inner conflict. They want to be like the other teenagers, yet they want to be adults. They will recognize authority that has proven itself.

Therefore, when you display authority over them, you should be loving but firm. At the same time, you should be tactful and direct. Be careful of laying down the law unless you have the resources to carry through.

2. *Give qualified approbation to all young people.*

Teenagers are very sensitive. They need great assurance in life. Many of them portray the apex of self-assurance, yet inside are fraught with self-distrust. They want approval from adults, and they demand it from their peers. Therefore, you must give qualified approval and acceptance to all teenagers. Find something in which all can be successful. Set goals that are attainable—not adult goals. Provide some personal satisfaction that will motivate them in worthy ambitions in life.

3. *Present Christ as the ideal.*

In junior high/middle school, teenagers are looking up to people. It is said that they are big hero worshipers. Therefore, hold up the person of Christ as the ideal. In high school they are beginning to think about work. They will do anything that will add to their reputation, and they will refrain from anything that will detract from their reputation. Present the work of Christ as ideal. In the college-age class they are beginning to think in terms of other people. Purposeful functions crowd in on their lives. Therefore, interest them in the service of Christ as the ideal.

4. *Provide information, interpretation, and example to help develop scriptural social attitudes.*

Teenagers display the extremes of life. They desire to be alone; they desire to be with others. They want to know people, and they need a knowledge of social graces, self-control, and poise. They need a wholesome attitude of social life that is evidenced in maturity. This life must be governed by rationality and a sense of social graces. Guide them in the formation of scriptural attitudes on social life. Knowing the right thing to do and how to do it creates self-confidence and adjustment.

5. *Identify and minimize gulfs created by different social and economic backgrounds.*

The youth worker should note individuals who do not conform to the church youth group and attempt to help them adjust both to themselves and to the young people around them. Be on guard for danger signals—social isolationists or the disenfranchised. The youth worker can help such guys and girls satisfy their social needs by encouraging them to join groups that will welcome them and to form friendships with other teenagers who have different interests, along with those who have similar interests.

CONCLUSION

Teenagers have a tendency to be rebellious against adult authority. They are trying to live as responsible adults without the facilities to do so. They have the physical maturity of an adult, yet the self-adjustment and security are not there.

The conflict of adolescents with parents frequently blocks easy communication about the problems that trouble teenagers. Still the teenager needs adult direction and understanding. The youth worker then becomes a crucial person in the adolescent's world, offering one of his first and most vital adult relationships. The way the youth worker responds can help or hinder the youth's development or progress toward maturity. He is a key figure for teenage identification and imitation. The young person is sensitive to the youth worker's behavior and how he treats him and his friends. He learns from adults—not only by what they say but by how they live.

The teenager wants to be treated as a mature person, whether he is or not. He responds to the attitude of trust and respect. He doesn't want to be told but wants to find out. It is the obligation of the youth worker and the church to provide him with this opportunity.

Being able to talk it through will help the adolescent more than anything else. This is not an easy period. The teenager is shy and reserved about things close to him. Sometimes the teenager actually has to learn how to express his innermost feelings and to put into words what is bothering him. The young person's sensitiveness about his emotions may hamper the youth worker in gaining the teenager's confidence. You must feel free and easy with him and draw him out. Sympathy and understanding are qualities that you must cultivate.

This, then, is the teenage period. He is neither child nor adult. He is far from understanding his own behavior and from being able to predict his own conduct. He cannot determine his own relationship with God. The teenager is experiencing a great period of insecurity. He has desires and drives that he does not yet understand. He is only beginning to understand himself. The teenager wants to be accepted, understood, loved, and exalted, but he is afraid of getting too close to others. The teenager has strong ideals and a sense of right. He is trying to find a coherent system of values that will reconcile his desires with his beliefs. The teenager is confronted with making serious plans about the future. These decisions demand that he assume responsibility and maturity that he does not yet have. The teenager has little desire to take this responsibility; he prefers to be told and sometimes to be led by the hand. You must draw the teenager out. He must be guided in the path of maturity.

NOTES

1. "Professor Robert Havighurst of the University of Chicago proposes that stages in human development can best be thought of in terms of the developmental tasks." According to Professor Havighurst, these tasks are a part of normal transition. He has identified "eleven developmental tasks associated with the adolescent transition."
   (1) The adolescent must adjust to a new physical sense of self.
   (2) The adolescent must adjust to new intellectual abilities.
   (3) The adolescent must adjust to increased cognitive demands at school.
   (4) The adolescent must develop expanded verbal skills.
   (5) The adolescent must develop a personal sense of identity.
   (6) The adolescent must establish adult vocational goals.
   (7) The adolescent must establish emotional and psychological independence from his or her parents.
   (8) The adolescent must develop stable and productive peer relationships.
   (9) The adolescent must learn to manage her or his sexuality.
   (10) The adolescent must adopt a personal value system.

(11) The adolescent must develop increased impulse control and behavioral maturity. http://education.indiana.edu/cas/devtask.html.

Source: "Developmental Tasks of Normal Adolescence," (accessed September 20, 2001).

2. "Adolescence," http://www.planetpsych.com/zPsychology_101/adolescence.html
3. John W. Santrock, *Adolescence,* 8th ed. (Boston: McGraw-Hill, 2001), 134.

6

Crisis of Identity

The question today's youth ask most consistently is "Who am I?" They are a searching generation. They are not willing to accept traditional answers and roles just because "that's the way it's always been done." They want meaningful answers, answers that can stand the test of careful scrutiny, answers to build their lives and futures on. They want to understand themselves and their world; they want to understand their role in their world. They are asking questions about themselves. This internal examination leads to a search for self, also labeled an "identity crisis." To affect today's youth, church leaders need to know the basics of identity crisis and self-identity. It is the purpose of this chapter to provide some of the basics youth leaders will need to know to properly cope with the questions of this present youth generation.

PUBERTY AND IDENTITY CRISIS

Psychologists are finding that a youth goes through an "identity crisis" as he passes through puberty. The word *puberty* comes from the Latin word *pubertas* (to grow hair), one sign of physical maturity. Puberty is the doorway to the mystical land of adolescent experience. Puberty is a physical renaissance. A flood of sensory phenomena descends upon the youth when he becomes aware of many facts and stimuli coming to him from the outside world of which he has been unaware previously. The child living in the sheltered protection of the home has never realized the inconsistencies of his parents. Suddenly, with an awakening of the reasoning power and the emergence of objectivity, the adolescent becomes critical of his parents. The young male teenager quarrels with his mother over his being late for dinner. The teenage girl disagrees with her father over allowance or the style of a new dress. However, later in the teens the girl tends to attack the mother more than she does the father and will usually disagree with her mother more than the boy will disagree with his father. Perhaps the mother is becoming the model for the teenage girl's growing identity, causing more difficulty as the girl attempts to escape "Mother's apron strings."

The word *adolescent* is derived from a Latin verb *adolescere,* which means "to grow into maturity" or "to grow up." For the purpose of this writing, the following definitions will be used:

1. Sociologically. Adolescence is a transition period from a dependent childhood to an independent, "self-sufficient" adulthood.

2. Sexually. Adolescence is the time leading up to and following the emergence of the youth's ability to reproduce himself biologically.
3. Emotionally. Adolescence is that age of self-awareness, when the youth realizes he has an inner nature and searches for an identification of that nature by asking the question "Who am I?"
4. Chronologically. Adolescence is the time span from approximately ten to nineteen years of age.
5. Culturally. Adolescence involves entrance into a subculture where the youth will usually identify with and accept value systems of others in his subculture (clique or gang), sometimes identifying with and accepting the values of the family, other times rejecting them.
6. Physically. The beginning of adolescence is marked by "pubescence" (a period of time of physiological development during which the reproductive functions mature). The exact time of puberty when the reproductive organs reach maturity varies greatly and seems to be related to socioeconomic as well as geographic factors.[1]

The emergence of puberty in the average teen arrived approximately nineteen months earlier in 1996 than it did in 1947. This means that the average youth of today is entering puberty almost two years prior to those of Second World War vintage. The physical changes of puberty take place in a time span of approximately two years that usually begins around the middle of the sixth grade for girls and the seventh grade for boys. "At perhaps no other period in human life, except birth, does a transition of such importance take place. And though physiological change takes place at all age levels, the rate of change during this period is immeasurably greater than in the years that precede and follow it."[2]

Many modern-day scholars believe that the elongated period of time called adolescence is the invention of a technically advanced society. The prolonged time of puberty is not a physiological necessity but a social invention. In many societies the transition from being a child to an adult is smooth, and society does not recognize the period of change. In some societies there are puberty rites to transfer a person from childhood to adolescence or from childhood to adulthood. Some of the primitive societies recognize that after puberty the young man or woman obtains adult responsibility and has adult privileges.

Characteristics of Puberty in Girls

1. Skeleton growth
2. Breast development
3. Straight pigmented pubic hair
4. Maximum annual growth increments
5. Kinky pigmented pubic hair
6. Menstruation
7. Appearance of auxiliary hair

Characteristics of Puberty in Boys

1. Skeleton growth
2. Enlargement of testes
3. Straight pigmented pubic hair
4. Early voice changes
5. Ejaculation
6. Kinky pigmented pubic hair
7. Maximum annual growth increments
8. Appearance of downy facial hair

9. Appearance of auxiliary hair
10. Late voice changes
11. Coarse pigmented facial hair
12. Chest hair

Any of the above characteristics (one or a combination of the above) could be used as an indication of the beginning of puberty. Obviously, puberty is not one of the above events, since in no case will all of them occur simultaneously. Neither do any of the above appear instantaneously. Consequently there is a lot of overlapping in the designation of puberty. When one speaks of teenagers today reaching puberty nineteen months earlier than 1947, he is talking about a statistical figure, primarily measuring when girls begin to menstruate as the characteristic age of puberty. If puberty is synonymous with the attainment of reproductive maturity, there is one qualification: Most girls have a period of one or more years of sterility between the first menstruation and the ability to conceive and reproduce.

Adolescence is a time of life when the individual is undergoing actual physical change. Because of this, he is concerned with his inner self-image. This whole issue is exacerbated when you add ethnicity. Although the establishment of identity is an important, complex task for all adolescents, it is particularly complicated for adolescents belonging to ethnic minority groups. Ethnic identity of the majority group of individuals is constantly validated and reinforced in a positive manner, whereas the minority group is regularly ridiculed and punished in a negative manner. What does this say for those adolescents who are the minority and not the majority? It is important to study or research ethnic identity, because it provides better knowledge and provides meaning for direction and meaning of ethnic identity.[3]

The outer physical changes trigger inner turmoil. Major choices—such as education, occupation, friends, as well as marriage—face the adolescent. The adolescent asks himself if he has the ability to perform in life. When such major decisions face the adolescent, the self-image is more likely to support his choice if he has a strong self-identity or to betray him if his self-identity is weak or rejecting. Self-identification begins to grow because adolescence is a period of unusual change. During puberty a boy may grow several inches or gain up to 20 percent in weight in a matter of a few months. When the adolescent looks in the mirror, he sees pimples and becomes emotionally perplexed. The flat-chested girl desires a figure and is embarrassed when people call attention to her lack of feminine characteristics. Sexual drives increase in intensity. New desires surge through the young person.

Perhaps one of the reasons self-identification is currently awakening during adolescence is that the teenager is young at a time when adults live in a society that worships "youth." The youth-oriented culture has made possible advantages, freedom, and training not available to previous youth. The adult expectations that are projected on teens tend to have both positive and negative effects. Parents are a significant part of the process.

"Due to the complexity of the task of identity formation the individual involved experiences any variety of four developmental statuses. These four statuses are based upon the dimensions of exploration, or examination of alternative identities, and commitment, or stable investment in the present state of one's identity. The four statuses are individually addressed below."

Diffusion

Lack of exploration of alternatives

Lack of commitment

Least sophisticated level of development

Typically the level at which identity formation is begun

Does not feel accepted by parents

Foreclosure

Lack exploration of alternatives

Commitment has been made, but without exploration of alternatives, identity is not attained

Developmentally unsophisticated level of achievement

Adopt parents' characteristics

Moratorium

Active exploration of alternative identities

Commitment is desired, but it is not yet attained

Sophisticated level of development

Achievement

Individual has explored alternatives

Commitment is at a high level

Most developmentally sophisticated status of identity formation

Perceive parents as supportive[4]

The young people, wanting to live up to expectations, still rebel in order to fit in their own life patterns. Self-identification grows because the adolescent begins following a different pattern of thinking. Memories are keen in the early teen years. With the onset of puberty, the ability of the preteen to memorize is curtailed. Not that he memorizes less, but the ability to memorize is not as productive as before. Memory is best in the preteen years because concrete or material concepts are used as thought patterns. After puberty, the teenager begins to think in abstracts and begins to use the ability to think by using concepts. He begins to rationalize as well as apply logical reason.

WHAT IS IDENTITY CRISIS?

The apparent pioneer of self-identification psychology, especially in relationship to a theory of adolescence, is Edward Spranger, professor emeritus at the University of Berlin.[5] He called his the *geisteswissen-schaftlichen* (cultural science) psychology. Spranger believed that the first pattern of adolescent development is experienced as a form of rebirth in which the individual sees himself as another person when he reaches maturity. The second pattern is a slow, continuous growth process and a gradual acquisition of cultural values and ideals held in society, without a basic personality change. Spranger's third pattern is a growth process in which the individual actively participates. The youth consciously improves and forms himself, overcoming disturbances and crises by his own energetic and goal-directed efforts.

According to Spranger there are three areas in which a structural change of the organization of the psyche can be observed. These are:

1. discovery of the ego or self
2. gradual formation of a life plan
3. the selection and integration of a personal value system

Spranger does not say that the child has no ego, rather that adolescence is a time when the ego is discovered and united. Prior to puberty the ego was present but divided. Now, the juvenile begins to reflect upon himself by directing his attention internally and analyzing himself. He discovers the internal ego and experiences it as separated from the external world. This results not only in loneliness but also in a need to experiment with one's own undifferentiated ego in order to establish ego unity. This brings about three effects:

1. A challenging of all previously unquestioned ideas and relationships. Thus there is rebellion against tradition, mores, family, school, and other social institutions.
2. An increased need for social recognition and interpersonal relationships.
3. A need to experiment with different aspects of one's own ego, trying out and testing one's own personality.

Many of the books treating youth work and/or adolescent development from a Christian perspective have not attempted to integrate identity crisis into a biblical perspective. The term *self* should not be confused with pride or egotism. Pride is a higher estimation of oneself than is actually true. Pride is also inordinate focus on oneself and looking down on others. Self-identity deals with accepting oneself as one is and recognizing the potential he can become.

Four Reasons That Self-Identity Is Imperative

The first reason for the importance of self-identity is the youth's special capacity to recognize and develop a self-consciousness that can think, evaluate, choose, love, hate, and live in this unique human manner. The self-identity is like a person who stands above the human body, observing the actions that go on within, yet remaining a part of that which is within. The development of a self-identity into a constructive and healthy reality looms as the greatest task facing the teenager. Psychologist John Schlien states flatly the position of the self-theorist on the matter. To put it very simply, self-theorists do not believe that the organism is wholly subject to the conditions of and conditioning by the environment. They believe that the organism (human) has a special capacity (which makes it human, and without which it is less than human) to develop a *self,* which is self-conscious and self-evaluating, and which, therefore, chooses, acts upon its environment, and has much responsibility because it has volition.[6] To act meaningfully an adolescent must develop an adequate self-image to guide in the construction of an adult personality.

The second reason for the development of self-identity is the number of problems facing the adolescent today. Psychologist Morris Rosenberg defined these briefly as follows:

1. Problem decisions, reasons for awareness of self-identity
2. Physical change, a reason for awareness of self-identity
3. Adolescence, a period of unusual status ambiguity[7]

These problems overwhelm the youth and demand answers, forcing the youth to identify himself.

Too often Christians think the major question facing young people is finding the will of God or making correct choices. The identity question is deeper. The young person who knows himself has a clear picture of what he is. He is the teenager who can make the correct choices, especially when he is in right relationship to God. He can find God's will and implement it for his life. Some young people who do not have ego strength—that is to say, they do not have self-identity—may be manipulated to make correct choices in the present. Yet when they are removed from parental influence, they will probably not be able to stand against outside pressure. The Christian young person who knows himself, his strengths, weaknesses, values, and aims in life, is the one who can properly guide his life.

The third reason for identifying self is the demand of finding a satisfying vocational path in life. The question of a lifework needs solutions quickly. In the immediate future the youth will be brought face-to-face with life's great choices. In the next few years he must make critical decisions that will irrevocably shape his life. Among these are vocational choices, educational choices, marital choice, and other choices of a philosophical and spiritual nature that become an indelible part of the realistic self-image of the now pliable youth. Rosenberg says that there are several reasons for this heightened awareness of the self-image during this period of adolescence (ages fifteen to eighteen). For one thing, it is a time of major decision; for example, the individual must give serious thought to his occupational choice. The individual must urgently think about what he is like if he is not to make a disastrous choice. He must also think about marriage. When an individual is faced with a serious and urgent decision and when a major basis for this decision is his view of what he is like, then the self-image is likely to move to the forefront of attention.

It is not difficult to see the vital role of the self-image if satisfactory choices are to be made in these critical years of development. To an adult—parent, teacher, or youth leader—"growing up" may mean nothing more than heavier, taller, bigger, increased appetite, outgrown clothes, another year, another grade of school! To the teenager, growing up is much more than this. He finds himself in a continuous search for himself. "Too often this search is fruitless," declares psychologist Carl Schneider.[8] Self-knowledge will guide the search for self. The young person will need to try to get as much information as possible about his interests, abilities, and the jobs he wants to consider. The more a person knows about himself, the more opportunity he has to make wise plans for his future.

Self-identity is not the same as maturity or independence. The teenager is searching; many times he does not know the object of his quest, but an inner disequilibrium drives his search for self-fulfillment.

An adequate self-knowledge will guide the teenager to maturity. Also, the teenager must in time cut himself off from parental control and form an autonomous responsibility for his life. This independence is achieved after self-identity is found. Many young people are geographically independent from their parents, but emotionally they are still tied to "Mother's apron string" because they never found themselves. People without self-identity are usually the extension of their parents' personalities. Therefore, independence and maturity are the goal of self-identity as stated by Schneider. This is, in a real sense, the crowning achievement of adolescent striving. Without self-identity, the adolescent does not know how to work toward independence. Without self-identity he finds it difficult to grow up and to continue moving toward the goal of adult responsibility.

Eternal consequences are a fourth reason making it imperative to help teens find self-identity. Many young people, and adults, are social derelicts; and their lives are useless to themselves, to society, and to God. Each person has a unique contribution to make in life, but many do not have the inner strength to give to others or to God. As a parasite, the person without identity lives off those around him. He is like a vacuum, and the law of nature teaches that the surrounding elements fill a vacuum. Schneider described these teens,

> Adolescents often manifest lack of self-identity which is one of the reasons why they are at times uncertain, confused, and extremely vacillating in their opinion, behavior, or goals. We see this clearly exemplified in the high school senior who cannot decide whether he should go on to college, go into the army, or get a job; and in the college student who cannot decide on a definite curriculum. We see it also in young adults, who, having left college, flounder from one position to another. We see it exemplified in the extremely large number of boys and girls who, after a period of one or several years, leave the convent or seminary because of a "lack of vocation," often bitterly disappointed, disillusioned, and more confused than they were before. There are countless instances of such vocational disorientation that has its roots in the failure to achieve self-identity.[9]

The teenager can "control" his life. God has not left the young person to aimless determinism, bumping into obstacles throughout life. God intends the young person to use the mental facilities, willpower, and energies at his disposal to direct his life. Obstacles should not determine his life, but the inner person who sees the obstacles should guide the outer life.

All experience is evaluated as friendly or dangerous, interesting or boring, possible or impossible, etc., depending not upon the nature of the experience so much as upon the self-concept of the experimenter.[10] Young people who do not find themselves lapse into what Erik Erikson calls *role diffusion*. They do not become themselves, but as the vacuum attracts the surrounding environment, these teens playact the lives of those around. A boy chews on a toothpick and plays the role of "tough guy." Another might attempt to play several roles, portraying the person who is nearest and exerting the greatest influence at present. Then other teens develop deeper psychological problems of role diffusion. As a teenager once yelled, "I'd rather be someone bad—to be no one is hell!" Erikson notes, "The danger of this stage is role confusion. Where this is based on strong precarious doubts as to one's identity, delinquent and outright psychotic episodes are not uncommon."[11] And again in the same context, after describing the cruel intolerance and discrimination in adolescent groups, Erikson adds: "It is imperative to understand (which does not mean condone or participate in) such intolerance as a defense against a sense of identity confusion."[12] Diffusion of self-image is another of the problems in the developmental tasks before youth. Perhaps all teens go through this stage of role diffusion before they find themselves.

Erikson aptly describes the adolescent in suspended ambivalence between past and future. There is a "natural" period of uprootedness in human life: adolescence. Like a trapeze artist, the young person in the middle of vigorous motion must let go of his safe hold on childhood and reach out for a firm grasp on adulthood, depending for a breathless interval on a relatedness between the past and the future, and on the reliability of those he must let go of and those who will "receive" him.[13]

EXAMINING SELF-IDENTITY

The definition of self-identity becomes vital if we are adequately to help teens find themselves. Self-identity must find itself in "Who or what am I?"

Some credit William James as the modern originator of the concept and importance of identity.[14] James equated I with *ego,* and in this reflection he called it *me;* together he called it *self.* A man's *self* is the sum total of all that he can call "his." This self is considered as being constructed from three constituents: a "material," a "social," and a "spiritual" self.[15] Theologically we can argue whether man is bipartite or tripartite (two parts—material and immaterial, or three parts—body, soul, and spirit), but of course it's better to have God, rather than psychologists, define what man is made of.

Carl Rogers defined the self-concept as a person's view of himself. The *self-structure* is a person viewed from an external frame of reference.[16] The ubiquitous observer stands within and views the many facets of personality, the many roles played in life, and the changing moods and, as the observer, perceives the internal person. He also controls the total person. The knowledge one has about his self is powerful, whether the knowledge is correct or not, for a person lives out the personality styles he perceives he possesses. Some live up to their perceived view of self-expectation; others fail. Some are aware of their perceptual self; at other times it is subliminal, but self still controls behavior. Self-perception not only controls actions but also controls the emerging self-identity and reinforces the idea of the emergence of the ego. The emergence of the ego plus the development of the self-concept and the self-ideal are closely correlated in adolescence with the development of the self-identity.[17]

Morris Rosenberg defined the self-image as a "self-picture"

or a mental "self-portrait"[18] as though the person visits the art gallery and views his portrait. Yet, just as no painted portrait is a perfect photographic reproduction, so the self-image is not identical to the real self. Self-image is the present attitude toward the self that one wants to become, what one knows he is not, what acts or attitudes one values, and how one wants to be perceived by others. Those who like what they see in the mirror of developing self-image are generally healthy persons. Those who reject what they see or those who have a hazy, imperceptible view are generally those who need help. (Keep in mind that the issues of the sinfulness of man and a God awareness have not been included here.)

Perhaps a change in self-perception is all that is needed, but like the old witch in *Snow White* who demanded from the mirror to be called beautiful, those with a weak self-image recognize themselves as not the "fairest of all." A change of self-perception takes time, exposure, and sometimes professional therapy. Many years are usually wasted in developing a distorted self-perception, and much energy is needed to change that image. The change begins with a shift in attitude, as writes Rosenberg: "We conceive of the self-image as an attitude toward an object. (The term *attitude* is broadly used to include facts, opinions, and values with regard to the self, as well as favorable orientation toward the self.)"[19]

The person who has established a clear and correct self-identity is usually a mentally healthy person. He has a proper grasp on the external world of reality, has identified life's goals and is pursuing them, and is accepting others as he is accepting himself. Self-identity is a quality of personal experience and of existence that is linked to the growth of the self-concept and the self-ideal, and means a clear awareness of one's role and status in life, one's goals and purposes, and one's relationships to reality, to society, and to a Supreme Being. (Of course one can only have a proper identity if that "Supreme Being" is God the Father.) The person with self-identity knows the answer to such questions as "What am I?" "What am I supposed to be or become?" and "Where am I going?" The person lacking self-identity, on the other hand, is confused and uncertain as to what he is supposed to be and where he is going.[20]

The present self-image is only one of a number of self-images, which might be considered. William James also mentioned the ideal self or what the individual would like to be or "stakes" himself on becoming.[21] The various writers are saying, then, that there are several self-images, each of which must be identified and accepted for what it is worth. Rosenberg does a rather complete job of compiling all of the ideas of different self-images. These are as follows:

1. Present self-image—what he really is
2. His committed self-image—the type of person he has staked himself on becoming
3. The fantasy self-image—the type of person he would like to be if unencumbered by reality
4. The ego ideal—the type of person he feels he should be
5. The future or possible self—the type of person he feels he will become
6. The idealized self-image—the type of person he most enjoys thinking of himself as
7. The presenting self—the picture the individual attempts to project
8. The accorded self—what other people hold of the individual
9. The inferred self—what the scientific investigator is able to learn about the individual.

CONCLUSION

The self is one of the important factors governing adolescent behavior. The adolescent is developing a "self-image," and the adolescent years will be important in determining his personality that will remain with him throughout life. The following chapters will examine the impact self has in every area of life.

NOTES

1. Ruth Benedict, *Pattern of Culture* (New York: New American Library, 1950). H. Remplein, *Der aujbaudes seelenlebens bei mensch und tier* (Nuenchen: Bayrischer Schulbuchverlag, 1950). V. V. Greulich, "Physical Changes in Adolescence," in B. Nelson, ed. *Adolescence: Yearbook of the National Society for the Study of Education,* vol. 43 (Chicago: Univ. of Chicago: 1944).
2. Rolf E. Muuss, *Theories of Adolescence* (New York: Random House, 1962), 6.
3. Margaret Beale Spencer, *Child Development.* 61, no. 2. (April 1990), 290–310.
4. Rita Varano, "Parenting Style and Identity Formation," http://www.personal.psu.edu/faculty/n/x/nxd10/adid2.htm#verano (accessed October 11, 2001).
5. A concise discussion of Spranger is found in Muuss, *Theories of Adolescence,* 46–47.
6. John M. Schlien, "The Self-Concept in Relation to Behavior: Theoretical and Empirical Research," *Religious Education,* 57 (July-August 1962); S-111.
7. Morris Rosenberg, *Society and the Adolescent Self-Image* (Princeton, N.J.: Princeton Univ. Press, 1965), 3–4.
8. Carl Schneider, *Search for Identity,* 144.
9. Ibid., 140.
10. Schlien, "Self-Concept," S-115.
11. Erik H. Erikson, *Childhood and Society,* 2d ed. (New York: Norton, 1964), 262.
12. Ibid.
13. Erik H. Erikson, *Insight and Responsibility* (New York: Norton, 1964), 90.
14. David J. De LeVita, *The Concept of Identity* (Paris: Mouton and Co., 1965), 29.
15. Ibid.
16. Schlien, "Self-Concept," S-111.
17. Schneider, *Search for Identity,* 139. Compare De LeVita, 29.
18. Rosenberg, *Adolescent Self-Image,* xiii.
19. Ibid., 5.
20. Schneider, *Search for Identity,* 139–40.
21. De LeVita, *The Concept of Identity,* 29ff.

How Self-Identity Is Formed

Self-identity is formed in relationships. The young person develops his personality in meaningful interactions. This chapter will trace the personal growth of self-identity, first in relationship to spiritual development, second in relationship to social adjustment, and finally in relationship to psychological growth.

SPIRITUAL DEVELOPMENT OF SELF-IDENTITY

The thought of being "nobody" is intolerable; and in general the adolescent prefers being a "bad somebody" to a "nobody." However, when a young person is searching for identity, or seeking for a "self," this does not mean he is becoming selfish. He simply wants to become his own person. The selfish person desires to become something he isn't. He grasps after glory or recognition. God "resists the proud, but gives grace to the humble" (1 Peter 5:5).

Pride tops the scriptural list of God's most-hated sins (Prov. 6:16–19). Anyone who is totally wrapped up in self-glorification certainly has a distorted self-image. The opposite extreme to self-glorification is total rejection of one's self. Reverse pride is denying what one is—to belittle oneself. This is as detrimental to the personality as egotism. A person should accept himself for what he is; this is self-respect and is not sinful. Jesus allowed for self-respect when He said, "Love . . . your neighbor as yourself" (Luke 10:27). Rejection of self will also lead a young person not to respect others. To belittle oneself falsely will not lead to an esteem of others. A person can love others only in direct proportion to a proper respect for himself. This is why self-identity is important for young persons. Dr. Cecil Osborne says,

> A proper self-love is the starting point for loving another person. If we do not love ourselves properly, we can never truly love anyone else; for we tend to project on our own disguised self-contempt. . . . Self-love does not imply narcissism, egocentricity, selfishness, or a warped self-interest. It does imply: I too, am a person loved by God.[1]

If a person's self-concept is distorted to either extreme, his actions will be either narcissistic or hostile toward self and others. If he believes himself to be a defeated, inferior, and inadequate person, then soon his actions will reveal these characteristics. "Whatever you feel yourself to be at the center of your emotional nature, that is what you really are existentially and your actions will be in harmony with your self-concept."[2]

Obviously neither extreme can lead to a healthy personality. Young persons should reject the extreme attitudes of "I am everything!" (egotism) and "I am nothing" (self-rejection).

Young persons find their self-identity as they receive love and learn to give it in a depth relationship. They begin to grow into a healthy personality when they realize they are worthy of love and another person wants their love in return. A loving mother can lead a child into a mature self. When the child reaches adolescence, his self-image continues to grow as he matures.

Happy is the young teenager who is the recipient of such loving acceptance. Love bartered across the bargaining counter of behavior or gotten in the backseat of a car will not give the adolescent a sense of being loved as a person. As the young person becomes conscious of God's eternal love for him, he gains self-awareness and self-respect. No single additional factor can contribute as much to one's sense of self-esteem as to be loved unconditionally.

Boundaries in Learning Self-Identity

God loves without conditions (Rom. 5:8), but He doesn't *accept* unconditionally—the Cross is His condition. The young person learns self-identity as he realizes there are limits and laws in life. The young person who wants to be absolutely free doesn't understand life or the universe in which he lives. God has placed us in a society that has laws and put us on a planet that is controlled by laws. The young person is loved enough to have fences set about him that keep him from hurting himself and others. No parental or societal jurisdiction is exercised over those on the outside, people who do not belong to them. Our God has set boundaries in the areas of sex and interpersonal relationships. He has further instituted the home, the church, and society, which also have boundaries separating acceptable from unacceptable behavior. God's love is demonstrated not only through the bounds He sets but also by punishing violations of them.

God has given the conscience as a radar to spot the danger zones of behavior. Parents play a major role in the conditioning and giving of a set of values to that conscience. Commenting on the restricting power of the conscience, author B. Blaine states,

> Adolescence is the period when the underlying core of the conscience laid down in the early years is most needed. This is a time of necessary rebellion—when superimposed values seem false and artificial. The individual self becomes all-important and the search for what comes truly from within, and therefore seems real as a consuming task. It involves experimenting with new ideas, new ways of behavior, and different ways of dressing, and the trying out of new goals and ambitions; but always as the limiter of action there remains the basic core of conscience provided by childhood training from the parents which prevents completely self-defeating and self-destructive behavior.[3]

Restrictions, discipline, and guidance give the young person a clear picture of who he should be. A child who is pampered and never disciplined will expect the same treatment later in his youth and on into adulthood. He does not understand himself nor society. "The young child is able to absorb into his self-regulating apparatus the prohibitions and restrictions of his parents and to make them a part of his permanent and irrevocable inner self. The parents' ability to influence their children's future is never again so great."[4]

The authority of the parents is but a prelude to the lifelong submission to the authority of school, society, the law, and God. Adjustment to the control by parents leads to adjustment to society.

While the young person finds himself by accepting controls, he must learn to deal with freedom. Often the young person desires freedom of the open road or open waterways. As a result, he feels that the lack of restraint signifies real freedom. The cultural heritage in the United States places a premium on freedom. The freedom of choice also brings with it the responsibility to accept the resulting consequences. In God's system, man is left free to choose, but God has graciously given "means of grace" to bring each person to salvation. But in the final analysis, man can accept or reject. True freedom is being committed to the Lord Jesus Christ. One need not be a slave to sin (Rom. 6:18–22) but can be free to be a servant of the Lord of the universe. Rousseau observed, "Man is born free, and everywhere he is in chains." Young people are free, but they reject that liberty. They are plagued by conformity in their dress, music they listen to, places they go, possession of the "right" things, and much more. They are slaves to the contemporary youth culture, yet they reject their parents' society. The young person who has a strong identity can break away from slavish conformity to other young people's mores. He can control his own life. The Christian young person is free to make his conformity God-ward rather than man-ward.

Biblical Truth in Developing Self-Identity

As the young person reads the Scripture, he identifies with those who have served God. The convictions of Daniel, the boldness of Elijah, the faith of Abraham, and the patience of Job all speak to him. When he views the experiences of men and women in the Bible, those experiences demand some interpretation. The Bible is not filled with empty moralisms or rusty clichés. Rather it deals realistically with life's problems. When the young person identifies with biblical personalities, he is doing more than learning factual information. He is building up an intellectual and emotional attitude (self-image), which will help him make right decisions.

A minister once claimed, "Ninety percent of the Bible deals with life situations, not theological standards—therefore, the Bible is related to life." The emphasis of this minister's remarks is correct. However, to say that only 10 percent of the Bible deals with theological standards is erroneous. Theological standards undergird the entire Scripture and reflect themselves in the everyday life situations of the Bible. Theological standards, both negative and positive, are the mortar that molds one's self-image. When the Bible teaches, "You shall not take the name of the Lord your God in vain; you shall not steal; you shall not murder; you shall not commit adultery," it is molding the young person's "negative self." The negative self in relation with the conscience determines the action of each individual just as much as the positive self.

A Christian young person has been taught at home or in Sunday school or church the Ten Commandments. He goes into the supermarket. Deep within his subconscious is a negative self that says, "I am not a thief." ("You shall not steal.") Therefore, although the clerk is in the back room filling an order and the only other customer is not watching, the young person does not walk out the front door without paying. Stealing is not in harmony with his negative self.

After the adolescent considers God's law and has found himself under authority, he reads God's Word, recognizes grace, and realizes he is free. The young person must consider God's claim upon his life. If man is truly created in the image of God but is separated from God because of his sin, then God must reestablish a relationship with man (as He has done). Here the young person finds true identity.

The adolescent must see himself as a unique person in four areas. First, he is created in God's image and likeness. God was preeminent in creation. Man is made in God's image and is preeminent above the world. Second, man is superior to all creatures of this world. God put man in dominion over all that has been created. Third, man, like his Master, is a rational being. He can think, reason, and express emotion. Fourth, man is spirit. This is not a psychological existence but a created reality. Man has an immaterial spirit that will live forever. The young person must come to see himself as an individual, uniquely himself, and see that there is something within him that separates him from all other people. That something that God as Creator gave to him is his soul. The adolescent will need to consider who and what God is. He must also determine what spiritual gift God, through His Spirit, has given to him. "In each of us the Spirit is manifested in one particular way, for some useful purpose" (1 Cor. 12:7 NEB). To know himself, the individual must know God's gift for him as a unique person. Through this recognition of his relationship with God, the adolescent will form part of his self-image.

SOCIAL DEVELOPMENT OF SELF-IDENTITY

Personal relationships are just about the most important aspects of life to a young person. As a person relates to others, he learns self-identity. The individual learns a set of expectancies from parents, peers, significant individuals, and society in general as he relates to these each day. The young person learns that he is good or bad, that he is accepted among peers or rejected, that he is a good student or a poor one, and that he is a part of society or an outcast. These relationships help to determine a young person's positive or negative feedback from society, resulting in a positive or negative self-esteem. Those who have received positive reinforcement throughout life usually have a good, strong self-image. Negative reinforcement results in self-rejection.

The self-image, whether good or bad, strong or weak, tends to reinforce itself. In a study by Mussen and Porter, a person was found to put his self-image into behavior. "Self-concepts are translated into action, and contributes further support to the . . . adequate social functioning."[5] When the individual is able to function adequately in society, the reward is positive. Therefore, as the young person relates to society around him, his self-image takes shape.

People with low ego strength usually like to put on a front or mask. Why do people wear masks? Basically, they fear discovery will lead to rejection, but experience has shown just the opposite. When a person frankly admits a weakness, he places himself in a category with all other members of the human race. Taking off a mask is different from striving for acceptance. Striving for acceptance by reading personality books or studying etiquette will not solve the problem for the mask wearer. Psychologist Morris Rosenberg found that young persons with weak ego strength tend to rate themselves lower than others in the possession of desirable characteristics, except the item "having a good sense of humor." Those who have weak ego strength think it can be hidden, but Rosenberg suggests, "They are, however, probably less successful in deceiving others than they think."[6] Rosenberg suggests that the young person doesn't like himself and is trying to hide that fact, but because he isn't successful at hiding his self-dislike he isn't well liked.

The work of Sigmund Freud indicates that the individual who loves himself *more* will thereby love others less. Freud believed that a person had a certain "capacity" of libido (energy). If the person expressed this on himself, he had little left for others. Erich Fromm disagreed: "The individual's attitude towards humanity, toward human nature, is one of the central axioms of his life theory. If he trusts and respects human nature, then he will trust and respect himself, since he is himself a member of the human race. If he hates and despises others, then he will have a fundamental concept for himself."[7] The problem is, we aren't supposed to "trust and respect human nature" but to see ourselves and others as (1) made in the image of God and thus valuable, but (2) fallen and thus not necessarily "trustworthy."

Rosenberg's studies of young people indicated that Fromm's relationship of people (if he trusts others, he will trust himself) was correct, but the order was reversed. Rosenberg felt that mistrust, hostility, or rejection of others began in a person's attitude toward himself. Those with weak ego strength were skeptical or rejecting in their relationship with other people.

Those with weak ego strength tend to keep to themselves. They put up a high wall between themselves and their friends.

It is all right to throw bits of information or to lean over the wall and talk, but nobody gets in. They don't have the strength of personality to let people "look around" inside their personality. Those with "strong ego strength" can also do this—they can be self-sufficient and choose not to let others inside.

IDENTIFICATION WITH TRUSTED OTHERS

The young person's identification with other persons is one of the basic means whereby he discovers his self-identity. Identification in personality development is not one person attaching himself to a second, as one might attach two pieces of cloth or two sheets of paper. A young person identifies with a prized person and emulates his basic traits. Identification is carried out in many ways. Some of these factors are:

1. The biological inheritance naturally leads to identification. The adolescent male most naturally will identify with a man, and the adolescent girl will have an "ideal self" with whom she identifies—a certain woman whom she admires.

2. The pressures of society upon children cause them to identify with their own sex. From the moment mother puts pink upon the baby girl, and the young father puts a ball in the crib of the baby boy, society begins to pressure a child to identify with its own sex. The distinct clothes, the different bicycles, and the separate bathrooms pressure the child to identify with his own sex.

3. The degree of love shown a child by the person with whom he identifies influences the degree of identification. The four-year-old boy who attempts to identify with his father is more likely to do so if his father shows love and acceptance to the boy. A young preadolescent boy may idealize a ballplayer. Yet, when the ballplayer brushes aside his request for an autograph, the young boy no longer wishes to identify with his hero. Identification is greater where there is love and a warm relationship.

4. Identification is greater if a child's needs are met by the

person with whom he is identifying. Identification will be greater between a young high school girl and a "Miss America" candidate if the potential Miss America has the attributes the high school girl needs. For instance, the candidate for Miss America is disciplined, dedicated, and excels in playing the piano. The high school girl has a desire to play, yet cannot force herself to the routine of practice. When the high school girl sees her "heroine" do what she cannot do, a need is met.

5. Identification is greater when there is a degree of acquaintance between the individuals involved. The unknown movie star will not have as much influence on a young high school girl as the homeroom teacher in high school who is in her late twenties, wears stylish clothes, and drives a sports car.

6. Identification is much easier when the ideal has a clear role in the perception of the young person. The older person who is confused in his Christian life will not have a positive influence on the young person who is seeking to identify. When the "hero" has a strong concept of "who am I," it is easier for the adolescent to identify with him.

7. The attitude of the "ideal" to the young person will affect the relationship. The young person is more likely to identify with someone who treats him as a person rather than someone who treats him as a nuisance or a child. Attitudes of respect, sharing, and love will make for a positive identification, whereas attitudes of belittlement or toleration tear down the identification process.

8. The natural abilities of the child to be like his "hero" determine the case of identification. When the young boy attempts to identify with a ballplayer, identification is easier if the young boy is athletically inclined. The beautiful model will not have much influence for a homely girl, because she "lacks" natural ability to be a model.

9. Identification is greater when the temperament of the young person is similar to that of the identified person. Studies are not sufficient to show whether young people identify with

those who are like them in temperament or they become like those with whom they identify. However, it is conclusive that when young people identify with those of like temperament, the identification process has the greatest influence. Identification may have a host of meanings. However, what happens in molding the young person's life is most important. It may mean some of the following:

- The young person and his model have the same behavior.
- The model has influenced the young person, who reciprocates by mimicking.
- The young person may mimic the attitudes, not the behavior of the model.
- The level of the unconscious personality may be affected. The young person's "self" may be constructed to become like that of the model.
- Only a part of life may be affected. The young person may attempt to become like the model in one specific behavior, rejecting other aspects of the model's life.
- Identification may be a superficial product. The young person's behavior is related to the model's outward behavior, but the internal persons are not similar.
- Identification may become a process. As the young person learns one action of behavior from the model, this leads to a second or to an accelerating series of acts.

Identification can be as simple as a young boy assuming his father's walk, posture, and the tilt of his head. It simply means that the adolescent's behavior is similar to his model's.

Negative Identification's Role in Self-Identification

Negative identification is similar in concept to the negative self. It results in self-identification but in a dissimilarity of behavior to the model. When a young person has negative feelings (that is, he dislikes the model), he has negative identification. He makes either a conscious or unconscious attempt to become opposite to the model.

Many young people claim to be "weak willed" when their problem is a weak ego. A person who has a poor self-image cannot see himself in the role of a strong, forceful, or directive individual. He sees himself as one who is carried along by the tide of society. Perhaps this person considers passivity a virtue (seen as surrender to the Lord). What he considers virtue may be nothing more than a projection of his own weak self-image. Though of course Christ values submission, this type of submission is more of a debilitating acquiescence.

Can the weak-willed person build a strong will later in life? Can the indecisive businessman become more decisive? Yes! The person who changes his self-view can become more decisive in handling decisions. Acceptance by others builds self-identity, and ultimately the person who knows himself can be confident. (Of course, the opposite is true: The aggressive person can become submissive because of Christ in his life.)

A person with weak ego strength is more likely to take criticism as an interpersonal threat. In Rosenberg's study the adolescents with weak ego strength indicated, "Criticism or scolding hurts me terribly." The same adolescent would be deeply disturbed "when anyone laughs at him or blames him for something he had done wrong."[8]

At the same time, some adolescents with weak ego strength have built in a defensive reaction. They indicated that it did not matter to them what others thought. Two-thirds of those adolescents who had weak egos confessed that criticism "bothered them very much." In another case where those with low ego strength were observed, the observer indicated these people's reactions to criticism was "touchy and easily hurt."[9]

On the other hand, young people with weak ego strength were hypersensitive to "dishing out" criticism, ridicule, and chastisement. Rosenberg gave the example of one girl with weak ego strength who indicated, "I don't want to hurt other people because I've been hurt, and I don't feel that I'd like to hurt others."[10] In addition, the young person who is usually the brunt of ridicule may feel that if he criticizes others, they may in turn criticize him. Fearing the retaliation, those with weak ego strength stay clear of confrontation. As a result these people place much value on "harmony" and getting along with people. "It's the Christian thing to do," stated a high school guy who would rather let people run over him than face an issue. Many people mistake meekness for a psychological adjustment to weak ego strength. The person with a strong ego does not mind facing the issue (truth), for truth is more important than feelings.

In Rosenberg's study those with weak ego strength found it awkward or difficult to meet new people or strike up a conversation with strangers. Those with weak ego strength tended to avoid meeting strangers and many times avoid their own friends. Social contacts seemed to threaten them. One adolescent male with weak ego strength answered Rosenberg's questions, stating: "When you are small it is much easier making friends because you don't feel you are going to embarrass yourself meeting new people . . . but when you get older it is not so easy. You begin to think what a fool you can make of yourself in the eyes of a person you don't know. I kind of become shy and withdrawn."[11]

The young person's opinion of himself is going to be significantly influenced by (1) his self-image and (2) what he imagines others think of him. Thus Rosenberg has found, "It is not surprising to find those people who consider themselves unworthy are more inclined to feel that others share this opinion of them."[12] At first glance one may say that young people who have low opinions of themselves should "think positively" because other people have high opinions of them. However, Rosenberg's study has not indicated this. The young person with low ego strength may be quite correct in assuming that others do not value him highly. Thus, if an adolescent feels he is not well accepted, he probably is not well accepted. He communicates this nonverbal attitude to others. People believe his message that he is unacceptable, and they reject him. This could be a vicious circle, but it could well start with others—people reject him, so he *then* feels himself unworthy of acceptance. For example, young people who aren't accepted often aren't loved by their own parents—and certainly that's not the young person who initiated that cycle.

Self-punishment becomes an important factor in understanding young people. Others reject the young person with low ego strength who rejects himself. Thus we can conclude that the path for good relationships with other people includes a good relationship with oneself.

Role Performance

Some young people might assume that the way to become friendlier is to force themselves into sociable contacts, thus learning interpersonal success. However, Rosenberg's findings point to the contrary. "The person with weak ego strength often makes special efforts to gain sociable qualities. His misfortune lies in the fact that those people are often most popular who do not strive for popularity." Role performance, or the roles played by young persons in their subculture, is still another factor that helps shape self-image. More attention is given to role performance today in understanding adolescence.

Role performance is simply defined as "that behavior of an individual which is performed in the fulfillment of a role, that is in accordance with the norm."[13]

The president of the student body does not always do as he wishes; he performs according to the demands and standards of his office. He performs the role of the class president. The star athlete, the cheerleader, the valedictorian, and the average girl dating an average guy all perform roles in accordance with the expectations of their position.

When a sophomore is playing the role of second-string tackle, is he really himself or is he wearing a mask? He may "kiss up" to the coach in an attempt to get the starting role, or he may go all out in practice to get into the starting lineup. In life the sophomore is sarcastic and "lips off" to adults. He is also lazy and indifferent about most things except football. Who is the real sophomore—the guy diligently playing football or the sarcastic student?

As you study the adolescent subculture, you become aware of the many roles that encumber each young person. The average young person plays more than one role at a time. Josh may be president of the youth advisors group at church, student leader of his homeroom class, and the star basketball player. These are formal roles, whereas his informal role may be dating Leanne. Jonathan is studying for the ministry, and he is the pastor's son. He is expected to be a better Christian than everyone else.

Formal roles are those that are placed upon a young person by recognized positions in our society. Formal roles might be class officers, club officers, positions on athletic teams, or other recognized positions with "power" and requisite standards. The informal roles of young persons are more difficult to define and describe. The informal role has clear standards, but they are usually never articulated. For instance, the girl who has been dumped by her boyfriend has a specific role to play in the high school subculture. She is not to look hurt and offended and is now free to flirt with all of the boys. When she sees her former boyfriend she either smiles or nods her head while underneath she may feel embarrassment or contempt for the former friend. The formal role is more understood by the adult society than is the young person's informal role. Adolescents understand its (informal) requirements, while adults stand off and shake their heads in bewilderment. As the young person plays his different roles, he learns to see himself in light of the roles he plays or does not play.

PSYCHOLOGICAL DEVELOPMENT OF SELF-IDENTITY

Self-image is determined largely by what both God and society think of us. However, the person will help determine what he does with the information coming to him from the outside. It is the self that accepts or rejects the information fed to him. The self is a unique creature. The self is the only creature that can continuously help to create itself. Many natural endowments are given at birth. The Creator determines the plant and animal world. However, man alone continuously assists in the fulfillment of his nature. The poet Wordsworth describes the process, "So build we up the being that we are."

Since the self-image is key to understanding human personality and human behavior, growth in self-image produces growth in the young person's personality and his behavior. Norman Vincent Peale has said much about the power of positive thinking. This may have some merit, but there is also much error. Put a young boy on a bicycle and tell him to "think positively" as you give him a push down the street. He may end up in an accident. It takes more than correct thinking. Yet the boy who has been diligently practicing and has conquered his fear may, through the power of positive thinking, actually ride a bicycle for the first time. The power of positive thinking *cannot* work when it is inconsistent with the circumstances. Yet a person through positive thinking may bring about growth in his self-image, and his self may apply the rules of life and ultimately change life.

The ability to discover oneself may mean the difference between success and failure in life. What may be success to one person is failure to another, so each person must know his capacities and abilities and from these formulate his own goal. Each of us carries a mental blueprint of his life. We are our own creative architects. The blueprint was in the drawing process in a nonverbal way throughout our preadolescent years.

With the arrival of adolescence the job of draftsman is taken over more and more by the young person. A person's self-image has been built up over the years from his own beliefs about himself. Maxwell Maltz has observed concerning self-image, "We do not question its validity, but proceed to act upon it just as if it were true."[14]

Whether one's image of himself is true or false, he acts upon it as if it were without error. A musician may teach piano for thirty years, feeling he is a good musician because his self-image has told him this. However, the same person may have had more natural gifts to become a teacher in the public school. Most people "act out" the sort of person they conceive themselves to be. The man who conceives himself to be "not very gifted" may end up in a 9:00 to 5:00 job and be happy that he is employed. If this person had the willpower, or even the opportunity, he might have become a stockholder and board member in the company. The high school student who sees himself as "dumb" in English but smart in arithmetic will usually "act out" his image of himself. In class he may have a mental block to literature and as a result receive a "D." Because he sees himself as exceptional with numbers, he may score well in calculus or physics. No doubt the report card will bear out his self-image.

One psychologist speaking of self-image indicated that self had three principle elements: (1) the imagination of one's appearance to the other person, (2) the imagination of one's judgment of that appearance to the other person, and (3) some sort of self-feeling, such as pride or mortification at one's appearance.[15]

Each person has more than one ego. The following points indicate the type of ego that each person has.

EGO IDEAL

Each person has a conception of himself as he wants to be. The graduating senior sees him or herself as a humanitarian, whereas another high school graduate sees herself married to a rich businessman, living in the prestigious section of town. Each of us should honestly face the question, "What do I want in life?

What is my ideal? Do I want a loving relationship with another person more than anything else? Do I want the applause of people more than anything else? Do I want security, ease, and freedom from fear more than anything else? Do I want to serve God and people?" We can't ignore the spiritual implications of career decisions.

Ego as Others See Us

The poet Robert Burns said, "O . . . to see ourselves as others see us." This might strengthen some personalities, yet shatter others. Some people imagine themselves as well liked by their friends, when really behind their backs they are laughed at. One youth pastor who thought he was successful was unaware of the fact that the board had called a secret meeting to discuss how to get a resignation without hurting the youth pastor's feelings.

The Self-Image

The self-image is how a person sees himself in his honest moments. When he lies on his bed at night and sleep escapes him, he sees himself as he really is. This self-image can be divided into seven categories.

Content

When a person thinks of himself, what is the content of the self-picture? Does he see himself as intelligent or a loving human being? Some may think of themselves as being interested in sports, while others feel they have good human relations. An artist? A businessman? An athlete? Or a grumpy old man? All these form the content of one's self-image.

Direction

Direction means consideration of one's self-image as favorable or unfavorable. Does a person have a favorable attitude toward his self-image? Some see themselves in the "best light," while others have an unfavorable attitude.

Intensity

A person may feel very strongly about either a favorable or unfavorable attitude toward himself. The high school boy who has a strong, favorable attitude toward himself may be called an egotist. One such egotist was overheard, "I may not be the best in the world, but you won't find anyone better." In the same way a person may be intense in his self-hatred. He may hate himself enough to commit suicide, yet not have the courage to do so. Also, there may be weak feelings toward one's self-image. A young person may have a positive or poor image of himself, but the intensity of his feelings about himself are weak.

Importance

This involves a consideration of how important the individual is in his own thinking. A person may have a weak or strong opinion of himself, yet thoughts about his self may not take up much of his thinking. His self-image is not important to him. On the other hand, some young persons are so important to themselves they are egotistical; they think of nothing else.

Stability

Some people have a consistent, firm attitude concerning themselves. "I know I'll make good in business someday," expressed a young person. This was a stable self-image he held throughout life. Even through several setbacks, he saw himself being successful in business and eventually one day he succeeded. Stability of self-image deals with the intensity, importance, and direction given the self-image. Am I strong in my feeling of self-esteem? Do I consider myself as an important subject? Do I have a favorable attitude toward myself? If the answer is a stable yes, then the person has a stable self-image.

Consistency

Consistency deals with the content of our self-image. Do I usually see myself in the same role? If the young person vacillates from truck driver to college professor to airline pilot, he is inconsistent. However, if his self-image remains in the area, say, of technology, then he is consistent in his self-attitude. Consistency deals with continuity of self-image. Stability deals with intensity, direction, and importance.

Clarity

Some people have a clear, sharp picture of themselves. Others have a vague, hazy, and sometimes blurred self-image. It is as though they were viewing their lives through a rain-spattered glass. One cannot generalize about people and call them introverts and extroverts as has been done in the past. These seven categories indicate the personality can have many dimensions. Thus, if one can learn what the individual sees when he looks at himself, he may determine better how this individual will function in life.

Negative Ego

Most people not only know who they are, but they may know who they are not, as well as who they do not want to be. The negative self is like the stabilizer of an airplane, giving a straight course through turbulent winds. There seems to be a type of vicious circle in determining one's real ego or self-esteem. What one is, or what he sees himself as, determines what he does. And what he does determines how he sees himself, which in turn determines his basis for self-esteem. With no attempt there can be no failure; with no failure, no humiliation. So our self-feeling in this world depends entirely on what we *back* ourselves to be or do.

LEARNING SELF-VALUES

Rosenberg makes a distinction between *self-estimate* and *self-value*. Self-estimate is how the individual actually rates himself with regard to a particular personality characteristic. The term "self-value" indicates how much the individual cares about the quality of his personality. Rosenberg indicates that the term "self-esteem" refers to the individual's overall self-acceptance or self-rejection. Therefore, self-estimate and self-value are part of the bricks and mortar of self-esteem.

Since self-values are of such importance to the individual, they raise the broader question: What social and psychological factors influence the selection of self-values?

The motivation in selection of self-values is wide and variant. For example, a young adolescent girl identifies with her mother and values those qualities in her mother that are outstanding or emphasized by the mother. However, if the young adolescent girl is rebellious to her mother, she may mimic or identify with those qualities that the mother lacks or disdains.

One motivation for selection of self-values cannot be disputed. People select self-values that maintain or enhance their self-esteem. A person selects a system of self-values that build his self-estimates. If a girl thinks she is good at sports, she may decide that athletic qualities are important to her. If a boy thinks he is poor at music, he may decide that he does not care about artistic expression. Rosenberg concluded, "In the long run, we would expect most people to value those things in which they are good, and to try to become good at those things they value."[16] However, there is always the person who strives in the face of disappointment and physical impossibility to be good at the thing he knows inwardly he cannot attain. This "martyr" needs help to understand his own self-image. I would not suggest that only immature and foolish people keep striving for things. There are definitely things worth striving for, even if we can never reach perfection in them—especially from a biblical perspective, for things such as spiritual disciplines, but also in life pursuits, such as academics or paying taxes.

Rosenberg makes another observation: "If each person can choose his own values, we are led to an interesting paradox of social life, namely, that almost everyone can consider himself superior to almost everyone else, so long as he can use his own system of values."[17] A boy who is a good football or basketball player considers himself to be better than the other boys on the youth committee at church. The three other boys consider themselves superior to other committee members. One is on the honor roll at school, another has excelled in the school orchestra, and the last considers himself physically good-looking. Each boy may acknowledge the superiority of the others in qualities that he considers unimportant. This feeling of superiority is not necessarily wrong (not an unbiblical pride that says I am superior to others); sometimes it may build strong ego strength and add worth to life. But in other students it may build pride and poor relationships with other people. Many young people get into trouble because their self-values are not equal to their ability. A high school junior envisions himself making the first-string basketball team while he does not have the skills, coordination, or physiology. A high school senior with limited ability plans to enter music in college and ultimately make her living through music. Now the question remains as to how young people get the wrong self-values.

How People Arrive at Wrong Self-Values for Life

1. *Self-values are acquired long before the opportunity to test them adequately.*

A child from a musical family may learn to value and desire musical skill, but only later in life does he become aware that he has insufficient talent for his desire. He must change his self-image and self-values. However, Rosenberg points out a problem. "Self-values, particularly if established early and reinforced by 'significant others,' may be quite difficult to change even if, at a later time, it is the individual's interest to do so."[18]

Many people have had to change their life's occupation after age forty, even though they were happy in their present occupation. Changing their occupation could be viewed as rejecting themselves.

2. *Self-values relate to goals as means relate to ends.*

The young student in college sees himself as a physicist (goal), yet he has no value or desire to study algebra (means). This boy has grown up in a home where his father was a teacher of mathematics in middle school, and the aspirations of the father were implanted into the self-image of the son. The boy cannot give up his self-image of becoming a physicist because that would be denying himself. Yet he has no love for algebra. In the same way a girl has a self-image of being a wife and homemaker (goal). The church she attends tells her to give little if any importance to physical or social attractiveness (means). Since physical and social attractiveness are relevant means for attaining the goal of marriage, they are important to her and cannot be easily dismissed from her mind. She does not want to give up her goal of being married; therefore, she has conflict with her church over her journey to marriage.

3. *Self-values are derived from the community norms and may not be in keeping with the self-image of the individual.*

Fred is a college freshman who sees himself as a good Christian. He is from a Christian home and at an early age learned what is right and wrong, what is important and unimportant. Now, as a Christian away from home and attending a secular college, he finds himself in conflict with the university morals. He finds that he desires the approval of his classmates. He wants to excel in terms of their values, not his own. He can enhance his own self-esteem by abandoning their values that are not appropriate to his self-image. However, he is likely to call down upon himself the disapproval and contempt of the university crowd. Rejection by the university crowd probably would diminish his self-esteem and bring worse conflict.

Changing One's Self-Values

Self-values cannot be changed just to suit the convenience of the personality. Self-values are a part of the personal philosophy or orientation to life. To change one's life, one must change his self-image. But how does one change his self-image? There must be some motivation for deciding that the old picture of oneself is in error and that the person needs a new picture. Many factors can cause a person to decide the present self-image is inadequate. First, his experience may show that he is not happy or cannot produce by the present self-image. The college professor sees himself as an excellent instructor in English literature. Yet not a single sophomore signs up for his elective, and his required course is taken only because students cannot get into other sections. The dean calls the college instructor in and tells him perhaps teaching is not his gift. Experience shows him that he must change his self-image. Perhaps he is better at research.

A second reason for changing one's self-image is "new

knowledge" about oneself. Jerry, a high school sophomore, had a self-image of himself as second-rate academically. After taking an IQ test, Jerry was told that he had an IQ of 130. For the past four years Jerry had been telling himself that he was not able to do high school work, and therefore, he was going to take a vocational course. After hearing that he "had it," Jerry began to apply himself and was soon scoring above average.

Third, one's self-image changes because of new relationships. Through a meaningful relationship one can learn a new worth of himself. Vanessa had been a high school junior classified as a "loner." She was slightly overweight, yet cute. Because she had few close friends, her life was wrapped up in reading novels, doing homework, and serving as a nurse's aid. Nic noticed her and dated her. Vanessa's life changed because of the new relationship. When Nic told her that she was cute, she tried to become the girl that he wanted her to be.

In life, many act and feel not according to what they really are like but according to what their imagination tells them they are like. Twelve-year-old David finished a piano recital, and his ability was average. However, parents, friends, and buddies told him that he was great. In actuality, he made several mistakes, and his nervousness put the audience on edge. Yet the compliments of friends and parents convinced David that he was good. Next time he played at a recital, his nervousness was gone because he thought he was good, and he performed without error—just as he had done in practice. Eleven-year-old Mike stood up before the Christmas pageant to recite Luke 2:1–20. He supposed that his buddies in the back row were sitting there laughing at him. In actuality they envied him because they wanted the part. But he imagined his buddies in rollicking laughter. Therefore, his emotional and nervous reactions were the same as if he had faced peer ridicule. It follows that if one's ideas and mental images concerning himself are distorted or unrealistic, then one's environment will likewise be inappropriate. Therefore, what should be done?

1. *Be sure you are right, doing the right thing, then go ahead.*

If a person sees himself doing the right thing, he will have confidence and self-esteem.

2. *Give others the break that you want from them.*

The average person on the street is not a cruel, vindictive criminal looking for opportunities to kick us in the face or knife us in the back. Most people will give us the opportunity that we give them. Still, one cannot generalize about human nature. There is always the hot-tempered, loud-mouthed person who will criticize everything.

3. *Picture yourself mastering each situation.*

Most of us tend to do this. This can be called "mental role-playing." One simply imagines himself in various situations, then acts out in his mind what he will do and say whenever the situation comes up in real life. This will give one poise when the situation finally arrives. Also, a person will realize that his actions and feelings are the result of his own self-image. This gives a person a level of confidence that is needed to change a personality and life.

4. *Know your strengths so you are less vulnerable to hypothetical fear.*

Too many are dependent upon other people's applause and support. These people become hurt by tiny pinprick criticism or so-called "omissions" by their friends. Those who are most easily offended and those who rely heavily on other people are those who have the lowest self-esteem. However, young persons who have strong self-esteem can take the criticism because they have a true or strong picture of themselves. If a person feels undeserving, doubts his own ability, or has a poor opinion of himself, he will usually crumble at the slightest criticism.

Dr. Maxwell Maltz gives the following advice to patients: "Relax away emotional hurts." He explains his cure as follows:

> I once had a patient ask me: "If the forming of scar tissue is a natural and automatic thing, why doesn't scar tissue form when a plastic surgeon makes an incision?"
>
> The answer is that if you cut your face and it "heals naturally," scar tissue will form, because there is a certain amount of tension in the wound and just underneath the wound which pulls the surface of the skin back, creates a "gap" so to speak, which is filled in by scar tissue. When a plastic surgeon operates, he not only pulls the skin together closely with sutures, he also cuts out a small amount of flesh underneath . . . so that there is no tension present.[19]

The incision heals smoothly, and there isn't a distorting scar. It is interesting to note that the same thing happens in the case of an emotional wound. If there is no tension present, there is no disfiguring emotional scar left. Have you ever noticed how easy it is to get your feelings hurt or take offense when you are suffering tensions brought out by frustrations, fear, and/or depression? This simple everyday experience illustrates very well the principle that we are injured or hurt emotionally not so much by other people or what they say or don't say, but by *our own attitude and our own response.*

There is a difference in the self-values of adolescent males and females. In the process of males identifying with males and females identifying with females, there is a good bit of similarity, but there are also important differences. In Rosenberg's test, girls consistently gave importance to such self-values as interpersonal harmony, friendliness, sociability, pleasantness, ability to get along well with people, and virtue. The list of self-values of males included physical courage, toughness, athletic ability, interpersonal control, dominance in their relationship with others, ability to get people to do what they wanted, freedom from naïveté, and versatility (males are likely to care about being good at many different kinds of things).[20] Even though males have certain self-values that are different from females, boys and girls have some similar characteristics. Both groups tend to consider it important to be intelligent, to be sociable and well liked, to be dependable and reliable, to have "interpersonal courage" (i.e., to stand up for your rights), to be independent and self-reliant, and to be mature (i.e., not to behave childishly).[21]

NOTES

1. Cecil G. Osborne, *The Art of Understanding Yourself* (Grand Rapids: Zondervan, 1967), 197.
2. Erich Fromm, *The Art of Loving* (New York: Harper & Row, 1956).
3. B. Blaine Jr., *Youth and the Hazards of Affluence* (New York: Harper & Row, 1967).
4. Ibid.
5. Boyd McCandless, *Children: Behavior and Development* (New York: Holt, Rinehart and Winston, 1967), 265.
6. Morris Rosenberg, *Society and the Adolescent Self-Image* (Princeton, N.J.: Princeton Univ. Press, 1965), Chapter IV, 1.
7. Erich Fromm, *Man for Himself* (New York: Rinehart, 1947).
8. Rosenburg, *Society,* 169.
9. Ibid., 170.
10. Ibid.
11. Ibid., 174.
12. Ibid., 176.
13. Robert Welch, *Identification and Its Familial Determinants* (Indianapolis: Bobbs-Merrill Co., 1962), 17.
14. Maxwell Maltz, *Psycho-Cybernetics* (New York: Prentice-Hall, 1960), 2, 116.
15. Charles Horton Cooley, *Human Nature and the Social Order* (New York: Charles Scribners Sons, 1912), 152.
16. William James, cited in Rosenberg, *Society and the Adolescent Self-Image,* 309–10.
17. Ibid., 251.
18. Ibid., 301.
19. Maltz, *Psycho-Cybernetics,* 143.
20. Rosenberg, *Adolescent Self-Image,* 301.
21. Ibid., 254.

A Biblical Perspective of Identity

The biblical concept of self in the Christian is one of the most important issues in helping a young person, or any other person, discover and establish his self-identity. If our faith is in Christ, then our identity is in Christ. There are a number of characteristics that come with this identity. Each of the following characteristics can become more meaningful and evident in our lives if we believe and act on them.

I am a child of God (John 1:12).
I am part of the true vine, a channel of Christ's life (John 15:1, 5).
I am Christ's friend (John 15:15).
I am chosen and appointed by Christ to bear His fruit (John 15:16).

I am a slave of righteousness (Rom. 6:18).
I am enslaved to God (Rom. 6:22).
I am a son of God; God is spiritually my Father (Rom. 8:14–15; Gal. 3:26; 4:6).
I am a joint heir with Christ, sharing His inheritance with Him (Rom. 8:17; Gal. 4:6–7).
I am a temple—a dwelling place—of God. His Spirit and His life dwell in me (1 Cor. 3:16; 6:19).
I am united to the Lord and am one spirit with Him (1 Cor. 6:17).
I am a member of Christ's body (1 Cor. 12:27; Eph. 5:30).
I am a new creation (2 Cor. 5:17).
I am reconciled to God and am a minister of reconciliation (2 Cor. 5:18–19).
I am a saint (1 Cor. 1:2; Eph. 1:1; Phil. 1:1; Col. 1:2).
I am God's workmanship—His handiwork—born anew in Christ to do His work (Eph. 2:10).
I am a fellow citizen with the rest of God's family (Eph. 2:19).
I am righteous and holy (Eph. 4:24).
I am a citizen of heaven, seated in heaven right now (Eph. 2:6; Phil. 3:20).
I am hidden with Christ in God (Col. 3:3).
I am an expression of the life of Christ because He is my life (Col. 3:4).
I am chosen of God, holy and dearly loved (Col. 3:12; 1 Thess. 1:4).
I am a son of light and not of darkness (1 Thess. 5:5).
I am a holy partaker of a heavenly calling (Heb. 3:1).
I am a partaker of Christ; I share in His life (Heb. 3:14).
I am one of God's living stones, being built up in Christ as a spiritual house (1 Peter 2:5).
I am a member of a chosen generation, a royal priesthood, a holy nation, a people for God's own possession (1 Peter 2:9–10).

I am an alien and stranger to this world in which I temporarily live (1 Peter 2:11).
I am an enemy of the devil (1 Peter 5:8).
I am a child of God, and I will resemble Christ when He returns (1 John 3:1–2).
I am born of God, and the Evil One—the devil—cannot touch me (1 John 5:18).
By the grace of God, I am what I am (1 Cor. 15:10).[1]

Neil Anderson says in his book *The Bondage Breaker,* "If you don't fully understand your identity and position in Christ, you will likely believe there is little distinction between yourself and non-Christians. Satan, the accuser, will seize that opportunity, pour on the guilt, and question your salvation."[2]

THE SIGNIFICANCE OF OUR SALVATION

In discussing biblical identity one would have to take an abbreviated look at soteriology. (The word *soteriology* is a derivative of the two Greek words, *soteria* and *logos,* which literally means "a word, idea or study of salvation.")[3] The word *regeneration,* used in Titus 3:5, simply means that change has occurred as a result of the work of the Holy Spirit in a person's life. The apostle Paul uses the term *adoption* (Eph. 1:5). Paul was familiar with the process of adoption under Roman law. It involved appointing an heir and that heir's being transferred to an adoptive father, with all the privileges and legal standing of a natural son and his father. *Sanctification* is another aspect of soteriology. To sanctify means to set apart. Sanctification is that process of being set apart for the service of God, because we belong to God. *Justification* is another critical part of soteriology. Justification involves our legal standing. Simply put, our legal standing has been changed in heaven and before God. We are no longer condemned individuals, and we have also been restored to "most favored" class. Positionally, we have been made perfect in the sight of God. We did not become perfect, but God has declared us to be perfect. The eternal benefit of this is the fact that we will not face eternal judgment.

SELF-IDENTITY AND CHRISTIAN TRUTH

The question "Who am I?" may or may not be a question that a teenager consciously asks himself. But it underlies some of his most basic actions and emotions in the process of self-identity. He is bombarded with this question from all sides, and the answers are varied. In science class, he is declared the result of an accidental arrangement of atomic elements. Marketers view him as a potential customer. The IRS sees him as a future taxpayer. Politicians see him as a future voter. The sociologist views him as a member of society.

A young person's identity does not depend on pure psychology, human goals and achievements, or societal labels. Each young person's identity, and ours as well, comes because we are held in high esteem by a sovereign God who has informed us of sin and forgiveness. Every Christian—every person who has received Jesus Christ into his life—is a new and different person (2 Cor. 5:17). God has added to his life. He has given us the only reason to have a good identity, and that reason is because we have been redeemed by Christ. (This is in total opposition of the nonbeliever who, generally speaking, sees humans as a little more than intelligent animals.)

> In the Genesis narrative, the concept of "image of God" appears at the consummation of all creation. At each stage of progress, Genesis notes punctiliously, God looks back on His creation and pronounces it "good." But creation still lacks a creature to contain God's own image. Only after all that preparation: "Let us make man in our image, in our likeness, and let them rule over the fish of the sea and the birds of the air, over the live-

> stock, over all the earth, and over all the creatures that move along the ground" (1:26).
>
> Among all God's creatures, only humanity receives the image of God, and that quality separates us from all else. We possess what no other animal does; we are linked in our essence to God. . . . Killing an animal means one thing; killing a fellow human is an entirely different matter, "for in the image of God has God made man" (9:6).
>
> . . . Adam was already biologically alive—the other animals needed no special puff of oxygen, nitrogen, and carbon dioxide to start them breathing, so why should man? The breath of God now symbolizes for me a spiritual reality. I see Adam as alive, but possessing only an animal vitality. Then God breathes into him a new spirit, and infills him with His own image. Adam becomes a living soul, not just a living body. God's image is not an arrangement of skin cells or a physical shape, but rather an inbreathed spirit.[4]

Within the church, Christians should learn that we can love ourselves because God loves us and has made us His children.

> Man is the apex of the creative works of God. As male and female, man was made in majesty to reflect the glory of God on earth. Man is the bearer of the very image of God; this is his differentia—that which marks him out from all other created things.[5]

We can acknowledge and accept our abilities, gifts, and achievements because they come from God and with His permission. We can experience the forgiveness of sins because God forgives unconditionally, and believers can praise God for what He is doing in and through our lives. No institution comes closer than the biblical church in educating people toward a more realistic self-concept.[6]

The New Nature and Christian Identity

God has created, or actually re-created, the person into a new being with a new nature. When Jesus Christ spoke of this process, He called it a birth from above, a spiritual birth or rebirth produced by God the Spirit (John 3:3ff.). The old manner of life for the Christian has been left behind, and a new one has taken its place. Therefore, the Christian has, or should have, a new lifestyle and a new mind-set—a new way of thinking and looking at things. Therefore, the Christian is a new and different being or self.

The Christian is also an individual who is loved totally and unconditionally by God. Nothing can ever separate the Christian from this love, according to Romans 8:31–39. Nothing he does in this life ("neither death nor life," v. 38), nor anything that is alive will ever separate him from God's love. Because God's love for him is assured, because he does not have to earn love, the Christian can have a deeper security than others. God loves the Christian as he is, whatever his true self may be. This is not to say, however, that God does not expect the Christian to become more Christlike. He does expect that. The Christian can rest secure in the knowledge of God's love, while discovering his true self. When God re-created the Christian, He added a new dimension, a new potential, to the Christian's self. This new dimension is Jesus Christ's power in the Christian (Phil. 4:13). The Christian is now able to conquer whatever situation he encounters (Rom. 8:37). The Christian has the strength to face and overcome his circumstances and surroundings because Jesus Christ is producing in him the power to do so. Therefore, the Christian can have a greater confidence than his contemporaries—confidence in Christ.

God has provided for the Christian all that is necessary to be a total person. The Christian can be a person with real love, not only for his friends but for his enemies as well; he can express the very love of God (Rom. 5:5). He can have that deep, inner joy that remains through trying circumstances because it is the joy of Jesus Christ Himself (John 15:11). The Christian can also have an unshakable peace of mind, totally incomprehensible to those around him, which remains even when things go wrong; it is Jesus Christ's peace (John 14:27). The same applies for the rest of the fruit of the Spirit (Gal. 5:22–23): patience, kindness, faithfulness, gentleness, and self-control. These are qualities of life that the Holy Spirit produces in the Christian's life. These qualities characterized the life of Jesus Christ Himself. God has provided these so that the Christian can be a complete, Christlike being.

The Holy Spirit and Christian Identity

The pertinent question at this point is how these characteristics and their potential can be integrated into the individual and realized in daily life. The key is the Holy Spirit, who produced the new life in the Christian (John 3:5–6), and He is the One who energizes the new nature of the Christian (Gal. 5:16, 25; 3:3–5). The Holy Spirit is also the One who helps the Christian realize more fully the love of God (Rom. 5:5). The Holy Spirit is the One who produces the power and dynamic of the new life (Eph. 3:16). He is also the One who produces the qualities of the Christlike life (Gal. 5:22). This is why the Christian is commanded to allow himself to be continually filled by the Holy Spirit (Eph. 5:18). The word *fill* means the person is so full of what fills him (the Holy Spirit) that he is completely under its control. In this case, He provides both the direction and power for the person's actions.

Three conditions are necessary for the filling of the Holy Spirit. The Christian must confess sin that is in his life, because sin hinders the work of the Holy Spirit (Eph. 4:30; 1 Thess. 5:19) as well as hindering the Christian's fellowship with God (1 John 1:5–9). The Christian must also yield his life to God, turning it over completely to God's control (Rom. 6:11–13; 12:1; Eph.

5:18). Finally, the Christian is filled by the Holy Spirit and lives his life under the Spirit's control by faith (Gal. 5:25; cf. Gal. 2:20; Col. 2:6). This last aspect is most vital and is the key to the consistent Spirit-filled Christian life (Rom. 14:23b; Heb. 11:6; Gal. 5:5–6). Faith in this respect is an utter and total dependence on the Holy Spirit's power, as well as the certainty that this power is in operation in his life, in every situation the Christian faces.

The Spirit-filled life is not only vital in the realization and integration of everything God has intended for the Christian as a new and total person; it is also absolutely necessary for the Christian in order to discover what his new self-identity should be and become, as God intended it (1 Cor. 2:12). The Holy Spirit assists the Christian in seeing who he is, who he has been made, what he has been given by God, and who he can and should become as a person. The Holy Spirit enables a person to recognize his actual self and empowers him to realize his potential self (John 16:13; 2 Cor. 3:18). This knowledge helps close the gap between these two "selves" and assists to harmonize the various aspects of self-image. In fact, not only does the presence of the Holy Spirit mean the Christian's potential self can be more effectively realized; his potential self has been increased since he has become a new person.

Biblical Identity and the New Life

So how does one develop the right biblical identity? A young person must begin with a personal relationship with God. In youth ministry, we cannot assume anything here, and we must begin here. It is God who has given us our appearance, parenthood, ethnicity, and personality. We must thank God for His workmanship thus far. We must acknowledge that God is not finished with us and that we are in process. Henry Morris and Martin Clark, in their book *The Bible Has the Answer*, explain it this way:

Meditation on Scripture passages that describe a believer's unchangeable position in God's sight will renew one's mind to think correctly. Such verses as Ephesians 1:3–14, I Peter 2:9, and II Peter 1:3–4 may provide a beginning, and frequent reflection to the same truths in other passages. Mental discipline is required to think repeatedly on these truths, and this discipline results in new thinking patterns that glorify God.

Christians can end confusion about their significance by thinking about themselves in the same manner as God does. As Christians, we cannot think correctly about ourselves without thinking about God, and our identity is determined from our position, our relationship with Him, in Christ Jesus.[7]

There are benefits to understanding a proper biblical identity. We will begin to view ourselves as God views us. This includes our sins and failures but also includes our position in Christ. Our value is determined by our relationship with Christ. This type of thinking will keep us mentally balanced with regards to personal piety and false humility. Another benefit is being able to weather the most difficult storms in our lives. Without this spiritual underpinning, we will experience the main brunt of life's storms. Matthew 7:24–27 reinforces this.

Therefore everyone who hears these words of mine and puts them into practice is like a wise man who built his house on the rock. The rain came down, the streams rose, and the winds blew and beat against that house; yet it did not fall, because it had its foundation on the rock. But everyone who hears these words of mine and does not put them into practice is like a foolish man who built his house on sand. The rain came down, the streams rose, and the winds blew and beat against that house, and it fell with a great crash. (NIV)

BENEFITS OF THE NEW LIFE

Other benefits include a boldness in our Christian service and an ability to fend off discouragement because of our position in Christ. If we are in Christ, then the following is true, by the grace of God:

I have been justified—completely forgiven and made righteous (Rom. 5:1).
I died with Christ and died to the power of sin's rule over life (Rom. 6:1–6).
I am free forever from condemnation (Rom. 8:1).
I have been placed into Christ by God's doing (I Cor. 1:30).
I have received the Spirit of God into my life that I might know the things freely given to me by God (I Cor. 2:12).
I have been given the mind of Christ (I Cor. 2:16).
I have been bought with a price; I am not my own; I belong to God (I Cor. 6:19, 20).
I have been established, anointed and sealed by God in Christ, and I have been given the Holy Spirit as a pledge guaranteeing our inheritance to come (I Cor. 1:21; Eph. 1:13, 14).
Since I have died, I no longer live for myself, but for Christ (II Cor. 5:14, 15).
I have been made righteous (II Cor. 5:21).
I have been crucified with Christ and it is no longer I who live, but Christ lives in me. The life I am now living is Christ's life (Gal. 2:20).
I have been blessed with every spiritual blessing (Eph. 1:3).
I was chosen in Christ before the foundation of the world to be holy and am without blame before Him (Eph. 1:4).
I was predestined—determined by God—to be adopted as God's son (Eph. 1:5).
I have been redeemed and forgiven, and I am a recipient of His lavish grace (Eph. 1:7).

I have been made alive together with Christ (Eph. 2:5).
I have been raised up and seated with Christ in heaven (Eph. 2:6).
I have direct access to God through the Spirit (Eph. 2:18).
I may approach God with boldness, freedom, and confidence (Eph. 3:12).[8]

The Spirit-filled life is not a cure-all for identity crisis, but it is an absolute necessity for the proper solution of it. If the Christian young person is living the Spirit-filled life, he will be able to more readily discover and more effectively establish his self-identity. This is true because he is following God's direction and using God's power; it is also true because he is allowing the Author of the Bible to use the Bible to help him understand and achieve self-identity. This last statement cannot be overemphasized. It is in the Bible that the Christian, under the Holy Spirit's guidance and teaching (John 16:13–15), finds the facts and materials from which he needs to establish a Christian self-identity.

NOTES

1. Neil T. Anderson, *Victory over the Darkness,* 2d ed. (Ventura, Calif.: Regal, 2000), 51–53.
2. Neil T. Anderson, *The Bondage Breaker* (Eugene, Oreg.: Harvest House, 2000), 48.
3. Elmer Towns, *Theology for Today,* 2d ed. (Lynchburg, Va.: Elmer Towns, 1994), 301.
4. Dr. Paul Brand and Philip Yancey, *In His Image* (Grand Rapids: Zondervan, 1987), 21–22.
5. Ronald B. Allen, *The Majesty of Man* (Portland, Oreg.: Multnomah, 1984), 199.
6. Gary R. Collins, *Christian Counseling,* rev. ed. (Dallas: Word, 1988), 324.
7. Henry M. Morris and Martin E. Clark, *The Bible Has the Answer* (Green Forest, Ark.: Master Books, 1996), 216–17.
8. List from Anderson, *Victory over the Darkness,* 64–65.

The Purpose of Youth Ministry

This is the most important chapter in this volume, because a ministry's aims determine and define not only its purpose but its accomplishments and shortcomings as well. If youth leaders have being "relevant" to today's youth culture as their only aim, then the programming will consist mainly of coffeehouses, rock music, or street demonstrations. "Cultural relevance" raises the question, "How much of the contemporary culture should be adapted into a youth ministry?"

This chapter has a simple thesis: *The aims of youth work are no different than the aims of a local church.* The youth are part of a local church, but that does not mean their aims are *partial* rather than *wholistic.* Many traditional youth programs have had partial church aims;

i.e., they have adapted some but not all of the aims found in Scripture. The catalyst of ministry to youth has been a Bible knowledge "training" approach that centered on Sunday afternoon programs. Most Christian educators now agree that this approach produces limited results. At one time Christian Endeavor dominated church ministry to youth. The catalyst of Christian Endeavor was a worship approach. The Christian Endeavor approach, like the training approach, only had partial aims rather than incorporating all the aims of Scripture.

THE NEED FOR DELIBERATE AIMS

This chapter maintains that "wholistic aims" are needed in youth work. When a youth leader plans his program, he should attempt to fulfill every biblical command. This goal can seem intimidating; however, we should strive to be as obedient as possible in all of our ministry undertakings, whether they be with youth or as a corporate body. We are not free to choose which commands we will or will not obey.

This chapter makes a distinction between aims of youth work (aims guide our activity) and the goals of youth work (a goal is the ultimate purpose toward which the process is moving). Some educators claim there is no distinction between aims and goals. However, the careful student will discover that, just as there is a distinction between the two, so there is a correlation. A valid aim points in some direction; it is directed to a goal. For the most part, aims are active and goals are passive. Aims are likened unto the bow and arrow held in the hands of the archer; he must give proper direction. Goals are likened unto the target; they give perspective to the process called archery. The archer aims, and when the arrow misses the target it reveals the aim was wrong. A youth worker needs clear aims to give purpose and direction to his energies. Vieth said, "Aims . . . are the outcome of one's philosophy of Christian Education."[1]

The correct philosophy of youth work grows out of the Word

of God and is not a creation by man. Biblical youth work obeys the commands of the Word of God; therefore, the aim of youth work is to carry out the aims of the New Testament. Eavey states, "An aim is attention brought to focus to make possible expenditure of energy for achieving a predetermined purpose."[2]

Many youth workers are not clear in their aim, and as a result they "spin their wheels" and accomplish little for God. Neither hard work nor sincerity will accomplish eternal results if the youth leader is not guided by biblical aims. Correct and clear aims are vitally important, for with them more can be accomplished by the youth worker in the lives of young people. Therefore, this chapter is an attempt to give clear New Testament aims for youth work. Fallaw notes, "Aims are immediate steps taken one after the other in class sessions toward goals which keep the teacher and pupil moving on the way to achievement of the final goal."[3] Therefore, there are many aims for youth work. But each aim should interrelate to give direction to the process.

In a Sunday school class, the youth worker has several aims: He wants to communicate biblical content, he wants teens to respond to the Gospel, and he wants teens to have Christian fellowship. These are several aims, leading to a definite goal—the maturity of the young person. One broad goal of all Christian activity is "to glorify God." This is the predominant theme of the Psalms and should control all that is done by the Christian teen. The Westminster shorter catechism asks, Q. "What is the chief end of man?" A. "Man's chief end is to glorify God and to enjoy Him forever." Christian teens should glorify God; however, it is sometimes difficult to know *how* to glorify God. The best way to glorify God is to carry out the aims of the New Testament, which advocate living a life of obedience to God. When we fulfill the biblical aims, we give our attention to the biblical goal, which is to glorify God (the end result).

Eavey gives a definition of a goal: "A goal is the ultimate purpose or destination towards which the educational process is moving. Aims assist in achieving the goal(s). Goals are the objectives which one seeks to attain."[4] The aim of all youth work is the aim of Calvary: to bring lost people into a right relationship to God through salvation and then to disciple them into a life of obedience. The ultimate goal is that God is glorified through obedience to Him. There is no better way to glorify God than through salvation and discipleship of the lost. Steps to be taken in accomplishing this goal come from many directions and lead to one goal—the glory of God.

THE AIMS OF YOUTH WORK

There is no place in Scripture where God spells out a different set of aims for young people than for all Christians. Also, there is no place in Scripture where God spells out a different set of aims for the youth program than for the local church. These aims can be found in the Great Commission. This is the last command Jesus gave before returning to heaven, and it has been characterized as the strategy for the church. "Go therefore and make disciples of all the nations, baptizing them in the name of the Father and the Son and the Holy Spirit, teaching them to observe all that I commanded you; and lo, I am with you always, even to the end of the age" (Matt. 28:19–20 NASB).

The Great Commission is one command, but it has three aspects: (1) evangelism, (2) baptism, and (3) teaching. Christian young people cannot choose what aspect of the Great Commission they will or will not obey. Hence we must structure our ministry in such a way so that the opportunity to obey each aspect of the Great Commission is given. Since it is one command, to disobey one part makes one disobedient. If a youth worker only emphasizes teaching and neglects evangelism, then he is not carrying out the Great Commission. God's strategy is evangelism, baptism, and education. Youth programs that do not include baptism are not biblical youth programs, although what they may be accomplishing may be good (the exception here would be parachurch organizations, which delegate baptism to the local church).

The first aspect of the Great Commission is found in the word *teach* (v. 19), which is translated "disciple." We are commanded to go disciple all nations. Implied in the word *disciple* is reaching the lost, communicating the Gospel to them, and leading them to Jesus Christ. When we are evangelizing, we are causing teens to begin to follow Jesus Christ and live for Him. True New Testament evangelism gets people to follow Jesus Christ and His commands. Therefore, youth work involves more than presenting the Gospel to the unsaved or explaining salvation to them. We should attempt to persuade them to become Christians, causing the unsaved to follow Jesus Christ. The youth worker should get his young people to follow Jesus Christ, and when they do, the youth worker has a successful youth ministry. There can be no ultimate success in the Lord's work without a series of small successes along the way. Therefore, we want more than large crowds of youth to follow Christ. We want youth to become His disciples.

The following outline gives the full scope of a biblical youth program. Your youth program will be successful if you apply all the aims of the New Testament. Even though these aims are for the entire body of Christ, we will communicate these principles as they relate to youth work.

Aim One: Discipleship (Matthew 28:19)

Overall Aim: To make disciples out of as many teens in the world as possible. Discipleship begins with evangelism, for we cannot grow someone spiritually who is spiritually dead.

1. *Show compassion to the needs of teens.*

The first aim in youth work is a heart of compassion for teens. When Jesus saw the multitudes, He was moved with compassion

(Matt. 9:36). This is love translated into action. You reflect compassion by getting up at 2:00 A.M. to counsel with a teen who has run away from home or by giving up a favorite television program to meet with a teen.[5] The first biblical criterion for effective youth work is a love for God and of course a love for teens.

2. *Have a vision of what God can do for the lost teen.*

The second step in evangelism is vision. You must have a vision of what God can do in the life of your young people and through your youth group. First, vision involves faith. You must believe God can change their lives; therefore, you work to that end. You believe God can bring revival to the youth of your city; therefore, you plan outreach programs. Before you can have a great youth group, you must have vision. Second, vision involves foresight, and this lies in the youth leader. As a person of God, you must have the ability to (1) see first, (2) see the most, and (3) see the farthest into the future. Just as the Old Testament prophet was called a seer, you must be the eyes of God and see the world as God sees it.

> Jesus went about all the cities and villages, teaching in their synagogues, preaching the gospel of the kingdom, and healing every sickness and every disease among the people. But when He saw the multitudes, He was moved with compassion for them, because they were weary and scattered, like sheep having no shepherd. (Matt. 9:35–36)

If you want to build a great youth work, you must have a great vision of what God can do through your teens. The third aspect of vision is insight into young people. You must see the degradation of sin and the damnation of sin. The degradation of sin ruins their lives now, and the damnation of sin will send them to hell in the future. The final aspect of vision concerns seeing God. You must have a correct vision into the nature and person of God. God wants to work through you; He loves teens, and He can transform their lives. You must have a correct view of Scripture to have a correct vision of God. Since the Bible is the foundation of correct doctrine, you cannot build a biblical youth work without building on the principles of Scripture.

3. *Bring the Gospel to lost teens.*

You cannot assume that young people want to come to a youth activity or a Bible study. It is your duty to reach them. Reaching is "motivating a young person to give an honest hearing to the Gospel." You have not evangelized the young people in your community until you have reached them for Christ. This is simply using every acceptable means to (1) make contact with lost young people, (2) motivate them to come under the Gospel, and (3) have an attractive program to present the Gospel. The apostle Paul defines reaching as "to the Jews I became as a Jew, that I might win Jews; to those who are under the law, as under the law, that I might win those who are under the law; . . . to the weak I became as weak, that I might win the weak. I have become all things to all men, that I might by all means save some" (1 Cor. 9:20–22).

Reaching is using every acceptable means to communicate the Gospel to young people: radio, newspapers, visitation, activities, retreats, outreach services, mailings, telephone, tracts, testimonies, television, videos, Internet, concerts, etc. Regardless of which methods you use, reaching must be controlled by a New Testament aim and accomplish a New Testament goal. Reaching must not compromise the Word of God. A pastor recently said, "I will do anything to get people saved!" Anything? Would he lie and coax people to church by promising something he couldn't deliver? Obviously, not every technique is acceptable to the youth worker who attempts to live by the standard of Scripture. Principles and techniques must be controlled by biblical aims and accomplish biblical goals. If not, they are rejected as being unbiblical (see a sample goal sheet at the end of this chapter).

4. *Talk about one's Christian experiences with lost teens.*

Young people love to share their testimonies with others. The New Testament calls this witnessing. "You shall be witnesses to Me" (Acts 1:8). The witness is one who tells his experience. A person who sees an accident and is called into the court as a witness is not expected to give his opinion of who caused the accident. He testifies to what he has seen or experienced. His opinion or interpretation of the accident is not allowed. Just so, teenagers should witness to others what Jesus Christ has done for them. They should witness to (1) what they have seen of Christ, (2) what they have heard of Christ, and (3) what they have experienced.

The changed life is the best testimony for Jesus Christ. When Peter and John were called before the council concerning their preaching, they gave the following witness: "For we cannot but speak the things which we have seen and heard" (Acts 4:20). This was a witness and not a sermon to the council. In the same trial, the healed man who had been lame from birth stood with Peter and John. He told the council what had happened to his life: "And seeing the man who had been healed standing with them, they could say nothing against it" (Acts 4:14). His testimony was an effective tool of evangelism. Give your young people many opportunities to tell their testimony when winning souls or when just "shooting the breeze" with other teenagers.

5. *Communicate the Gospel to all teens.*

Teens love to witness, but they need to go further than giving their subjective experiences. They need to give the factual content of the Gospel. The Gospel gets lost teens saved. This is preaching, whether the Gospel is given to one or to a multitude. Preaching gets teenagers saved. Dr. Lewis S. Chafer, past president of Dallas Theological Seminary, often said, "You haven't preached the Gospel until you have given people something to believe." Jokes and deathbed illustrations make teenagers laugh or weep, but the content of the Gospel (biblical truth) saves the soul.

Preaching is simply a clear and complete presentation of the content of the Gospel to lost people. It is more than teaching. Teaching gives the facts of the Gospel; preaching gives biblical content with persuasion and compassion to convince the audience to become Christians. Many American churches talk about evangelism, proclaiming the Gospel to the lost. New Testament churches talk about soul winning, proclaiming the Gospel with persuasion. The Gospel is twofold. First, it is *propositional truth,* the fact that Jesus died for sins. He was buried and He rose again the third day. Everyone should hear this message because Christ died for all. However, the second aspect of the Gospel is *personal truth:* Jesus Christ is the Gospel. A lost teenager may understand the propositional truth of the Gospel, i.e., the fact that Jesus died, was buried, and rose again, yet not be converted. Salvation is more than understanding. The lost teenager must receive a person—Jesus Christ. Jesus Christ saves the teen from sin. Christ must live in the heart of the teenager for him to become a Christian (John 1:12).

Some youth groups are satisfied to have a small intimate coffeehouse ministry, because this fulfills their aims. Other youth groups have a dynamic evangelistic outreach aimed at evangelizing every teen in the city. Whatever method suits your aims, use it to reach the youth in your community with the Gospel of Christ.

6. *Persuade the lost teen to receive the Gospel.*

Persuasion is a conscious attempt to motivate lost people to accept Jesus Christ and repent of their sins. The youth pastor urges teens to repent and believe. Some people dislike the invitation at the end of a Gospel message, where young people are invited to come forward and receive Jesus Christ. An invitation may put teenagers on the spot, but it is biblical persuasion, inviting them to be saved. The lack of persuasion in today's youth ministry reveals a weakness in the church. Paul indicated, "Brethren, my heart's desire and prayer to God for Israel is that they may be saved" (Rom. 10:1). In this same desire to persuade Israel, Paul said, "I have great heaviness and continual sorrow in my heart. For I could wish that myself were accursed from Christ for my brethren" (Rom. 9:2–3 KJV).

Youth directors do more than tell the facts of the Gospel to teens; they use all the motivational devices at their command to get the youth to accept Jesus Christ. When the youth director preaches to youth, he may use humor, illustrations, and "current lingo" to encourage youth to make a positive decision for Jesus Christ. However, emotional persuasion must be based on an intellectual communication of Bible content and the working of the Holy Spirit in the life of the teen. The primary purpose of a church is discipleship, which begins with evangelism, reaching a town for Christ. Since the youth program should reflect church aims, the primary purpose of a youth group is to evangelize and disciple the youth of its community.

Aim Two: Baptism (Matthew 28:19)

Overall Aim: To identify each Christian teen with a local church.

The second major thrust of the Great Commission is to baptize the new convert after salvation. Baptism is an outer symbol of an inner change. The converted teen is identified with Christ in His death, burial, and resurrection. When the new Christian is placed under water, he is identified with Christ in His death and burial; when he is taken out of the water, he is identified with the resurrected life of Christ (Rom. 6:4–5). In the

New Testament, when the believer was baptized, he also was added to the church (Acts 2:41–47). Just as baptism marks our being placed in Jesus Christ, so baptism marks our being placed in the body of Christ—the local church. Therefore, when Christ commanded the disciples to go and "baptize," He was commanding to go and "church" people, that is, get them identified with a local church. The key to successful, growing Christians is the continuous ministry of a local church.

We live in a day when it is fashionable to attack the local church for its hypocrisy, lethargy, failure, or lack of relevance. Interdenominational agencies have risen to public attention because many people believe the church has failed. But the church, with all of its failures, is still the institution founded by Christ. The local church still has priority in God's plan of evangelism, education, and edification.

The American economy emphasizes the independence of the individual. Teens are told to "be your own god." Society has made each teen the "focus" of all decisions, meaning the youth is told he has the right to choose what is best for him within his own perspective. This influence has led to license on the part of many Christians. Many young people feel the church has no rightful claims upon their life. When Christian teens are not under the authority of the church, they are easily led off into doctrinal tangents, and they live unproductive lives and are slothful in service. True, the Christian teen has freedom in Jesus Christ, but this liberty is exercised within the framework of the local church under the Word of God. The church is never pictured in the Scripture as a social club; it is an organized army, equipped for battle, ready to charge the enemy. A good soldier is known for his discipline; he follows orders and is personally armed for battle. Christian young people should be under the discipline of the Word of God, which means also under church discipline. The local church has the following aims for all believers. These aims should be applied to the youth ministry as well.

1. *Bring each believing teen under the discipline of the Scriptures.*

The word *discipline* has a positive and negative connotation. Positive discipline is simply the constructive commands of the Word of God, preached and taught. In this way the Scripture edifies, exhorts, and comforts the believer. The Word of God sets doctrine straight and gives the teenagers a basis on which to live. Negative discipline corrects false doctrine and false living. When the youth pastor points out the sin of teenagers in his preaching, he is exercising negative discipline. He may counsel with a young person concerning attendance at a questionable event; this also is negative discipline. Discipline is not always found in consensus of the deacons or elders or in a congregational meeting. A disciple is disciplined, and his standards are found in the Word of God.

The main reason a youth worker wants to get teens to attend church every Sunday or to come to a youth outing is to get them under the teaching of the Word of God. Some might criticize that youth workers only want to count "heads." Some youth directors emphasize attendance to swell their ego or to win the praise of a congregation. These are wrong reasons to stress church attendance. Teens should be in the house of God so they may hear the Word of God and grow thereby (1 Peter 2:2). One weakness of many youth ministries is their reflection of the freedom movement of America and their acceptance of the philosophy that people should do as they please. Since the local church was instituted by Christ (Matt. 16:18), every teen believer ought to be identified with a New Testament church that has oversight over his spiritual welfare.

2. *Use the total abilities of each Christian teen for God's purpose.*

The second purpose for attempting to get teens into a church is to help involve them in Christian service. Every Christian ought to be involved in service, for every Christian has a gift.

Paul indicated, "Each one has his own gift from God" (1 Cor. 7:7). A gift is an ability to serve Jesus Christ and accomplish spiritual results, thus bringing glory to God. God gave these abilities to be used for His glory. Like the parable of the talents, if we don't use our abilities, God removes our opportunities. Therefore, an aim of churching people is to use their ability in service to God. If every young believer becomes involved, first the teen grows, and then the local church grows and is built up (Eph. 4:13).

The aim of a youth ministry is to have every young person spiritually trained and every young person active in service. Since God has given everything to the believer, Christian teens should be taught to give to God in return. First, it should be a priority to attend the primary services: Sunday school, morning and evening church services, and youth activities. This is a biblical stewardship of their time. Christian young people do not have the right to choose whether or not they will miss church services; they should attend services unless providentially hindered. Christian teenagers should be taught to give their money to God, as well as their time. Giving is the stewardship of their treasury. The stewardship of talents is where every Christian young person serves Jesus Christ with the gifts that are his. Youth should be ministering (using their gifts) to the community, the church, and each other.

3. *Encourage fellowship among teens so they may strengthen one another.*

Christians are urged to have fellowship for the purpose of edifying one another and supporting one another in their faith (1 John 1:3–4). When youth tell their testimonies, both the defeats and victories, they encourage others and are thereby encouraged. Many youth groups place small-group fellowship as the main purpose for their existence. Although fellowship is biblical, it is not the main purpose for a youth ministry. Groups that minimize evangelism or the power of the Gospel can never have biblical fellowship. The Gospel makes teens one in Jesus Christ, and He becomes a center around which they can have fellowship.

4. *Produce corporate worship and motivate Christian teens to private worship.*

Worship is not an optional choice for teens; it is their obligation. They should worship both privately and publicly. Jesus noted, "But the hour is coming, and now is, when the true worshipers will worship the Father in spirit and truth; for the Father is seeking such to worship Him" (John 4:23). Worship must be in spirit (enthusiasm or with one's total being) and in truth (accurate according to God's standards). "True worship" implies the possibility of false worship. Jesus knew people would worship in the wrong way. You should be sure that your teens worship according to the Scriptures. Since God wants worship from man, it is the teen's duty to worship God. (See chapter 19 on worship.) Worship is not man-centered; it is God-centered. Worship is not concerned with the needs of teens; it is the teens' concern with magnifying God. The phrase *worth-ship* defines worship, for it is giving God the worth due to Him.

5. *Become the focus for an organized outreach into the community.*

The unstable teen needs the stability of a local church. The church is a community of believers who exercise watch-care over the spiritual development of the teen. The human (sinful) nature does not like discipline, so some teens will find it difficult to follow the leadership of the youth leader. Elmer Towns defines the church: "The church is a group of baptized believers in whom Christ dwells, under the discipline of the Word of God, organized for evangelism, education, fellowship, worship and the administration of the ordinances."[6] The church should have an organized evangelistic program. Paul reflects an organized outreach: He had "taught [the elders] publicly and from house to house" (Acts 20:20). As a result of this spread of the Gospel, "All who dwelt in Asia heard the word of the Lord Jesus, both Jews and Greeks" (Acts 19:10).

An organized evangelistic program is complete in *kind* and *coverage*. Various forms of organized outreach should be included in a youth program: for example, personal evangelism, mass evangelism, mailing evangelism, rest home and hospital evangelism, beach evangelism, and radio-TV evangelism. Complete evangelistic coverage includes house-to-house visitation, rural evangelism, summer mission trips, and outreach to foreign mission fields. A church is indwelt by Christ in a unique way (Rev. 1:13; 2:1), different from an interdenominational gathering, different from when two Christians gather for fellowship (Matt. 18:20). Christ is the light of the world (John 8:12), who shines out of a gathering of Christians into the darkness of this age. The youth group is an extension of the church and should reflect the light of the Gospel into the youth community. Since God desires that the church do all things decently and in order (1 Cor. 14:40), the evangelistic outreach of the youth group should be systematic and comprehensive. When evangelism is haphazard (left to the inclination of each believer), there is omission and overlapping in reaching the community. Some needy sections are overlooked and the popular "in" cause receives all the evangelistic attention.

6. *Administer the church's ordinances.*

Both the Lord's Table (1 Cor. 11:23–26) and baptism (Matt. 28:19) are commanded. These are church ordinances and are administered by the church. Individuals and interdenominational agencies do not have the authority to administer these ordinances. If Christian teens have not taken advantage of these symbols, they are not obeying the commands of Scripture.

Therefore, a well-rounded program to youth will include the correct use of the ordinances as part of the youth program and the corporate body as well.

Aim Three: Education (Matthew 28:20)

Overall Aim: To teach each Christian teen to obey the Scriptures.

The third aspect of the Great Commission is teaching. The church is given the responsibility of carrying out the example of Jesus the Teacher. He spent time with His disciples. The Sermon on the Mount begins with this observation: "His disciples came unto Him and He taught them" (see Matt. 5:1–2). After He taught the disciples and the multitudes, we find this explanation: "He taught them as one having authority, and not as the scribes" (Matt. 7:29). The content of Christian education is suggested in the Great Commission: "Teaching them to observe all things that I have commanded you" (Matt. 28:20). A youth group is first aimed at evangelism, reaching the young people in the community for Jesus Christ. After the unsaved become Christians, they must be taught the Word of God. Those who have grown up in a Christian home must also be taught the Word of God. Therefore, a youth program must have a strong teaching ministry. The following points describe the teaching aim of youth ministry.

1. *Communicate the content of the Word of God.*

The first educational aim of youth work is that every pupil should know the core doctrines contained in the Bible so that he will be protected from the contamination of sin, he will be built up in the Christian life, he will understand God's will for his life and become a productive Christian, and he will win others to Jesus Christ (Titus 1:9; 2:7). The thrust of Christian education is Bible indoctrination, "teaching them to observe all things that I have commanded you" (Matt. 28:20). The word *doctrine* is simply the noun form of the verb *to teach*. Therefore, when we are teaching the Word of God, we are indoctrinating young people with the Scriptures. Jesus spoke concerning the subject matter of the Holy Spirit's teaching, "all things that I said to you" (John 14:26). As a result, Christian education is transmissive in nature.

Some complain against indoctrination, indicating it lacks compassion for the student and is not experience-oriented. Indoctrination is usually interpreted to mean "rote learning" or simply "parroting" facts without understanding. However, the Scriptures indicate biblical teaching leads to understanding and that pupils should have experience with the Word of God (see chapter 14). A biblical program of teaching young people aims at a complete, comprehensive, consistent attempt to communicate all of the Bible, meeting the students' needs while being relevant to their lives.

2. *Train each Christian teen to use his skills to carry out God's plan for his life.*

If teaching content is the first step of education, then training in skills is the second. Training puts into operation content that has been communicated in proposition form. Some make the discipleship programs the catalyst of their youth ministry and ignore evangelism. To do so is to neglect the balanced ministry as seen in the Great Commission. However, other youth works have swung away from the "unworkable" discipleship and have left out training altogether. This extreme also is wrong. Training puts into operation what has been taught through theory. Jesus indicated in the Great Commission that the aim is "teaching them to observe" (Matt. 28:20). The aim of a church is to train members, including young people, to be able to adequately carry out their responsibility of evangelism, worship, and service, in and out of the church. The aim of training is good churchmanship where teenagers are good productive members of the house of God. Paul says his reason for writing was "that you may know how you ought to conduct yourself in the house of God, which is the church of the living God" (1 Tim. 3:15). That is a good motive for our teaching as well.

3. *Teach Christian values and attitudes to all teen believers.*

The first aim of education has to do with content and the second aim has to do with skills. The third aim has to do with the attitudes of life, an area that has been ignored by many educators until recently. Teens' attitudes will reflect the quality of their Christian life. The church should aim to communicate Christian values and attitudes in accordance with the standards of the Scriptures. A teen's attitude is based on his knowledge of Scripture, and his knowledge is usually based on the completeness of the church youth program. First, build positive biblical attitudes as reflected in the fruit of the Spirit (Gal. 5:22–23) and reinforce the danger of negative attitudes so they will abstain from all appearance of evil (1 Thess. 5:22). Strive after internalization (habits of the heart) over contextualization (head knowledge). The teens must live what they believe.

4. *Motivate Christian teens to live a godly life as called for in the Scriptures.*

Teaching biblical content without understanding will not produce growth in Christian teens. "The god of this world hath blinded the minds of them which believe not" (2 Cor. 4:4 KJV). The unsaved cannot understand spiritual things (1 Cor. 2:14); after salvation some of this inability remains. Therefore, biblical teaching takes away blindness and causes teenagers to grow in Christ. The youth leader can only impart limited (natural) insight into the Word of God. The Holy Spirit is the one teacher who takes away spiritual blindness and causes teenagers to understand (supernaturally) the Scriptures. "But the Comforter, which is the Holy Ghost, whom the Father will send in my name, he shall teach you all things, and bring all things to your remembrance, whatsoever I have said unto you" (John 14:26 KJV). You want to give your young people more than Bible content; you want them to be fully mature in Jesus Christ. Paul told his young babes in Christ that he wanted to give them his soul: "We were willing to have imparted unto you, not the gospel of God only, but also our own souls, because ye were dear unto us" (1 Thess. 2:8 KJV). This is the ultimate aim of a youth leader, that every young person would be as spiritually mature as he. Paul expressed it this way, "Be ye followers of me, even as I also am of Christ" (1 Cor. 11:1 KJV).

5. *Support the aims and sanctity of the family.*

The youth program cannot neglect the home, Christian or not. Your teens are exhorted, "Obey your parents in the Lord, for this is right" (Eph. 6:1). Therefore, your program is an extension of the influence of a good Christian home. The center of all that is taught in the youth program is to respect the authority of parents and recognize the dignity of the family. "'Honor your father and mother,' which is the first commandment with promise" (Eph. 6:2). Many homes have failed the teen, but that does not give a teen the right to disobey God and deny the sanctity God requires for the home. Parental wishes concerning curfew, dress standards, music, and other issues must be respected. The leader will have to build into the youth a respect for their parents, unconditionally, because it is commanded by God.

CONCLUSION

Aims give direction to the youth worker; the goals are the outcome you desire. Aims give purpose to the youth worker planning a program; he uses goals after the program is finished to judge his results. Techniques are the "way we operate" to accomplish youth work. The youth worker is not left to create techniques on his own. Results do not justify using any technique. A technique must flow out of biblical aims and meet the demands of biblical goals. A contest may be a gimmick that makes attendance grow, and kids may attend because of its novelty, but they may not give an honest hearing to the Gospel. Actually, the kids may feel the gimmick cheapens God. Therefore, it is not a biblical technique, even though attendance swells.

The youth worker who attempts to follow the Great Commission will have clear aims for his ministry. First, God expects successful evangelism, that the youth leader win young people to the Lord. Next, converts must be baptized, which involves identifying them with the local church. Finally, teenagers should be taught the Word of God, be trained for Christian service, understand the meaning of Scriptures, and assume the values and attitudes of the New Testament in everyday life. Simply, everything we do (including the programs) must reflect the biblical goals of the church as left for us in Scripture. As we establish biblical aims and goals we must work to see that our programs mirror these principles. As you read over the following aims and goals for youth ministry, establish the standard that whatever you do with teens will support at least two of the goals listed below. This may cause us to be creative in incorporating these goals into our programs.

Goals/Aims for Youth Ministry

For the youth to:

A. KNOW:

They have salvation through Jesus Christ and the redemptive power of the Cross (John 3:16; 10:9).

They are loved (Matt. 10:28–31).

They are valuable (Gal. 4:6–7; Eph. 2:10).
They are not alone (1 Peter 5:7; Heb. 13:5; Matt. 28:20).

B. DO:
Live a life in response to salvation (2 Cor. 5:17).
Love God (Mark 12:29–30).
Go on mission trips (Matt. 28:16–20).
Evangelize (Matt. 28:16–20).
Conduct service projects (Matt. 25:42–46).
Use their gifts (Rom. 6:13).
Obey the will of God (Luke 12:31).

C. EXPERIENCE:
The love of Christ (John 15:9).
The joy of service (Matt. 25:21).
Fellowship with other believers and God (1 John 1:7).
Life change (2 Cor. 5:17).

D. BECOME:
Everything that God would have them to be (1 Cor. 9:24–27).
Unmovable in faith, walk, and lifestyle (Col. 2:7).
Leaders in the church, home, school, and work (Ps. 37:23–24).

NOTES

1. Paul H. Vieth, *Objectives in Religious Education* (New York: Harper & Bros., 1930), 45.
2. C. B. Eavey, *An Introduction to Evangelical Christian Education,* ed. J. Edward Hakes (Chicago: Moody, 1968), 55.
3. Wesner Fallaw, *Church Education for Tomorrow* (Philadelphia: Westminster, 1960), 146.
4. Eavey, *Introduction to Evangelical Christian Education,* 56.
5. Discernment and common sense must be used in these situations. Make sure that you understand all state and federal laws as they pertain to adolescents (i.e., harboring a minor).
6. Elmer Towns, *Successful Biblical Youth Work* (Nashville: Impact Books, 1973), 149.

The Youth Worker as a Pastor-Shepherd

There still seems to be a reluctance in certain circles to use the term *youth pastor.* I (Steve) am not arguing the title (even though I prefer the elevated title of "youth pastor" before "youth director," "youth leader," "director of student ministries," etc.). I am arguing position and application. It is almost an uneasiness about elevating the person in charge of adolescents to a position recognized publicly as "pastor." It is true that "when the pages of the New Testament are examined, the position of the minister of youth or youth pastor is not found."[1] Yet Scripture is obviously aware of the crucial nature of the individual's youth. Plenty of Scripture indicates the importance and significance of adolescence, with all of its critical decisions that would color or taint an entire lifetime with digital clarity. Verse after verse reflects either a positive or negative aspect of the adolescent years.

> "The imagination of man's heart is evil from his youth." (Gen. 8:21)
> "He has been a warrior from his youth." (1 Sam. 17:33 NASB)
> "Do not remember the sins of my youth." (Ps. 25:7)
> "You are my trust from my youth." (Ps. 71:5)
> "Remember now your Creator in the days of your youth." (Eccl. 12:1)
> "I remember you, the kindness of your youth." (Jer. 2:2)
> "This has been your manner from your youth." (Jer. 22:21)
> "Moab has been at ease from his youth." (Jer. 48:11)
> "It is good for a man to bear the yoke in his youth." (Lam. 3:27)
> "Let no one despise your youth, but be an example to the believers." (1 Tim. 4:12)
> "Flee from youthful lusts." (2 Tim. 2:22 NASB)

With so many foundational habits and values being formed in the adolescent years, whether they be positive or negative, the youth minister is more needed than ever before. From a Christian education perspective, this "window" of adolescence is approximately six to ten years in duration (give or take a year if your school district includes sixth grade as middle school; it could and should include those few years of college for students, even though the demands of school and employment begin to force adultlike maturity and responsibilities upon them, distracting them even more from spiritual considerations), from the time they enter middle school until at least the time they graduate from high school. This "window of opportunity" is more like a "door of opportunity" when considering the magnitude of adolescent decisions that will have lifelong implications. Tom Beaudoin, an author who is a theological combination of Baptist, Catholic, and Pentecostal, describes the reasons for the plight of adolescence today:

> There are plenty of reasons . . . to feel deeply sad. . . . When a generation bears the weight of so many failures—including AIDS, divorce, abuse, poor schools, recessions, youth poverty, teen suicide, outrageous educational and living expenses, failure of government and religious institutions, national debt, high taxes, environmental devastation, drugs, parents that need to be parented, violence, unstable economic security, premature loss of childhood —how can suffering not be an important part of one's identity?[2]

In George Barna's book *Generation Next,* Barna deals with the spiritual aspect of Generation X, giving the church a report card on its progress in the area of outreach to this generation (e.g., there is a perception of inflexibility; there is no room in the church; and the two are on different bandwidths). The bottom line is that the church must upgrade its efforts or be forever irrelevant with this perceived lackluster effort for God. Barna also states that close to 85 percent of decisions made for Christ will be made before a person's eighteenth birthday. This sobering statistic has been consistent over the years since it was first introduced by Campus Crusade for Christ in the mid-1970s. Luke 19:10 states the very reason that Christ came to this earth, "For the Son of Man has come to seek and to save that which was lost." This includes adolescents.

With this present-day younger generation having a sense of spirituality, regardless of how irreverent or misguided, teenagers often receive a sense of achievement and well-being. Many challenges of spiritual lostness become moot. Evangelism classes have always taught a fundamental principle when trying to challenge people to find faith in Christ . . . they must first be lost. There is scriptural evidence that our ministry efforts should be where there is some kind of "return" or receptivity. If a younger generation has an acute sense of spiritual need, perhaps this is where ministry emphasis and concentration should be.

Christ Himself gave His disciples instructions in Luke 10 as to where to focus their evangelistic efforts. The chapter gives some clear instruction. They were to make plans to go to towns and villages. A closer look at the word *towns* and *villages* has a meaning that indicates the inhabitants of a particular topography or region. From a figurative perspective, adolescence would certainly fit this description, being a sociological grouping of young people who make the landscape they inhabit distinct and adaptable to their liking. Luke 10 is also explicit in its instructions when a disciple is rejected. He is to leave and take his endeavors elsewhere. So if this is the case, it certainly builds upon the fact that ministry emphasis needs to be where it is accepted and not where it is rejected. Why waste our precious time where the message is not wanted? This is not to sound preclusive. It is, however, a call to frugality with our resources of time, people, and money.

It is clear to me that if a body of believers, a local church or Christian organization, has a mandate for evangelization, there should be a corresponding correlation in its efforts and resources aimed at the age group of adolescence. Dawson McAllister, prominent youth speaker and radio talk show host, said, "If a church tells me that they are serious about evangelism, I ask them to show me their youth budget."[3]

THE GENERAL CALLING OF BELIEVERS

Eugene Peterson has sharpened the whole meaning of the word *calling*. His perspective of ministerial calling consists of three duties: prayer, Scripture, and spiritual direction. He claims in his book *Working the Angles* that ministers have abandoned their calling. What many are doing, according to Peterson, has nothing to do with pastoral ministry. It has morphed into something like shopkeeping . . . keeping customers happy, luring customers from competitors, and using the right packaging to keep customers shelling out more money. Scathing as this may be, Peterson is driving home a point. The call of ministry is the prominence, power, and prescription of prayer. What better spiritual dynamic is available to pastors of young people and to the young people themselves? For a generation that values privacy and confidentiality, talking to God is a practice they can appreciate.

The call of ministry involves the Scripture, not the mere reading of it but getting to know the Author of it. The greatest compliment one can give to an author is "I read your book." Adolescents need to be challenged to read the Scripture with the intent of getting to know the Author better. Who better to make the stories of the Bible come alive than the person who has a relationship with adolescents, the youth pastor?

Spiritual direction is also a part of this calling. It is that shining of light in a dark situation. An individual who is lost needs directions or a road map. Directions can only come from someone who has been there or knows where the right turns are and which turns to avoid. The youth pastor's calling becomes clearly relevant and applicable at this juncture. The experience and maturity that come with age can be a huge asset here. (I have noticed a trend among churches to request older, more mature youth pastors.) A knowledge of and sensitivity toward adolescence that comes with ministering to adolescents can only add credibility and, most important, a hearing. (A hearing is a difficult aspect of youth ministry simply because of the visceral nature of young people . . . checking their e-mail while listening to their CD player and watching TV, and doing their homework at the same time.) But when relationships are the number one interest of adolescence, it is the relationship of youth pastor and adolescent that will prevail.

All callings are sacred. In John Duckworth's book *Joan 'n' the Whale,* he illustrates the call by the following story[4]:

There was a Sitter, and there was a Stander. The Sitter was smiling contentedly, reading a book as he sat at a sidewalk café. His sunglasses, Panama hat, tropical-print shirt, Bermuda shorts, and spotless white running shoes matched his mood of permanent leisure. An umbrella kept him in the shade; on the table at his elbow sat a tall glass of iced tea—and a shining white telephone.

Yawning, he slowly turned a page in his well-worn book. He was about to take a nap when he heard a voice.

"Hey!" cried the voice. He looked up. It was the Stander, and she was approaching his table. He frowned, but only for a moment, and went back to his reading.

"What do you know?" the girl greeted him, putting her hands on her hips. "Is that really you? Long time no see!"

"MMMM," went the Sitter, not looking up.

"So what have you been doing all this time?" the girl asked.

The Sitter nodded toward his book, which he continued to read. "Studying, of course," he said proudly.

The girl scratched her head. "Studying? Well, I guess that's—" Glancing across the street, she gasped. "Hey!" she said. "What's going on over there?"

"MMMM?" the Sitter murmured.

"An old man just fell down in the crosswalk," she said urgently. "Come on, we'd better go help him!" She ran off, leaving the Sitter reading in the shade. Slowly he turned a page; it was his only movement.

A minute later the Stander returned, panting from her dash. "Well," she said between breaths, "he's okay." She frowned. "Hey, how come you didn't give me a hand?"

Irritated, he looked up from his book. "Because I'm waiting, of course," he said.

"Waiting for what?" she asked.

"For the Call," he replied, nodding at the phone on the table.

The Stander shook her head. "What's the—" Just then she happened to look down a nearby alley. "Look!" she cried. "That kid just snatched a lady's purse. Come on—we can probably catch him!" Off she ran again, and the Sitter just sat.

Two minutes later she was back, huffing and puffing. "Hey," she said. "What kind of neighborhood is this? People falling in the streets, kids snatching purses . . . What's the matter with you? Why didn't you come with me?"

The Sitter lifted his head and glared. "Because I didn't get the Call!"

"What Call?" the girl asked, exasperated.

"The Call," he answered, looking skyward.

The girl threw up her hands. "I don't—" All at once she noticed something else down the street. "Oh, did you see that?" she asked, putting her hand to her mouth. "That car just took a left and plowed right into the motorcycle. Now, come on! Don't just sit there; we've got to get help!"

The Sitter sipped his iced tea. "I'm sorry," he said, unconcerned. "But I'm just not called."

The girl started to run in the direction of the accident. "What are you studying, anyway?" She shouted at him over her shoulder.

"First aid," he said placidly and returned to his reading.

Three minutes later the girl was back, so exhausted she could barely stand. "I've got to use your phone," she asked, gasping for breath.

"What?" the Sitter cried, suddenly alert.

"I've got to call an ambulance for that guy," she panted and reached for the shining white telephone.

The Sitter leaped from his chair, wrestling the phone away. "You can't do that!" he said, his eyes panicky. "Why, the Call could come at any time! I might get the Call any minute now!" *Whatever the call or wherever the mission or whoever the group of people, we are to enter that calling with a sense of divine mission.*

Oswald Chambers said,

We are apt to forget the mystical, supernatural touch of God. If you can tell where you got the call of God and all about it, I

> question whether you have ever had a call. The call of God does not come like that, it is much more supernatural. The realization of it in a man's life may come with a sudden thunder-clap or with a gradual dawning, but in whatever way it comes, it comes with the undercurrent of the supernatural, something that cannot be put into words, it is always accompanied with a glow. At any moment there may break the sudden consciousness of this incalculable, supernatural, surprising call that has taken hold of your life—"I have chosen you." The call of God has nothing to do with salvation and sanctification. It is not because you are sanctified that you are therefore called to preach the gospel; the call to preach the gospel is infinitely different. Paul describes it as a necessity laid upon him.
>
> If you have been obliterating the great supernatural call of God in your life, take a review of your circumstances and see where God has not been first, but your ideas of service, or your temperamental abilities. Paul said—"Woe is unto me, if I preach not the gospel!" He had realized the call of God, and there was no competitor for his strength.
>
> If a man or woman is called of God, it does not matter how untoward circumstances are, every force that has been at work will tell for God's purpose in the end. If you agree with God's purpose He will bring not only your conscious life, but all the deeper regions of your life which you cannot get at, into harmony.[5]

Mary Francis Preston said, "Without exception the leaders who continually achieve most and are happiest in their work are those who possess an abiding sense of the presence of God and an unshakable conviction that He has called them to the task. Theirs are lives with a mission."[6] Galatians 1:15 says, "Even before I was born God had chosen me to be his, and called me" (TLB). The word *call* means to summon. The apostle Paul is explaining to the Galatians that his radical change has transformed his vocation of persecuting Christians to a calling of an apostle of Christ. In Ephesians 4:1 the apostle Paul reminds the Ephesians to "walk worthy of the calling with which you were called." In his book *Leading from the Inside Out,* Samuel D. Rima says, "Our calling as people far exceeds in importance and purpose any possible job or career in which we might engage. . . . Our vocation as Christian leaders . . . is to be a holy nation, a royal priesthood, God's own special possession. Our calling is to be reflectors of the wonderful light of God."[7]

In determining the calling of God in our lives, we have already mentioned the scriptural evidence that as Christians, we have a special calling on our lives. It is from here that the individual considering pastoral youth ministry must determine if the age group of adolescence is the best platform for him in which he can live out most effectively this calling. Samuel Rima suggests the consideration of previous experiences, present circumstances, possible opportunities, personal gifts, the prompting of the Holy Spirit, personal passions, and the wisdom of private counsel. Once these have been considered, there should be a relatively clear indication. So in speaking with the person who senses a calling to pastoral ministry among adolescence, we should do our best to encourage the fruition of that calling.

THE CALL TO THE PASTORATE

Some schools of thought hold to the idea that to be the pastor of a church is the highest calling God could give. A look at Scripture will reveal that the youth minister is of an equal calling. The office of pastor is found in Ephesians 4:11, "And He gave some as apostles, and some as prophets, and some as evangelists, and some as pastors and teachers" (NASB). The offices of apostles, prophets, and evangelists were given to the universal church. Apostles and evangelists had the responsibility of planting the church everywhere they went. Prophets exhorted the church. The phrase "pastors and teachers" is linked together by the same Greek article. The pastor and teacher are ministers of the local church. Being equipped with the appropriate gifts, they are responsible for the day-to-day building up of the local church. The word *pastor* literally means "shepherd." His duties are to feed the local "flock" with spiritual food and to protect it from spiritual danger. The pastor is answerable to the "Arch-Shepherd" or Archbishop, the term by which Christ is described in 1 Peter 5:4.

Other words include *bishop,* originally the principle officer of the local church, the other being the deacon or deacons (1 Tim. 3:1–7). The title "elder" or "presbyter" is generally applied to the same man, "elder" referring to his age and dignity, and "bishop" to his work or superintendence. The Scripture talks about "elders," probably plural within a church, and puts all of them on equal footing—and the youth pastor would fit there as long as he qualifies biblically to be an elder. As the churches multiplied, the bishop of a larger church would often be given special honor, and so gradually there grew a hierarchy, all the way from presiding elders to bishops (over groups of churches), then archbishops.[8]

First Peter 2:25 says, "But now you have returned to the Shepherd and Overseer of your souls" (NIV). The words *overseer, pastor,* and *bishop* refer to the same person. They are alternative names to be used for men in the ministry of overseeing the local church. Exercising pastoral care over the local flock is the responsibility of the bishop or pastor. Acts 20:17 reveals that certain congregations had more than one elder: "From Miletus he sent to Ephesus and called to him the elders of the church" (NASB). In any given local church, there are various age groups or "flocks." If the senior pastor cannot minister effectively to the adolescent "flock," he needs to find someone who can. This is where the youth pastor comes in.

God did not designate by name every ministry in which the church was to engage herself. When specific and unique needs arose, men called of God would attempt to meet those needs. Just as God raises up individuals to specific tasks at certain periods of time, so also He raises individuals to minister to specific age groups. The youth pastor specializes in ministering to adolescents. His flock is the adolescents in the local congregation. As their pastor, the youth minister has the same responsibility of day-to-day building up of the adolescent flock and their spiritual protection. This building up and protection is administered with the same dedication that the senior pastor ministers to his congregation; the youth group is a subgroup of the whole church. Being sensitive to the needs of the young people, the youth pastor should attempt to meet the needs of this young congregation. The youth minister's calling is equal to and just as important as the calling to be the senior pastor of a church.

THE CHARACTERISTICS OF A SHEPHERD

In order to be an effective youth pastor, the person will need to have the characteristics related to shepherd-leadership. The whole concept of shepherding has the connotation that he is looking after and caring for a particular flock. Eugene Peterson put it this way. Jesus said,

> Let me set this before you as plainly as I can. If a person climbs over or through the fence of a sheep pen instead of going through the gate, you know he's up to no good—a sheep rustler! The shepherd walks right up to the gate. The gatekeeper opens the gate to him and the sheep recognize his voice. He calls his own sheep by name and leads them out. When he gets them all out, he leads them and they follow because they are familiar with his voice. They won't follow a stranger's voice but will scatter because they aren't used to the sound of it.[9]

Even though this passage is describing Christ and His shepherd-like characteristics, Scripture has already indicated that we are to be shepherds of our flock.

We would do well to identify the truths from this passage for our own ministerial effectiveness. Some of these would include:

These sheep are in the pen of a shepherd; the shepherd calls them by name; the sheep follow the shepherd as he leads them; the sheep are familiar with the shepherd's voice; the sheep will not follow the voice of someone they are unfamiliar with; sheep have to get used to the sound of the shepherd's voice. Each one of these characteristics has an adolescent ministry parallel. Adolescents are in a special group (age group) that makes them feel comfortable. It should come as no surprise that adolescence is a time when there is a distancing from the family and the building of meaningful relationships with friends. Knowing the name of an adolescent is a significant aspect of identification. In a sea of young humanity and the importance of being with a group, an adolescent can still be internally lonely. His name is the best word he knows in the mother tongue. A shepherd-leader of young people must be able to call his young people by name, or, at the very least, someone who is a part of the ministry team knows and calls them by name.

The shepherd-leader of adolescents leads his young flock because they recognize his voice. Part of this voice recognition comes with familiarity. Tenure among adolescents is critical. Even though he is making commentary about Generation X, author Tom Beaudoin illustrates this in his book *Virtual Faith:* "That is why I boil down the religious quest of GenX pop culture to one question that begins on the most intimate level possible and in the midst of profound ambiguity. Our most fundamental question is 'Will you be there for me?' We ask this of our selves, bodies, parents, friends, partners, society, religions, leaders, nation, and even God."[10] The shepherd-leader knows his young flock. He is conscious of any idiosyncrasies. He knows about the world they live in and the cataclysmic changes they have to deal with. (The most significant, even cataclysmic, change has been the change in the family.)

Approximately 40 percent of this nation's children will go to bed tonight in a house where their fathers do not live.[11] More and more children and teens are victims of family violence. Most of the abuse comes from the hands of a parent (including a step-parent), sibling, or close relative. Violence is a part of life for 15 million families in America.[12] The shaping of values has moved away from family to other value-shapers, being music, movies, and friends.

It is from this framework of understanding that the shepherd-leader of this young flock will have to pastor. Proverbs 1:4 tells one purpose of instruction: "To give prudence to the naive, to the youth knowledge and discretion" (NASB). In other words, the wisdom of Proverbs (along with the rest of the Scriptures) will provide the awareness and discernment adolescents will need in order to mature to men and women of understanding (v. 5). This understanding has the connotation of thinking for themselves, knowing where to look, and having the ability to mentally distinguish between good and evil. These are characteristics that appear to be on the decline in this present culture. The shepherd-leader will have to lead by instruction and example in these areas for the sake of his young flock's development.

Following the Chief Shepherd

One final aspect of leading a young flock is an important element of following the Chief Shepherd. Much has been written on leading. Little has been written of following. Yet the very command of Jesus is for us to follow Him. In his book *The Power of Agreement,* Brian Molitor says,

> Our followers . . . deserve respect and guidance from leaders. We should remember that they, too, have choices about where they will work, worship, and live. If leaders become oppressive or inherently unfair, followers often exercise their option to leave. Therefore, a leader must act in ways that encourage followers to align with his vision rather than waste time trying to force followers to submit to his will.[13]

Without followers, a shepherd-leader is merely taking a walk. Even though the mental characteristics of adolescents include argumentation along with being critical and cynical, the wise youth pastor must look beyond these exercises of mental shaping. He must involve methods of teaching and instruction that demonstrate the subject of followship. Just as there is a cost of leadership, there is a cost of followship. Adolescents can be challenged with this subject, giving them practical applications that show what followship looks like. Brian Molitor lists self-motivation, team player, positive attitude, flexibility, and trustworthiness as qualities of effective followers. Adolescents can be led to take followship seriously.

CONCLUSION

In conclusion, there is no question in my mind that the youth pastor can be and is to be a shepherd-leader. The flock he leads requires the same love and care that any other age-group flock would need. Surely this person in charge of kids is a pastor in the truest form of the word. It is a position that has all the benefits and responsibilities of a true elder or bishop. Pure pastoral care with adolescent distinctives is not only needed but demanded.

NOTES

1. Elmer Towns, *Successful Biblical Youth Work*, rev. ed. (Nashville: Impact Books, 1973), 171.
2. Tom Beaudoin, *Virtual Faith* (San Francisco: Jossey-Bass, 1998), 104.
3. Dawson McAllister, interview by author held during meeting of youth pastors in Lynchburg, Virginia, 1 April 2000.
4. Reprinted by permission from *Joan 'n' the Whale* by John Duckworth, published by Fleming H. Revell. Copyright 1987 by the author.
5. Oswald Chambers, *My Utmost for His Highest* (Westwood, N.J.: Barbour and Company, 1963), 201.
6. Mary Frances Johnson Preston, *Christian Leadership* (Nashville: Sunday School Board of the Southern Baptist Convention), 15.
7. Samuel D. Rima, *Leading from the Inside Out* (Grand Rapids: Baker, 2000), 58.
8. Merrill C. Tenney, ed., *Zondervan's Pictorial Bible Dictionary* (Grand Rapids: Zondervan, 1967), 126.

9. Eugene H. Peterson, *The Message* paraphrase of John 10:1–5.
10. Beaudoin, *Virtual Faith*, 140.
11. "Various Forms of Father Absence," National Center for Fathering, http:/www.fathers.com/research.trends.html (18 December 1997).
12. "Child Abuse and Neglect Statistics," National Committee to Prevent Child Abuse Page, April 1997, http:/www.childabuse.org/facts96.html (18 December 1997).
13. Brian D. Molitor, *The Power of Agreement* (Nashville: Broadman & Holman, 1999), 202.

The Goal of Youth Ministry

God wants each teen to grow spiritually: "Desire the pure milk of the word, that you may grow thereby" (1 Peter 2:2). Growth is not only the process of physical life but also of our spiritual life as well. Children grow, plants grow, animals grow; each grows in its own way and in its own time. But growth alone is not the goal of youth work—maturity is. Growth is the means to an end; that end is one of maturity. Thus the goal of every believer (including adolescents) is to become mature in Christ.

Maturity has a specific goal, "For the equipping of the saints for the work of service, to the building up of the body of Christ; until we all attain to the unity of the faith, and of the knowledge of the Son of God, to a mature man, to the measure of the stature which belongs to the fullness of Christ" (Eph. 4:12–13 NASB). Hence the goal of youth ministry is to *produce spiritually maturing adolescents.* This goal may seem simple; however, it must be further explained through the examination of all the innuendoes and assumptions of spiritual maturity, and how this is cultivated in teens. For if we are to achieve and operate a biblically based ministry to youth, then we must cultivate spiritual maturity within our teens.

SPIRITUAL MATURITY

Our stated goal of youth ministry is to "produce spiritually maturing adolescents." Much could be written and discussed as to what spiritual maturity looks like in the life of the average teen. Spiritual maturity as our goal is misunderstood or ignored by many youth leaders today. In a recent survey of our students, we discovered that from the students' perspective 70 percent of youth leaders in ministry today do not plan for or cultivate spiritual growth in their teens. We must understand that our goal as stated describes "maturing adolescents," giving the idea of a process, not a final destination. We are not advocating as our goal that each youth must be at the same place spiritually when he departs from our care. We are not after cookie-cutter Christianity. Spiritual maturity is a developmental process that takes time and that will be different for each teen you minister to. However, although teens will mature spiritually at different rates, we as youth leaders still must have an impression of what spiritual maturity looks like. We must have a prototype or standard by which we set some particulars as they pertain to this important subject.

Our standard of spiritual maturity is Jesus Christ, and our biblical reference for this standard is found in 1 John 2:6, "The one who says he abides in Him ought himself to walk in the same manner as He walked" (NASB). Here John is simply saying that anyone who claims to be a Christian (a believer, one who has been born again) must emulate and imitate the character of Christ in lifestyle, thoughts, and attitude. As believers we are to incorporate the example of Christ in all that we do (Rom. 8:29; 13:14). We must be striving for our teens to progress in spiritual maturity by incorporating the attitudes and actions of Christ. If this is our goal, then the question becomes, "How did Christ walk?" John is not asking us to consider the physical nature of Christ's stride but rather those attributes that Christ exhibited as He ministered while on earth. The question remains, "How did Christ walk?" The answer is found within the pages of the New Testament. Jesus modeled:

1. Prayer—Luke 5:16; 6:12; 11:1; 22:31–32; John 11:41; 17:9, 15–17, 20–22
2. Compassion—Matthew 20:34; Mark 6:34; 8:2–3; Luke 19:41–42
3. Purpose—Matthew 5:17; 15:24; 18:11; 20:28; Mark 1:38; 2:15–22; Luke 1:79; 2:49; 4:18–19, 43
4. Servanthood—Matthew 20:28; Mark 10:43; John 13:3–10
5. Understanding/knowing Scripture—Matthew 7:29; 22:16
6. Disciple making—Matthew 10:1
7. Unconditional love—Matthew 8:17; 18:11–13; John 10:3–4, 11, 14–16; 13:1
8. Pure motives—John 5:30; 8:48–50
9. Holiness—Luke 1:35; 23:47; John 7:18; 14:30
10. An example for others to follow—Matthew 11:29; John 10:4; 13:5, 13–15
11. Meekness—Matthew 11:29; 27:12–14; Luke 22:27
12. Unity among the body—John 17:14–23

13. Intercession—Matthew 6:9–13; Mark 4:35–41
14. Wisdom—Matthew 4:1–11; Mark 12:13–17; Luke 6:20ff.
15. Obedience—Matthew 26:39; John 4:34; 5:30; 6:38; 8:29
16. Proper zeal—Luke 8:1; 12:50; John 2:17

Spiritual maturity in teens will take time. However, as we minister to those whom God brings our way, we must help them to progress in their walk with God. We must help them "put on" the new and remove the old way of life. The characteristics listed above are not optional for those who claim Christianity. They must be painstakingly developed within the life of teens. Think of it this way: If you had a tableful of marbles, which method would you use to claim as many as possible? You could walk up to the table and scoop up as many as possible at one time. You would drop a few and leave some on the table, only gathering a fraction of the total number. Or you could approach the table, take your time, pick up one marble at a time, and place each one into your pocket. This method takes more time, but you would be able to gather each marble and hold on to it. None is dropped or left behind due to haste. The same concept applies with helping teens progress in spiritual maturity. If we rush, some important aspects of what it means to be spiritually mature will be left on the table.

Growth takes time, effort, and energy. Don't rush teens to a location (spiritual maturity) that they are not ready for. Move each one into a deeper relationship with Christ according to his ability to receive and implement the truths of Scripture. Modeling the attributes of Christ is the only place to start. This dictates that we have programs established that will enable the youth to mature in this fashion, consistent with Scripture. Why this emphasis on spiritual maturity? Consider the following:

It is God's design for today that we become progressively

more like our heavenly Father. From the beginning of creation to the Cross, the nation of Israel was to conform to the Law as a means of being set apart from other nations. Relationships were built around the *mentoring* of persons to live under the Law. From the Cross to the return of Christ we are under grace, as we work out our salvation with fear and trembling. This process, as modeled for us by Christ, is one of discipleship as we learn the faith through the reading of the Word and the application of the same. Thus the method that we should use today is that of discipleship. A discipleship program with the main focus on the learning and application of Scripture in the life of teens is not simply mentoring.

HISTORY OF MAN

C			
R		C	Discipleship conforming →
E	Mentoring under the Law	H	by Grace
A		R	
T		I	
I	Moses — Joshua	S	Christ — The 12
O	Elijah — Elisha	T	Paul — Timothy
N			

This application of the faith is evident throughout participating in the work of the ministry. The work of the ministry is multifaceted in description and application. Spiritually maturing teens are to fulfill the Great Commission, going out into their world and presenting the Gospel message to their peers and their schools and communities. Additionally, they are using their gifts in ministry, resulting in God being glorified (John 15:8) and the body being "built up" (Eph. 4:11–16). As teens spiritually mature, they will be able to reproduce themselves in others through Bible studies, small group leadership, ministry teams, and one-on-one discipleship. We should strive to see the youth mature through conforming to the image of Christ and the work of the ministry being fulfilled through their hands. This means that as youth mature we must have opportunities and avenues for them to use their gifts.

As teens strive to conform to the image of Christ and use their gifts in a manner consistent with Scripture, the methods we implement must be acceptable to the culture of the church and the community in which we find ourselves. This "culture" will dictate to us what programs we may use in guiding our teens to spiritual maturity. In a traditional conservative church, liberal methods will be out of reach and off limits as you try to reach teens. Likewise if your church is liberal in methodology, conservative methods will not be acceptable to the church. This concept in helping teens reach spiritual maturity is a decisive factor in determining how effective you will be in achieving the stated goal. You will only be able to reach youth through those vehicles, methods, and techniques that are acceptable to both the church and the teens in your community.

Our goal is simple: to produce spiritually maturing adolescents. The path to achieving this goal is based on the goal itself.

The Bible teaches adjustment (the fine-tuning of one's standards to the standards of Scripture) or satisfaction (the satisfaction achieved when obedience to Scripture is accomplished). This is seen through several scriptural qualities. These qualities are available for all believers and applicable to teenagers. Since these qualities are expanded in many other sources, the following explanation is not comprehensive but shows the relationship between the scriptural qualities of life and adjustment, which leads to maturity. Spiritual maturity is being rightly related to the will of God and the Word of God.

THE FIRST GOAL OF ADJUSTMENT—*PEACE*

Peace in the Bible is seen in at least two ways:

a. Peace with God—the work of Christ on the Cross, into which the believer enters at conversion. This truth is seen in Ephesians 2:14–17 and Romans 5:1. The teenager must enter into the "peace with God" relationship before he can enter into the "peace of God" relationship.

b. Peace of God—the inward tranquility or satisfaction of the believer who commits his anxieties to God. The youth worker should realize he cannot lead the teenager to true peace of soul until the question of salvation is settled. The peace of God is promised to the believer as a result of surrendering anxieties to God. "Be anxious for nothing, but in everything by prayer and supplication, with thanksgiving, let your requests be made known to God; and the peace of God, which surpasses all understanding, will guard your hearts and minds through Christ Jesus" (Phil. 4:6–7). Youth workers should attempt to lead teenagers into the peace of God. Note that the realm of peace is "through Christ Jesus." The means of peace is through the release of prayer, and the results of peace come after anxieties are satisfied. Therefore, the peace of God and steps to maturity are the same thing.

Note that the peace of God has no equal in worldly adjustment. Christ promised peace that the world could not give. "Peace I leave with you, My peace I give to you; not as the world gives" (John 14:27). Beware of trying to bring satisfaction into the youth's life apart from spiritual adjustment. Spiritual maturity is being rightly related to the will of God and the Word of God. If the teenager is divorced from the ministry of the Lord and the Word of God, there can be no peace. "These things I have spoken to you, that in Me you may have peace. In the world you will have tribulation" (John 16:33). Here Christ indicates that the young person will have inner anxieties, frustrations, and misery apart from living according to the Word of God. There is no true peace living outside of Scripture. Some workers have counseled young people apart from spiritual truth and dynamics. These youth leaders have felt inclined to deal with mental doubts only in philosophical terms, or inappropriate intimacy only in terms of biological reactions. On these occasions, they failed the teen seeking help by not throwing the light of the Word of God on the problem. Christ has promised that peace comes through Him.

The youth worker should keep the goal of maturity always before him. The youth need inner peace and satisfaction, which leads to maturity.

THE SECOND GOAL OF ADJUSTMENT—*SATISFACTION*

A Christian is commanded to find satisfaction in his Master. "Delight yourself also in the Lord, and He shall give you the desires of your heart" (Ps. 37:4). The drive to have satisfaction or delight must be filled in every life. The teen demands satisfaction. This drive for satisfaction was placed in his psychological and biological makeup. Don't blame the youth for these urges; they are following the compelling urges of the inner man. The question is, How do they satisfy their urges? Perhaps some responsibility falls on the shoulders of youth leaders for not providing the biblical means of bringing satisfaction to the teen. When the teenage student is rightly adjusted to the will of God, the result is satisfaction. It can be said of them what was said of the Israelites' Sabbaths: "Not going your own way and not doing as you please or speaking idle words, then you will find your joy in the LORD" (Isa. 58:13–14 NIV). The teenagers should have Jesus Christ at the center of their lives. Therefore adjustment is seen as rightly related to God's words, not our words; rightly related to God's pleasures, not our pleasures. Adjustment and satisfaction lead to maturity when the teenager delights in the realm of God's provision for his life.

THE THIRD GOAL OF ADJUSTMENT—*JOY*

The Christian teen should live a life of joy, happiness, and satisfaction. Joy comes only as a result of the Christian being in right adjustment to God—the source of joy. "The joy of the Lord is your strength" (Neh. 8:10). Joy is the positive reaction of fulfilled desires and drives. "You will show me the path of life; in Your presence is fullness of joy; at Your right hand are pleasures forevermore" (Ps. 16:11). The Christian is commanded to have joy and express it to others. "Rejoice in the Lord always. Again I will say, rejoice!" (Phil. 4:4). The youth leader must understand the source and secret of joy if he is going to help teenagers. Young people demand and need happiness. This does not mean we are to give in to their selfish demands or treat the young people as children. But true obedience brings joy, and perhaps a youth leader can help a teen find joy and satisfaction in obeying the commands of God's Word.

CHRISTIAN MATURITY

The aims of Christian education of young people are ultimately the aims of the church. These aims are clear and give direction to the youth leader. The goals are sometimes difficult to verbalize or implement in a life. But goals should nevertheless remain the constant guidepost. Between the immediate ministry and the ultimate goal are years of heartache and pain. The youth leader may get lost from one youth meeting to the next unless there are clear ultimate goals. The following checklist is based on material suggested by Dr. Lois LeBar to evaluate maturity.

OUTLOOK ON LIFE

1. Is all of life integrated around Christ, who is revealed through Scripture by the Spirit?

2. Is concentration on Christ, rather than on work or people, so that we can live above circumstances?
3. Are we able to see life as a whole and the relationship of parts to the whole?
4. Is all of life sanctified, even to the smallest detail and most humdrum routine?
5. Do we take every circumstance that the Lord sends as an opportunity for learning?
6. Do we see problems as challenges because we have faith in what God can do in us and in others?
7. Do we discern God's part and ours—what can and should be changed, and what cannot be changed?
8. Are we free to be natural and spontaneous, disliking masks and walls that separate and deceive?
9. Are we free from attitudes that poison the spirit—doubt, guilt, self-pity, resentment?
10. Can we face and accept reality as it is, openly, honestly, heartily?
11. Are we progressively developing depth of insight and experience?[1]

Relation to Work

12. Do we spend our limited time and energy on and get excited over the things that count most?
13. Have we strong drives from pure motives, yet without being so serious that we can't laugh at ourselves?
14. Have we spiritual courage to work for convictions, though risks are involved?
15. Do we suspend judgment until all the facts are in, then make wise decisions and abide by them?

16. Have we an experimental, creative spirit that is open to new ideas in an exploratory, evaluative way?
17. Do we consistently work for high standards, yet remain flexible in our thinking?
18. Do we work consistently without yielding to moods or waiting for prods?
19. Are we known as dependable people who can carry projects to completion?
20. Have we sufficient discipline to control deep longings over a period of time and postpone present satisfactions for future good?
21. Can we take disappointment in stride and keep from depressed moods?
22. Do we derive intrinsic satisfaction from everyday work and simple pleasures, with a continually fresh appreciation for what life brings?

Relation to People

23. Have we a healthy respect for the individual rights and contributions of other people?
24. Can we identify with the needs of others, going out to them, forgetting self?
25. Are we ready to take the role of humble follower or "up-front" leader, according to the need?
26. Can we be comfortably related to people above and below us in authority?
27. Do we enjoy being both conventional when conformity is important and unconventional in making a unique contribution?
28. Are we ready to graciously admit our own failures as well as commend others?

CONCLUSION

Maturity is a measure of quality. It is not *how much* one does that determines maturity; it is *what* one does with the opportunities at hand that determines maturity. Maturity is not how old the teen looks on the outside but what he looks like on the inside. He is as mature as the way he sees his life. Maturity is not measured by observation of physical features; maturity is measured by our view on life and other people as seen through the lens of Scripture. The goal of our youth work is that the teens progress in spiritual maturity. Blessed are the unsatisfied when they have a proper goal. Many of our teenagers are unsatisfied, and their lives are filled with frustration, because they focus on the wrong goals. Christianity does not have a goal for teenagers—it is a goal. Young lives should be productive for Christ, satisfying to teens, profitable to the church, and counting for eternity. They could be, if youth leaders understood the biblical goal of maturity and then translated it into challenges for teens.

NOTES

1. Dr. Lois LeBar, unpublished material. Printed by permission.

What's Going On With Sunday School

Contrary to popular belief, Sunday school is alive and kicking; however, it's not the same Sunday school that our fathers knew and experienced. Further, that Sunday school is alive doesn't mean to imply that what is happening in Sunday school is effective. The simple fact is that a majority of churches provide a specific time for youth to meet on Sunday morning or during the week for lessons and general Bible knowledge. Thus, before we proceed any further, a definition of Sunday school needs to be established, for the term "Sunday school" means many different things to many different people. A working definition for the purpose of this chapter needs to be presented. By the term *Sunday school* we mean training and Bible study outside of the main worship service of the church, anytime that takes place during the week, including Sunday morning. Whether this time consists of flannel graphs or praise bands, for our purpose these are considered Sunday school. And of course our focus is on Sunday school for youth.

Over the past twenty years a sweeping change has taken place in the Sunday school hour. This change is reflected in the curriculum (a 37-million-dollar-a-year business), the methodology used to reach today's youth, and the avenues presented for using the teens' gifts. However, not all changes in this methodology of today's "Sunday school" are meeting the needs of today's youth. The teaching environment, lesson aims, student history and needs, teacher preparation, and learning environment determine what teaching techniques and methods will be used to achieve maximum effectiveness through this time. No two teaching times are the same, and the needs of students vary deeply. Thus, a knowledge of the youth is paramount to success. This chapter will examine both the positive and negative aspects of today's Sunday school, and it will present ways of improving upon this important time.

THE PROBLEMS WITH TODAY'S SUNDAY SCHOOL

A few major problems exist within today's Sunday school that have little or nothing to do with the youth; rather, the problem exists within the leadership of the group and/or the church. The responsibility for the overall effectiveness and programming of this time rests with the leadership of the group, not the youth. There seem to be several basic causes for problems.

YOUTH CURRICULUM

First, as mentioned, this is a 37-million-dollar-a-year business. Published curriculum has replaced youth leaders' time in the Word, seeking the guidance of the Holy Spirit as they prepare lessons according to the needs of their youth (2 Tim. 2:15).

The leaders miss the thrill of self-discovery and dependence on the Holy Spirit, while the youth miss the blessing of receiving teaching that is real and meaningful. In essence we put more trust in the curriculum writers' ability to know the needs of our kids than our own relationships with them. It's much easier to tear out or copy a sheet of paper than to be in the Word mulling over the planning, preparation, and presentation of lesson material.

Second, major curriculum houses appeal to a broad base of churches. As a result the message becomes watered down and the application of biblical truth becomes nonexistent. Each year I have the honor of teaching around four hundred students on how to do youth ministry. Each semester I conduct an informal survey on the values and aims of their perspective youth ministries. One question I ask is "Were any of you trained in how to apply Scripture to your life?" Out of the hundreds of students that come through our program, no one has ever responded "yes." However, when the question is whether the youth program was fun and full of activities, 95 percent of students raise their hands. Even though this is a very informal sampling of our students, the comparison between the two (application vs. fun) cannot be ignored. The fact remains that each year none of my students (ministry majors) confess to ever being instructed on how to apply Scripture to their lives. Without that, it's hard to understand the importance of living what they believe.

Have you ever stopped to think how a Catholic, Methodist, Southern Baptist, and General Association of Regular Baptist church can use the same curriculum when they are on different ends of the theological spectrum? Simply, it is nonoffensive to any group; therefore, key issues such as the inerrancy of Scripture, total surrender, servanthood, and biblical application are never talked about, because those subjects could alienate a denomination, and thus sales would suffer. Ultimately the youth are the ones who suffer in their relationship with God.

FIGHTING WITHIN THE BODY

Too much internal fighting and disagreement is taking place with regard to Sunday school and its methodology. One denomination dislikes praise bands and feels any music that does not adhere to a four-four time scale is of the devil. Some believe that drama is the most effective way to reach this young generation for Christ and they fail to believe that others would not capitalize on this valuable asset. Some suggest that a return to ancient forms of worship, including biblical meditation and chanting, will deliver the greatest amount of success.[1] We are not advocating one method over another; simply, if lives are being changed and youth workers are reaching their kids based on their needs, then the methodology matters little as long as the method does not violate Scripture. In other words, if the principles of Scripture are not being compromised and youth are being reached (saved and discipled), then there is no argument.

We must give each other the freedom to minister according to God's calling on our hearts and the needs of our particular group, as long as what we do does not violate Scripture in the process. This lack of courage to stand firm on the uncompromising principles of God's Word is producing a generation that is content with mediocrity and missing the essential foundational principles of Scripture.

The Confusion Between Being Relevant to Culture and Conforming to It

The dictionary defines *relevant* as applicable, pertinent to the purpose. *Conform* or *conforming* means to make or become similar, to act or be in agreement, to have the same form. As we relate to youth and establish our ministry, in an effort to be relevant we have often fallen on the side of conformity. Look closely at the definitions. To conform means to act or be in agreement with, while relevant means simply to be meaningful.

We have become dangerously close to conforming our time

with youth to the world's ways. Our youth dress alike, talk alike, act alike, and in some cases the youth leaders try to be too close to the world themselves and they become pseudoteens. I have seen too many youth leaders who try to "relate" to teens through the use of their lingo, fashion, and actions. The middle-aged accountant who dyes his hair and wears thirty-six-inch pipes (baggy-legged jeans that are the same width all the way down), chains, and nose rings does not relate to youth any better than those who are real. In fact those who adopt a pseudoteen mentality actually hinder the ministry to teens. Teens are not looking for leaders who are not real.

It is essential that we as leaders possess a genuine love for our youth and be who we are. Youth meetings have taken on the air of the world in an effort to attract youth and have crossed the line over to conforming. The result of this confusion is that youth are being saved but are not being transformed. Many desires, thought processes, and attitudes continue to progress in the same manner as before salvation, producing a generation of youth that except for salvation are not different than the world. A delicate line must be drawn between these areas so that we do not fall on the wrong side of the line. Scripture is very clear as to

- *the nature we are to achieve after salvation:* "Whoever claims to live in him must walk as Jesus did" (1 John 2:6 NIV).
- *the proof of our new life:* "By this all will know that you are My disciples, if you have love for one another" (John 13:35). "Therefore, if anyone is in Christ, he is a new creation; old things have passed away; behold, all things have become new" (2 Cor. 5:17).
- *the progress we are to make in Christ as believers:* "We have much to say about this, but it is hard to explain because you are slow to learn. In fact, though by this time you ought to be teachers, you need someone to teach you

the elementary truths of God's word all over again. You need milk, not solid food! Anyone who lives on milk, being still an infant, is not acquainted with the teaching about righteousness. But solid food is for the mature, who by constant use have trained themselves to distinguish good from evil" (Heb. 5:11–14 NIV).

Lack of Understanding and Acceptance

This problem is easily remedied through the general acceptance of those youth whom God brings to your ministry. Remember, we are to love each one unconditionally as Christ loves us (John 15:12). We must build relationships with them regardless of the way they look, talk, or smell, and not solely for a decision. If we "cozy" up to youth solely for a decision, what occurs if they reject the Gospel? Typically the relationship is shut down or totally cut off, leaving the youth feeling rejected and the youth leader looking like a hypocrite, becoming one more person who "wants something" in the eyes of the youth.

As kids walk into your Sunday school, they must be accepted for who and what they are, even if you disagree with it. Our job is to love and nurture them to Christ while the Holy Spirit works on their hearts. In a former youth position I was involved with, God saw fit to bring a group of "nontraditional" guys to a very traditional church. These young men were the "poster boys" for adolescent punk rock. They wore baggy jeans, big T-shirts, chains, and baseball hats, backwards of course. Needless to say, the church was not comfortable with their presence and in fact was shocked at their appearance. The kids were the center of controversy within the church even though they all were believers. However, through the unconditional acceptance and love of the youth leadership team and personal discipleship, these young men became leaders within the group, growing and blossoming into godly young men. If we as leaders had rejected these teens based on appearance, we would have missed the blessing of seeing them grow into mature men. Five years later the bond of love and acceptance is still there. In fact they have become like sons to my wife and me and brothers to our children. Who are we to withhold love and compassion to youth based on external factors? We rob ourselves and the youth of the blessing of ministering to each other in the love of Christ. By the way, they still dress the same.

All of these problems can be overcome, and they are not listed here to imply a defeatist attitude. They are simply stated to call attention to a few areas that must be addressed in order to have the greatest impact possible with the youth that God brings our way.

THE POSITIVES OF TODAY'S SUNDAY SCHOOL

NUMBERS OF YOUTH ATTENDING SUNDAY SCHOOL

Without question we are experiencing greater numbers of youth attending weekly meetings and showing an interest in spiritual matters. How effective we are in leading these youth to Christ and discipling them into a deeper walk with Him is yet to be seen. However, the truth is simply that more youth are returning to the church. Thus Sunday school or its facsimile must be meaningful to the youth in the culture that you minister in.

CURRICULUM

Even though curriculum was mentioned above as a problem with today's Sunday school, it also is a blessing for those who work with youth from a "lay staff" position. We realize that a majority of churches cannot afford the services of a full- or part-time youth pastor and they depend on the laity of the body to minister to the youth. It is from this perspective that the increase in variety of curriculum publication has benefited the church. However, we suggest that these publications be used as a blueprint for the teaching of the Word of God rather than teaching the curriculum verbatim with no thought to the relevance to the needs of the youth. In other words, the leadership should change and adapt these lessons to better fit the needs of the youth in attendance. A deeper impact will result. Think of it this way: The furnace in your apartment has been stuck at ninety degrees for three days, the cat's sweating, the pictures are melting off the walls, and you just can't breathe from the heat. You call the landlord so that the problem can be fixed, and a few hours later a plumber knocks on your door. He can't fix the furnace, but he can take care of the drip in the kitchen faucet. Great, the drip in the kitchen is finally taken care of, but your greater need was to have the furnace fixed. Something was accomplished, but not what you needed. So many times this is our tendency with youth. We do something but miss the greater need.

Becoming More Relevant

Growing youth ministries are ones that are relevant with today's teens. They understand the problems, needs, likes, and dislikes of the youth in their community and adapt their ministry accordingly. They reach out with new and different methods while not compromising the Gospel in the process. They play contemporary Christian music, serve coffee, play extreme sports, and provide a safe zone while reaching the youth with the message of Jesus Christ. These churches also provide avenues for youth to use their gifts and abilities and experience the joy that comes from ministering to others through them. They have learned to combine the Bible lesson with hands-on application of truth.

PAYING ATTENTION TO YOUTH NEEDS

The leaders of any given Sunday school class must become acquainted with the needs of their youth. Today's youth carry more baggage and heartache than previous generations. Consider the following: The annual divorce rate has doubled since 1960 to 4 percent, and the percentage of kids living with one parent has more than doubled since 1970 to 28 percent.[2] In a recent study[3] youth ranked their worries and concerns in the following order:

CONCERN	RANK
HIV and STDs	1
Drinking/Driving	2
Casual sex	2
Pregnancy	3
Weapons	4
Suicide	5
Car accidents	6

In addition there are many issues and many ways in which today's teens are "growing up" too fast. Substance abuse, for example, sexual issues, having to fend for oneself while both parents work, or having to emotionally support mom ever since dad left her. In addition, this generation of kids has been consciously exploited since grade school years to be propagandists for such issues as environmentalism and tolerance. (It's one thing to tell kids something is right or wrong, another thing entirely to tell them, "Adults have messed up on this issue, so it's your job to save the planet, and your job to teach the adults around you the correct way to do this.") Because of this, those who work with youth must understand the deep heartfelt needs of those in their group and then minister to them accordingly.

Many good and exciting things are happening in today's Sunday school, no matter how you choose to define it. We must understand that the needs of the youth should drive us in our preparation and our methodology in reaching them and, in doing so, not compromising the Gospel.

WHAT TODAY'S SUNDAY SCHOOL SHOULD LOOK LIKE

Now that the positives and negatives have been discussed, the question becomes, "What should Sunday school look like?" As mentioned earlier, Sunday school means many different things to many different people. However, here are seven points that, regardless of the methodology chosen by various churches, should be included within Sunday school.

BALANCE

Simply put, do not go to any extreme. We don't want to go to the extreme of being so relevant that we actually conform to the youth culture and don't minister to the youth. However, we can't be so far removed from the current youth culture that we're not being relevant. If we move to either extreme, we won't be effective. We must strive to achieve balance within our group to reach the greatest number of youth possible. This balance also needs to be seen in our programming of the ministry, which will be discussed in a later chapter.

A SAFE ENVIRONMENT

As we develop our Sunday school, one of the most important things that can be done is to establish a safe zone. The youth must feel safe within the confines of the group. They need to have a place to hang out and relax with no fear of confrontation from peers and leaders, an environment where they can be who they are with no fear of being put down or looked down upon. They can relax, physically, mentally, and emotionally, and experience the grace not only to fail but also the grace to bloom into whatever God intends for them to be. When the environment is "safe," the youth are open to build and form relationships with those in leadership because they know they will not be judged or looked down upon by you. Remember, we are to love the youth that God brings our way and lead them into a personal, vibrant relationship with Him.

Friendly, Accepting Peers and Adults

Following on the above point, one way this "safe zone" can be established is through the leaders in the group. To operate a ministry to youth with individuals you really don't care for is not the best idea! Those who work with the teens must have a passion, a desire to do so. These leaders should be trained and educated about the present culture, and their personal gifts should be developed for the greatest impact possible.

Relevant Bible Lessons

Today's youth are interested in lessons that are "doable" in the world in which they live. They must be practical, meaningful, and relevant to help them survive in a world that has left them empty. They are not interested in lessons that have no meaning in their lives and that leave them searching for truth. Lessons in today's Sunday school must meet the needs, the deep heartfelt needs, of youth. The days of long, drawn-out Bible lessons that have no meaning in their lives are gone. Also, youth are not looking for soft pat answers, but they want the truth brought to them in a straight and honest fashion. Christian recording artist Rebecca St. James recognizes this need for relevant, real communication, saying, "Young people are wanting something that's real. They don't want to be messed with. They don't want to beat around the bush. They want to get the nuts and bolts of it and find the truth."[4] When we communicate the truth to teens we must do so in a way that answers questions and present it in such a way that they can take the truth and apply it in their lives. The truth, illustration and application, must be relevant to this present-day culture. This topic will be handled in upcoming chapters (it is enough here to state the need to be meaningful with the Word of God).

True Worship

No subject will produce more conflict within the church than the topic of worship. It must be remembered that true worship is a matter of the heart, and the proof of our love for Christ is found in our obedience to Him (John 14:15), not in our methodology of worship. Simply, the method of worship employed should be relevant to the culture of the church and the culture of the youth you are trying to reach. Worship will be discussed in later chapters. However, Sunday schools that are reaching youth use methods of worship that coincide with the trends of their respective communities.

A Good Fit into the Overall Goal of the Ministry

In addition to the above points it is paramount that the goals and purpose of the Sunday school time fit into the overall mission of the church. Youth Sunday school should not be viewed as a separate entity or a stand-alone ministry. It should fit into and come alongside what other various ministries are trying to accomplish within the church. Communication must be taking place between the senior pastor, minister of family, Sunday school superintendent, and the youth leaders. As the overall mission and vision of the church is understood, then a proper understanding of the function of youth Sunday school will become apparent, producing freedom to minister accordingly.

A DEFINITE AIM AND OBJECTIVES

This aspect of Sunday school is a natural outcome of the above point. Once an understanding is gained of the mission/vision of the church as a whole, then the aims and objectives for the youth Sunday school can be established. Youth Sunday schools that are on the move are those that have established and adhered to the aims and objectives for the group. These aims and objectives function as the tracks that keep the group moving in the proper direction. Youth leaders must be asking, "Why are we doing what we're doing?" If this question cannot be answered through the lens of the stated aims and objectives, then it shouldn't be done. Everything that we do within the context of Sunday school must have a purpose: that of achieving our goal found in the aims and objectives of the ministry.

Sunday school is still an important part of ministry to youth. In fact it is essential to the overall health of the ministry. Even though there are many different opinions as to what Sunday school is and what it should be today, the fact remains that this time of communicating truth cannot be taken lightly or taken for granted. Time, energy, planning, and methodology must be thought out and implemented according to both the culture of the church and youth in the community. As people called of God to work and minister to this generation, we must make every effort to do so as effectively and efficiently as possible.

NOTES

1. "Ancient-Future Youth Ministry" *Group* (July-August 1999).
2. Walter Kirn et al., "Should You Stay Together for the Kids?" *Time Canada,* (25 September 2000): 42.
3. *USA Today,* 13 September 2000.
4. *Faithworks,* January/February 2000.

Philosophy of Teaching Young People

The time has come for you to communicate the Bible lesson to the youth. As a leader, you have studied well. Your lesson plan is written. You have spent time looking for illustrations and have some practical ones from the fields of sports and current events, and even some humorous ones. You have spent time in prayer, asking God to use you to reach the youth who are waiting for your lesson. During the lesson you express yourself well and students seem to be attentive. You cover the material well and use several teaching aids. However, something is wrong. You discover the youth are not learning. The true test of teaching is a change in the lives of students. Are the youth under your care learning anything from your teaching? If students aren't learning, then you aren't teaching.

Teaching is a step of faith: faith in God, faith in His Word, and faith that the Holy Spirit will use us as instruments of righteousness (Rom. 6:13). However, faith by itself will not produce lifelong impact in the lives of students. The teacher must add an understanding of the principles of teaching, an understanding of the learning process, and skill in the planning, preparation, and presentation of the class session.

Teaching is far more than relating Bible stories, facts, locations, and events. It is more than week after week exhorting learners to conform to the image of Christ. It is far more than asking questions, giving lectures, utilizing the latest multimedia equipment, using illustrations or hot discussion topics. Our goal is that of impact and change. If we are not touching lives and changing those under our care to become more like Christ, why are we teaching?

Teaching is an art that is exacting and at times difficult. Teaching requires a well-prepared, touchable, alert, and creative individual who is willing to pay the price to be effective. Teaching also requires a person who can organize and mobilize students toward a definite and meaningful outcome. Effective teaching is not a matter of haphazardly putting material together or winging it, praying that by chance and/or circumstance the lesson will affect students for the kingdom of God. Teaching is not found in the diligence of following the rules of teaching or the strict observance of the laws of the learner. Teaching is simply the result of proper planning and leading students in events and activities that have meaning and purpose for them.

Successful teaching changes lives, encourages growth toward spiritual maturity, and conforms thoughts, behaviors, and lifestyles to the image of Christ. These cannot be left to chance but are premeditated through the planning, organizing, creativity, and timing of the learning experience. Thus the Christian teacher must combine this thoughtful and deliberate planning with spirituality. The quality and quantity of the planning process greatly determines and enhances the quality of the delivery of the teaching and ultimately the quality of learning.

A DEFINITION OF TEACHING

So a common definition of teaching needs to be established. Teaching means different things to different people. We will use the definition from *Webster's Classic Reference Dictionary:* Teaching is "to communicate skill or knowledge; to give instruction or insight." This definition is loaded, meaning that we must examine and explain key terms and make some observations within the definition to gain better insight as to the nature of teaching.

Six things must be discussed as they pertain to our definition for this chapter. It is important to remember that we are viewing this definition from a spiritual standpoint. Thus we must relate our observations back to the purpose of our teaching, which is the conforming of thoughts, actions, and attitudes to the image of Christ.

COMMUNICATION

Communication means simply "to make known." We communicate in many different ways and through many different methods. Four main areas of communication will be discussed here as they pertain to teaching youth. First, we communicate through verbal expression. We relay information through our speech, our choice of words, our tone of voice, our pitch, and our speed of delivery. Second, we communicate through the written word. Thoughts, ideas, and instructions are placed in written form for the learner to read and glean information. Scripture is clear as to the importance of the written word. Words are used for instruction, as a record (journaling), and as a means of encouragement. Third, we communicate through our actions. This includes both our body language and our lifestyle. We communicate an abundance of information concerning our beliefs and Christian faith, primarily through our lifestyle, in full view of the youth. Our words and actions must be in alignment; otherwise we will fail in our communication efforts with youth. Youth have the uncanny ability to see us when no one else is looking, and they will watch for our reaction in all life situations. As someone has said, "More is caught than taught." Fourth, we can communicate or "make known" through the guided activities we allow youth to experience. As youth experience the joy of service, the thrill and excitement of gaining victory over sin, and the wonder of answered prayer, we can enrich and enhance these special times of communication through evaluation of the experience at hand.

As we consider this list of four areas of communication, we may be stronger and more comfortable with one than another. However, when we communicate truth to teens we must strive to use all these four areas to deliver the truth. In Matthew 28 Jesus leaves the Twelve and the future church the Great Commission, "Go make disciples . . ." We are to make disciples, teaching those who come to know Christ how to live a life in obedience to Him. It will take all four of these areas to accomplish this goal. If words were enough to communicate the truth, then everyone who heard Christ would have put their trust in Him. Likewise if actions were enough, then all who saw the signs and miracles of Jesus would have been saved. We must have a proper balance when we communicate truth to teens, and we need to take advantage of the different ways we can communicate truth effectively. This will increase the possibility that the youth will assimilate the truth of Scripture into their lives.

Skill

Skill is ability, which can be sharpened through practice. Should we as leaders and teachers of today's youth be skillful in the handling and the application (living) of biblical principles? Without question, yes! Just as an athlete increases his ability to perform through proper practice, so do we.

To be a skillful Christian means that I am in the practice of living a godly life. I know and understand the deeper life, because I practice it on a daily basis. Thus I'm able to communicate it from a heart that has lived it. The things of God and His Word have become habits of the heart, deep-rooted values and morals, based on Scripture that flows out in a life lived in obedience to God and His Word. These life principles have become internalized in my heart, not simply placed in my head as rote facts and figures that have no bearing on my life. And through the practice of these principles I have gained an ability to live out what I believe and the ability to influence others.

KNOWLEDGE

Knowledge simply is the understanding of facts and information. This is head knowledge, the assimilation of facts, figures, and characters and general information of Scripture. This is contextualization of the information into the mind of the learner. Plainly stated, this is knowing and understanding Scripture.

INSTRUCTION

Instruction is a key element in the effectiveness of teaching. Instruction is not only knowing what you're going to communicate but also your method. It is purposeful planning, having a desired goal and establishing the order of direction. It is the road map you will follow to reach your teaching objectives. This includes the lesson plan, the teaching aim, organization of material, and activities that reinforce your subject matter. It requires thought and prayer.

The relationship between teaching and learning has often been misunderstood. Too many teachers participate in the "information dump." They take all they know about the topic at hand and present it in a thirty- to forty-five-minute time frame. The result? The students become confused and no better off from the barrage of facts. Too much information, in too little time, with too little instruction, causes confusion. This approach is far more concerned with the transmission of facts over learning, and the students being impressed with the knowledge of the teacher rather than affected with Scripture. Depositing all the Bible knowledge that you know on the youth at one time leaves them confused as they sort out and swim through all the information that has just been placed upon them.

Other teachers use the "shotgun approach." Have you ever seen the spray pattern of a shotgun blast? The shell is filled with pellets, so when the gun is fired the pellets spray over the target, hitting a larger area than a single rifle bullet. You don't have to be a good shot with a shotgun. Likewise in teaching, there is a tendency to be all over the target, spraying facts and knowledge over the students with no apparent aim or reason. This also results in confusion as the students struggle to tie together what they have just heard. They spend more time trying to figure out what just happened than applying the Word of God. As teachers we need to organize the material in such away that it will touch the hearts and minds of those under our instruction. The order of direction will allow us to hit the intended target with the appropriate amount of information.

INSIGHT

Insight is the perception into the true or hidden nature of things. This perception or insight comes from the handling and studying of Scripture. In Hebrews 5:11–14, Paul rebukes the audience for not progressing in their understanding of biblical truth. In fact he states that they are "slow to learn" (v. 11 NIV) and that they should have progressed to the point of teaching the way. But they are simply not at that point. Paul compares them to babies in the fact that they need "milk" and not "solid food," as they are not able to digest it. For the "meat" of Scripture, through continual use, leads to the ability to discern and distinguish good from evil. Likewise as teachers we need to have the perception and insight of Scripture that comes from the Holy Spirit working in our lives, not suppressing or ignoring the insight gained through the Spirit through a lack of obedience. We must be progressing in our own understanding so that we are worthy to be deemed teachers. We must be beyond the elementary things of Scripture and on to the meat of the Christian life. Remember, we will produce what we are. Thus we must strive to be as obedient as possible so the youth will follow our example.

The Supernatural

As mentioned previously, teaching must incorporate the ministry of the Holy Spirit. All good things come from above, and the Spirit will lead us into all truth. Thus we must fight the impulse to use canned or prepackaged material. We must rely on the Spirit to reveal insight of the passage or topic at hand that will relate directly to the needs of the group. Teaching must be a transfer of knowledge from heart to heart. It must be real and from a heart that has depended on the Spirit in guidance and application.

Let us review our definition based on the previous observations. Teaching is to make known (through a proper balance of the verbal, the written, actions, and experience) an ability gained through practice (habits of the heart, the practice of living out biblical principles that have been internalized) or facts and information (head knowledge, the knowing and understanding of Scripture, its contextualization): to give a lesson or order of instruction (planning with a purpose, not shotgun or information dump) or perception into the true or hidden meaning of things (progressing in our understanding of Scripture, moving from milk to meat) while depending on the guidance of the supernatural (the ministry of the Holy Spirit).

Now that a common definition of teaching has been established, we can move to some basic fundamentals of teaching. Three fundamentals need to be present in the life of the teacher that are paramount to reaching this generation.

THREE FUNDAMENTALS FOR THE TEACHER

Anyone who is to be effective in communicating biblical truth to youth must first understand and exhibit three basic fundamentals of teaching. These are not laws or rules that can be synthesized into a lesson plan or simply incorporated into a lesson aim. Rather, these three principles must be internalized into the heart and life of the teacher.

First, today's teachers must be *real.* This principle is found in Luke 16:10–12, where Christ says:

> He who is faithful in what is least is faithful also in much; and he who is unjust in what is least is unjust also in much. Therefore if you have not been faithful in the unrighteous mammon, who will commit to your trust the true riches? And if you have not been faithful in what is another man's, who will give you what is your own?

Christ is communicating a basic principle for all of us who are privileged enough to teach. Simply put, we must take care of the little things in our lives and be faithful in the area that God has chosen to place us. In other words, as teachers we must personally live out and possess what we are advocating. How can we expect to see the youth living with integrity and personal holiness, without gossip or backbiting, showing honesty, and exhibiting the fruits of the Spirit when these things are foreign in our own lives? Youth can spot a fake and a fraud with relative ease. As we minister and teach youth we must make sure that we are growing ourselves and living what we proclaim. If we don't, we become hypocrites ourselves. Learning will not take place if youth deem us to be people who don't live what we say we believe. In fact it will be hard to accomplish any ministry at all. As teachers of the Word of God directed toward youth, we must be *real,* living a life that's worth duplicating.

Second, today's teachers must be *in the Word* on a personal basis. This principle is found in Hebrews 5:12–14,

> For by this time you ought to be teachers, you need someone to teach you again the first principles of the oracles of God; and you have come to need milk, and not solid food. For everyone who partakes only of milk is unskilled in the word of righteousness, for he is a babe. But solid food belongs to those who are of full age, that is, those who by reason of use have their senses exercised to discern both good and evil.

Here we are reminded to make a progression in our learning and move from the milk (simple) to the meat (complex) in our relationship with God. Paul urges us to move forward and become skilled in the use of the Word so that we may distinguish good from evil. The Word becomes our standard for knowing right from wrong, good from evil, and it is what sustains us in our relationship with Him. As we look to communicate truth to the youth, we must do so from the vantage point of knowing and understanding Scripture ourselves. When we have spent time in the Word, the result is less judgment of the youth and more instruction based on Scripture. From what other source do we want our youth to live? If we remain on the milk of Scripture (the elementary things of God), we will be producing a group of students who will be the same, remaining on the milk and never progressing to the meat of Scripture. This relates directly to the actions, attitudes, and choices that the youth will make as they try to live out their lives according to the Word of God.

Third, today's teachers must possess *dependence.* The importance of this principle is seen in Proverbs 3:5–6: "Trust in the Lord with all your heart, and lean not on your own understanding; in all your ways acknowledge Him, and He shall direct your paths." As we teach and impart biblical truth to teens we must lean on the understanding that comes only from God and the insight that comes from the Holy Spirit. As we develop and organize teaching outlines, it must be done in a spirit of prayer and guidance from above. If we fail to rely on God and His leading and prompting in our lives as we study and plan, then we rest solely on our ability to communicate the truth. We have reduced our teaching to one of personal opinion and selfish motives. As we depend on the leading of God, we are able to relate truth in such a way as to meet the needs of the youth and help them to progress in their walk with God. Relying on the influence, illumination, and insight from God helps to guard our hearts from the temptation of teaching in the flesh, and we can be secure in knowing that we have developed an outline that is anchored in dependence on God and not our own ability.

These three fundamentals of being real, in the Word, and dependent upon God must be present and exhibited in the life of the teacher.

GENERAL GOALS FOR TEACHING—WHAT WE SHOULD ACHIEVE

First and foremost we should strive to help youth conform to the image of Christ (2 Cor. 5:17; James 1:22–25) and prove their love of God through obedience to the Word (John 14:21).

As teachers our general goals are found in Luke 2:52, "And Jesus increased in wisdom and stature, and in favor with God and men." We need to encourage our youth to conform to the image of Christ and grow in wisdom as they grow in stature, and to increase in favor with both God and man. These areas should be the standard to which we lead and about which we teach our youth. Wisdom is the ability to use sound judgment or prudence in life. Biblical wisdom is to be coveted (Prov. 4:5); wisdom is to be treasured more than riches (Prov. 8:11), and it is an attribute of God (Job 36:5). Wisdom is described as "first pure, then peaceable, gentle, and easy to be intreated, full of mercy and good fruits, without partiality, and without hypocrisy" (James 3:17 KJV). Wisdom is essential for today's youth. They must not only understand the life principles of Scripture but how to act according to what they believe in day-to-day situations. They must understand that Scripture is our guide to living a Christian lifestyle, and then apply that truth.

The second area in which Jesus grew was stature. Developing in stature means to come of age, to mature physically. As we work with teens we must add to our teaching of Scripture an understanding of the many physical changes that they are experiencing. In addition to the maturing of their bodies, teens also experience a change in their thought processes as well, moving from the concrete to the abstract. In our teaching these areas must not only be taken into consideration as we formulate outlines, aims, and lessons, but they also become topical areas to address in teaching youth how to live a life anchored in obedience to Scripture.

Third, Jesus grew in favor with both God and man. Today we're more likely to say that someone has a good reputation, that the person is known for integrity and deeds of kindness. Hence Christ was succeeding at living out what He believed. He modeled the Christian walk for us to emulate. As a result, He increased in the favor of God as He was obedient to the Father. As He lived daily in this grace, He grew in the favor of men as He lived out His faith in full view of His Father. We must help teens to grow in favor with God through obedience to His Word. As they live out the principles of Scripture, people will come to view them with favor. Their testimony among others will be a source of glory unto God. A measure of this goal is simply to recognize and evaluate the opinion of adults regarding the teens under your care. Even though this can be subjective, we can still learn much about the progress the youth are making in their Christian life. Who doesn't want to be surrounded by teens who are gracious, loving, and full of goodwill? This goal of teaching explains and achieves the difference between servanthood (want to) and civility (have to).

The question becomes, "How do we achieve these goals in the lives of teens?" We must have an understanding of our role as teachers, understanding different teaching styles, as well as know how students learn.

PREPARATION FOR TEACHING

Scripture is assuredly God's inspired Word for man. The Word's effectiveness is either aided or impeded by the hands of people. It is true that regardless of how poorly it is communicated, Scripture will accomplish something of worth. However, the teacher who spends time in proper preparation becomes an improved channel by which Scripture may work more fruitfully. As teachers should this not be the desire of our hearts? *What is necessary for proper preparation?*

TIME IN STUDY AND PLANNING

We are commanded, "Study to shew thyself approved unto God, a workman that needeth not to be ashamed, rightly dividing the word of truth" (2 Tim. 2:15 KJV). Let's break this verse down into its parts so that the emphasis can be clearly seen. First, the term *study* gives the notion of time to study a subject, concept, or text. It simply means to spend time with it, absorbing all that can be gleaned and observed about the given subject. A thorough study of any subject cannot be accomplished in a short amount of time. It takes work, effort, time, and sweat to reach mastery.

Second, "approved," "workman," and "ashamed" each describe the quality of the individual's study and preparation of material. Wuest explains it this way: "Approved is a workman who has been put to the test, and meeting the specifications laid down has passed the test."[1] Being a workman can include the work of one's hands as well as the work in his study.

Third, the descriptive phrase that follows not only describes but depends upon this factor of planning to study. Terms such as "rightly dividing" express the thought "that the Minister of the Gospel is to present the truth rightly, not abridging it, not handling it as a charlatan, not making it a matter of strife, but treating it honestly and fully in a straightforward manner."[2] This can only be accomplished through planned study, mulling over the text, and making observations, interpretations, and applications through prayer and a dependence on the Holy Spirit. If I am to "rightly divide" the truth, then I need to be in the truth, learning the truth, living the truth, and then presenting the truth.

The Environment for Proper Study

Every student is affected by his surrounding atmosphere. Professional sports teams battle all year long to carry "home field" advantage during the playoffs. Why? Because the hometown fans create an environment of excitement and anticipation. Many professional athletes will comment that they "feed" off the excitement and energy of the crowd. It helps them to perform better and more effectively. Likewise the teacher must take care that his environment for study is conducive to just that, study.

The surroundings in which the teacher prepares greatly influences the quality of his preparation. Elements including his zeal for study, attitudes toward students, quality of preparation, and tone of prayer are all affected by the physical surroundings. These factors all affect (positively or negatively) the quality of the lesson plan. Make no mistake, preparation and study are exhausting and take much intellectual effort. Thus any distraction, chaos, or disturbance decreases the quality of the lesson plan and distracts from its overall effectiveness in developing the lesson. In addition to an environment of uninterrupted contemplation, the study area itself must be well equipped. Furnishings, lighting, and materials (books, pens, paper, etc.) must be arranged in such a way to help facilitate the teacher's study. This takes planning and thoughtful consideration of the surroundings.

Preparation for Organized Teaching of Scripture

"All Scripture is given by inspiration of God, and is profitable for doctrine, for reproof, for correction, for instruction in righteousness" (2 Tim. 3:16). Notice the four areas that Paul tells us need to be addressed by Scripture in an orderly fashion: (1) doctrine—teaching, (2) reproof—conviction, (3) correction—upright or right state, correction or improvement, (4) instruction—the whole training (moral and mental) of individuals. We must plan to cover these areas as we prepare our teaching. Our teaching must have specific aims and purposes. These can only be accomplished through proper planning. If we teach the Word without these purposes as our goal, why teach?

Focusing the Message

According to Ken Davis, "The most important ingredient to dynamic communication is focus."[3] No matter what platform a person speaks from, if he is to be effective he must be focused. The principle here is if you don't aim at something, you'll hit nothing. A dynamic presentation is secondary to focus. Davis asks, "What good is it to be dynamic if no one can tell what you are dynamic about? Dynamics and theatrics without focus is only entertainment."[4]

Davis gives one method for preparation that can be of great value for a youth teacher or speaker. One should begin the preparation by choosing a single subject. The speaker must seek God's direction in prayer. He needs to look for the needs of his group, and he must consider if he has been directed to speak on a specific subject if speaking for someone else's group. He needs to ask himself if he knows enough on the chosen subject to speak intelligently. He also must ask himself if the way he approaches the subject is consistent with scriptural truth. Next, the speaker/teacher needs to choose a single aspect of the subject as a central theme. He then needs to clarify his objective by asking, "What am I trying to say?" A good question to ask here is "Why?" Now he should write a propositional statement, question it, and answer the question "Why?" or "How?" with a phrase that uses a key word. Third, the teacher needs to develop his rationale by answering, "What are the main points of my message?"

The fourth step is gathering and using resources—putting frosting on the cake. "Illustrations and anecdotes are the glitter and sparkle that make people want to listen to our message."[5] One good practice we need to develop is drawing illustrations out of our own everyday experiences to use in our messages. It is a good thing to keep a file of these illustrations to pull from. Finally, the teacher should evaluate the preparation. This simply means to go through it and remove the impurities and those things that are not necessary. It's important with students to remember that the more information they are fed at one time, the less they can recall.

It's important to take one's time by preparing in stages. The teacher should allow time to mull over the speech in his mind. He should also write down any new thoughts on the subject. Outside of the actual message preparation, the teacher should prepare the environment. If it is a small discussion session, the chairs may need to be set up in a circle. The lighting and temperature in a room should always be checked. It should also be determined if the speaker will need a mike and/or other equipment. These are always important to check in order to eliminate as many distractions as possible.

PRAYER THAT THE HOLY SPIRIT WILL ENLIGHTEN AND GRANT INSIGHT

The need of prayer is overlooked or totally ignored by most teachers, which in fact demonstrates a lack of dependence on God and the Holy Spirit in their teaching and preparation. The teacher who fails to pray before, during, and after lesson preparation is setting him or herself up for failure and inviting disaster into the classroom. Since teaching Scripture is a spiritual/supernatural matter, then as teachers we are mandated to depend and lean on the One who guides, convicts, and leads us into all spiritual truth (John 16:13). Further, the teacher who fails to seek the help of the Holy Spirit in preparation fails to experience the joy of working in fellowship with Him. What better peace is there than knowing that the same Spirit who inspired the authors of Scripture will assist in helping the teacher prepare and present the same Book. A teacher's preparation must include prayer for guidance and insight. As teachers of Scripture we will be held accountable for our teaching of the Word (James 3:1). We are dealing with people and issues that have eternal consequences and that are affected by the quality of our message. This is a responsibility that must be taken to heart.

PRAYER OVER THE CLASS

The effective teacher teaches to the needs of the students. Praying over the class goes hand in hand with the above point. As I pray over my students, considering their situations and spiritual condition, I will be better equipped to structure activities and lessons toward those needs. In addition, as I pray for dependence and guidance from the Holy Spirit, I am relying on His help to structure the lesson content and the words of my mouth in such a way that as a teacher, I will be as effective as possible (Matt. 12:36). This is where the supernatural aspect comes into play. If we pray for the Holy Spirit's help in revealing insight, truth, and creativity to us, and pray that we can communicate biblical truth to our students, He will help. God wants our students to be saved and conformed to His image more than we do.

Mastering the Passage

There is a marked difference between understanding what the lesson is and what the lesson is actually about. It is never enough to know what the curriculum writers or the commentaries have to say about a given passage or lesson. It is imperative that the teacher masters the Bible passage him or herself. To master the Bible passage two things must be accomplished: (1) A complete knowledge of the Bible passage must be achieved. This will include the specific passage itself and any "background" information of the given passage. (2) As the teacher masters the given passage, clear, understandable lesson aims must be formulated that correlate to the material structure. These two areas are paramount to formulating and presenting a high-impact lesson. The teacher may have an excellent understanding of Scripture but not comprehend or understand how to arrange a lesson for effective teaching. The following steps will help the teacher to master the lesson passage.

Read the Passage Three to Five Times

Nothing helps clarify a Bible passage as much as reading it over and over. While reading the passage, the teacher should be praying that the Holy Spirit will enlighten and reveal insights that will meet the needs of his students. As one reads and rereads Scripture, one cannot help but think and meditate on that passage. This leads to making observations and interpretations that otherwise would be missed. The more Scriptures consume the mind and thought process of the teacher, the more effective he will be in ultimately presenting the lesson. Lessons become more "real" to the students if they are first "real" to the teacher. It is the difference between a meaningful, self-discovered lesson and one that has been handed down from a third source. This practice of reading through the lesson passage should transpire each day preceding the teaching. The teacher will want to read the passage prayerfully and meditatively, looking for observations, the human element, key words, key ideas, and key persons.

Make Key Observations

Look for what the passage is saying—its key themes, doctrines, and events, and how these tie into the context of the entire book and of the larger picture of Scripture. Looking for key words is a good place to start. What words are used several times? How are they used? What words are clues to the meaning of the passage? The following chart suggests words that help establish a passage's teaching.

KEY WORDS

Commands:	do, do not, be, be not
Contrast:	but, however, nevertheless
Condition:	if
Comparison:	like, as
Summary:	therefore, so, that, so that
Reason:	for, for this cause, that
Emphasis:	how much more
Processes:	"-ing," might, ought, should, by
Key Ideas:	filled, cleansed, holy, justification, etc.
Key Persons:	Christ, Holy Spirit, God, any major or minor human characters (including the addressee of the letter or book)

The teacher should develop his own system for marking these key elements and cross-referencing the passage. In addition, the teacher should use a dictionary to look up any definitions and pronunciations that he is unfamiliar with. For additional understanding the teacher should read different translations and versions of the passage. A Bible dictionary is helpful for understanding the cultural events that surround the passage. The reading and rereading of the passage should continue until it becomes so alive and real that the teaching of it becomes a "release" for the teacher and delight for the students.

Outline the Passage

After the teacher has become familiar with the passage through the above steps, he should engage in producing a brief outline of the passage. Break the passage down into three to five main points with corresponding subpoints. This outline can be used during the lesson, but mostly it acts to reinforce that the teacher understands the logical flow of the passage.

Understand the Setting, History, and Context of the Passage

As mentioned previously, the teacher would be wise to gain as much understanding of the background of the passage as possible. This would include author, date, cultural conditions, problems in audience, positives with audience, and the geographic location of the recipient(s) as well as the author(s). These aspects all play a part in understanding the passage in question.

Not all of this information is to be used in the presentation of the lesson, though some will. It is simply to better equip the teacher in planning and preparation, thus giving the Holy Spirit a greater network of information to draw from as the teacher prepares and ultimately presents the lesson.

Summarize the Lesson

Writing out a brief summary of the lesson will benefit the teacher. A brief summary consists of the broad contents of the lesson. At this point the teacher should not include details, applications, or background material. This step is intended to simply help the teacher clarify and organize the material in question by forcing the teacher to state the lesson in a clear and concise way.

Verify Conclusions

Commentaries and books are used in this step to verify, support, and challenge the teacher's own "self-discovery" and conclusion formed during the personal Bible study time. Warning: Don't let commentaries and books become a crutch for your thinking. The danger here is to consult commentaries and books first, causing the teacher not to rely on the working of the Holy Spirit in and through his own personal Bible study.

Specific Goals and Purposes in Teaching

The purpose of Christian teaching can be summarized in two verses, but these verses in no way encompass all there is to being a Christian. As we have already seen from 2 Timothy 3:16, there must be purpose to do what we do. In addition to 2 Timothy 3:16, our purpose in teaching Scripture must incorporate the following:

> But you have not so learned Christ, if indeed you have heard Him and have been taught by Him, as the truth is in Jesus: that you put off, concerning your former conduct, the old man which grows corrupt according to the deceitful lusts, and be renewed in the spirit of your mind, and that you put on the new man which was created according to God, in true righteousness and holiness. (Eph. 4:20–24)

Very simply, Paul is stating to us that as believers we must continue to remove our old way of thinking and living and replace it with the things of God, knowing what is sin and removing it from our lives. Thus our teaching needs to have as a purpose that of helping or communicating to our students what is "new," to conform to the image of Christ as found in the Word of God. A second verse to help narrow our goals and purposes in teaching is found in 1 John 2:6, "Whoever claims to live in him [Jesus] *must* walk as Jesus did" (NIV, italics added). This verse is a command for everyone who calls Christ Savior, to imitate the actions, attitudes, focus, love, compassion, and other characteristics that He modeled for us. This of course means that we as teachers need to know Christ, live Christ, and instruct Christ to our students.

TEACHING AND LEARNING STYLES

Raye Zacharias has published a very concise and clear series of books entitled *Styles and Profiles*. His research will be the main source of information concerning teaching and learning styles in this section. In identifying one's teaching style, it is important to identify learning styles as well. Having a basic knowledge of how others learn will help one develop his/her teaching style to stretch and reach all those under the person's leadership. Zacharias has separated learning styles into four types: innovative, analytic, common sense, and dynamic.

Innovative learners learn through reason, and they like to be given the big picture. They are motivated to learn primarily through trust, which can only come through building a relationship with them. As we spend more time with these types of youth and we show integrity in all we do, they develop trust. They are normally very good with words and are creative. They see things as very simple. They like to know the goal(s) they are moving toward. Innovative learners are concrete thinkers and reflective. They usually work best when emotionally involved with others. Talking and listening are two of their favorite things to do, so a comfortable learning atmosphere is important. They will take what they see and generalize the information. Innovative learners like to ask "Why?" or "Why not?" questions. They also listen with an open mind and are very sensitive to other people.

The *analytic learner* feeds off of facts and information. This is how most teachers approach teaching, and as a result this is usually the student who walks away having learned the most. This person works best when the requirements, schedules, and standards are clearly understood on both sides. He will remember every detail, and each one is very important to him. He is committed to excellence and completion. Analytic learners love to learn and love school. They are dedicated and punctual. Their homework is always completed. Rarely are they a discipline problem. They do not function well when called to stand before others in a given session.

The *commonsense learner* comprehends by making decisions and trying things out. This person is motivated to learn by being given freedom to figure out how things work. He is looking for a way to use the teaching in a real-life application. Turn him loose; let his mind and hands work it out. To the commonsense learner, the process is much more attractive than the product, so feedback and praise should be on the performance, not on the product. These students are not much into preparation. They want to do it and do it now! They become bored and jittery when the demand for concentration increases. These are the people who are often labeled as hyperactive. This style of learning is out of step with the traditional setting.

The *dynamic learner* is a goal-oriented person. His motivation is in accomplishing and reaching a goal, not in rewards. However, compliments and feedback boost his ego and assure him that what he is doing is of value to others. This type of person values relationships. Being with and working with others is a natural turn-on. When someone tells him that something can't be done, it only increases his motivation to do it. Seeing, hearing, touching, feeling, and then doing it himself are all important to the dynamic learner. He often learns by trial and error and is flexible and ready for change. This learner is perceptive and at times may know the right answer without logical reasoning. He will respond to several methods at the same time. He is very much into doing and experiencing.

STYLES OF TEACHING

To see the relevance of this information, one must look at the qualities that each teaching style possesses in relation to the learning styles. First, *innovative teachers* have a very strong person-to-person communication. People follow this kind of teacher even if they don't know where he is headed. The innovative teacher is a nurturer and a supporter. Students will soon know who this teacher is, because the teacher is very open and builds strong relationships. The teacher can identify the problem or potential, but sometimes doesn't know what to do about it. Innovative teachers would prefer to do things themselves rather than delegate and develop people. They are good with words and like to talk and listen; communication is excellent.

Analytic teachers put their greatest emphasis on content, making sure each teen knows the facts. They have a tendency to ignore relationships and concentrate on the lesson. They are abstract and reflective and probably will not be overly aggressive, but are capable of leading with solid goals. They always think they are strong, complete, and right. They want to know where they stand in a given organization and will communicate effectively with others they are responsible for. They prefer a tightly structured atmosphere. This teacher's style in Bible study will most likely be expository preaching.

The second part of Stephen and David Olford's book *Anointed Expository Preaching* gives in-depth explanation and instruction in preparing an expository message. Their definition for expository preaching is "the Spirit-empowered explanation and proclamation of the text of God's Word with due regard to the historical, contextual, grammatical, and doctrinal significance of the given passage, with the specific object of invoking a Christ-transforming response."[6] The analytic teacher will thrive in such teaching. It is full of facts. Analytic teachers must be careful that they do not overwhelm their listeners with so many facts that students experience information dump and get their fill in the first five minutes of the message, which is usually the case.

Commonsense teachers are the ones who are always doing the unexpected to develop freedom and spontaneity with the students. They have a joy in performing. Their strength is in providing a variety of action experiences for the students. These are problem-solving leaders. They have a way of getting to the heart of the problem. To the commonsense teacher the process is the important thing, not the product. They usually prefer to work by themselves rather than in a group or delegatory role. They become easily bored doing routine tasks. Some other words to describe them are active, black and white, confrontational, tough, and quick. They need to be reminded to include reason, information, and reflective time in their teaching. They are good procrastinators and have a tendency of being late and not being prepared. However, they will act on impulse and their natural drives, and soon will be ahead of everyone else.

Dynamic teachers are what one might call ideal leaders. They are sensitive to an emotional climate in their teaching environment. They have a compelling personal charisma and a strong commitment to their students. They always use a variety of methods, groupings, visuals, and other activities in teaching their students. They constantly look for new ideas and materials. They enjoy taking charge. Dynamic teachers have vision and can easily enlist others and enthusiastically lead them forward. It is important for them to stay busy. They need challenges set before them. They are flexible and willing to change. They like to become personally involved with each student in the group. They can be confronting, but they go out of their way to avoid confrontations. They are usually weak in follow-through principles. They also need assurance of others' full support to do their best.

Application of Teaching Styles

There is great importance in understanding both the students' learning styles and one's own teaching styles. Without this knowledge a teacher may fail greatly at the tasks of putting God's Word and principles into a student's heart. One must remember that the target is never one or two students but the whole group. George Barna states, "A person is not a teacher because he or she has great knowledge and hopes to transfer that information to others. A teacher is one who has successfully transmitted useful facts and processes to students so that they are better informed and more capable than before they encountered the teacher."[7] How can one ensure this takes place? We can't always. However, we can most of the time. Raye Zacharias states, "When teaching takes place with learning styles in focus, pupils learn where they are most comfortable and where success comes easy."[8]

Those whom one is trying to teach not only need to hear the facts but how to apply what they know. For some students, to ensure they understand the truths being taught means they need a project. This will give them the proper perspective and will allow the teacher to bend in his or her normal teaching. For example, a teacher may be trying to teach the importance of putting others before one's self. He may give an excellent expository message on Jesus' teaching in Matthew. However, to reach some in the class he may have them write down a list of ways they can implement the teaching throughout the next week. Still for others he needs to allow them time to discuss and ask questions. For some he may even put a short skit together to give a visual of the teaching. He might even need to organize a project for the upcoming week for students to participate in, giving them opportunity to see the teaching in action.

This may be a stretch for some teachers, especially for the analytic. So if one identifies himself as an analytic, it would help to see the areas in his teaching that need adjusting. This does not imply that a teacher should change his teaching style or personality. When communicating with teenagers, it is vital that one is genuinely himself or herself. Ken Davis, in his book *How to Speak to Youth . . . and Keep Them Awake at the Same Time,* notes this important principle: "When it comes time to be touched by God's Word or when they need personal help and counsel, kids will want to communicate with someone who is genuine. The person the kids see when you are communicating God's Word should be the same person they see in everyday life."[9] One last note in applying these principles is that no one should classify himself into just one category, though one will dominate. No one is confined by these classifications. Identifying where one is weak gives the opportunity to use the creativity that God has placed within every individual. It will take creative thinking and planning to adjust one's teaching styles in the areas where the teacher is missing his audience.

The misconception here is that a select few have creative abilities. In his book *Color Outside the Lines,* Howard Hendricks writes, "You are a creative individual, whether you have ever thought of yourself that way, and whether you seem to be functioning that way. You are a creative individual! At least potentially."[10] He goes on to explain, "You learn to be creative by practicing the principles of creativity. One reason why many of us doubt our creative capacities is the large gap between our creative potential and our creative productivity."[11] It is a necessity to make a plan to exercise and stretch one's teaching style and then consistently implement that plan until those practices become as natural as the original way the person began teaching.

As a Christian leader and teacher, one's aim is not just to enable a student to hold on to information, but to get students to ingest it, to practice it, to let the "Word dwell in them richly."

The Word of God is not meant to be delivered as a motivational talk. It is meant to get into individuals' heads and hearts and change their thinking, direction, actions, and lives. There are dozens of methods of teaching, and the number will continue to increase as society changes. It must continue to increase, or we will get stuck only reaching a select few. If one is teaching in student ministry, he is teaching at the forefront of all societal changes. From attitudes to technology, teenagers are constantly grabbing at the next new thing. Therefore, it is imperative that as the teacher aims to reach them with the truths of God's Word, he must study and search for new methods of teaching students.

DELIVERY OF THE MATERIAL

After preparation comes the process and method of delivery. Beware of traditional delivery in student ministry. Getting in front of a group and talking to them in monologue is still effective if done genuinely, but one can get in a rut and take his listeners with him. The moment any tradition gets in the way of a lost soul hearing the Gospel and coming to Christ, that tradition becomes an obstacle. This does not mean throwing it out altogether, but merely noting that there are appropriate times to use it and times to do things differently. This is where creative teaching comes into play.

Student ministry demands constant change based on the constant change youth culture goes through. Wayne Naugal, youth pastor of Center Hill Baptist Church in Loganville, Georgia, said that he relies heavily on small group discussions when it comes to discipleship. He stressed that it allows his students to open up and talk with one another. As a result, the students are beginning to own their own faith.

A discussion session is just one of many formats to present a message or teach a biblical principle. Marlene D. Lefever gives a list of benefits of discussion in her book *Creative Teaching*

Methods: (1) Discussion stimulates interest and thinking, and it helps students develop the skills of observation, analysis, and logic. (2) Discussion helps students clarify and review what they have learned. (3) Students can sometimes solve their own problems through discussion. (4) Discussion allows students to hear opinions that are more mature and perhaps more Christlike than their own. (5) Discussion stimulates creativity and aids students in applying what they have learned to everyday situations. (6) When students verbalize what they believe and are forced to explain or defend what they say, their convictions are strengthened and their ability to discuss what they believe with others is increased.[12]

Another important method to use in teaching is based on what Bill McNabb calls the "Action-Attitude Principle": Kids believe what they do more than they do what they believe.[13] When kids publicly act on their beliefs, they come to believe more strongly in their actions. That is why it is important to plan such things as neighborhood workdays, mission trips, or nursing home visits. These give the students the opportunity to experience firsthand in real-life situations the reality and relevance of what you are trying to teach them.

When teaching, it is sometimes effective to not make the answer obvious. Students are more motivated to learn when they do not possess the answer. Research has consistently shown that learners remember answers to questions they themselves ask.[14] The method here is to give enough information to get their attention and get them thinking and not to answer questions they haven't asked.

One method of teaching is expository. This has its place in time as we have discussed under teaching styles; however, teenagers' lives are lives of topics. Calvin Miller, author of *Marketplace Preaching,* suggests a topical series should not exceed five messages. The steps he gives are as follows: (1) Enhance the text-meaning to bring it to life by vocal alterations or drama. (2) Pick the focal passage. (3) Obtain a sermon logo to help visualize the message. (4) Polish by adding illustrations and jokes for relief. (5) Be yourself.[15]

Creativity is always welcomed. No teacher is limited in the methods used as long as those methods are biblically sound, culturally acceptable, and effective. Other methods may include allowing students to help choose what they study. No one knows better than the students themselves the struggles they are facing and the answers they are searching for. One may teach in varied settings, perhaps using an on-site object to illustrate a point. Students get excited about learning new things when they actually learn something. A few more methods may include role play, simulation games, using songs that relate to the topic, and drama or skits. (It's amazing how sometimes a thirty-second skit can better express a principle than a thirty-minute message.)

Today there is available to those who teach, a tool that perhaps surpasses all others—the Internet. Teachers should become as familiar as possible with the Internet in order to reach the Net-Generation of students who will only continue to increase in their use of the Net for communication. Mark Hall said that with his youth group in Daytona, Florida, everyone uses the Internet. He has begun using it every day to disciple students. He said that many students find it easier to ask him questions by e-mail than face-to-face. Every day he answers students' questions about the Bible and topics they are struggling with. "The cyber-gap between adults and children is going to get worse before it gets better. Youth workers have an opportunity to speak the same computer language and the same internet dialect that their youth speak."[16]

TEACHING THAT FITS OUR GOALS

Leaders and teachers usually have a definite goal of producing other leaders who possess the same knowledge as themselves with a continual desire to grow further. John Maxwell states in his book *Developing the Leaders Around You,* "Leaders create and inspire new leaders by instilling faith in their leadership ability and helping them develop and hone leadership skills they don't know they possess."[17] It is a process called discipleship. Paul told the believers in Corinth, "Follow my example, as I follow the example of Christ" (1 Cor. 11:1 NIV). Therefore, it is imperative that one be effective in his or her teaching.

The methods that have been noted may or may not be effective in a given setting. It is a matter of discernment in when and where to use a certain method. Discussion is a great method, but not with an audience of 150 students. In a small group of no more than twenty, discussion seems to be most effective. Doing a drama is a great idea in a large group setting (more than twenty-five students). Some methods are effective in both large and small groups, such as asking questions without giving answers for them to chew on throughout the week. One should be creative in combining methods. For instance, one may meet in a large group setting, do a drama, deliver a message that ends with a challenging question, and then split into small groups to discuss what was seen and said. It's important that teachers of students use a variety of methods and determine to keep in touch with the changes of the youth culture in order to change their methods. The goal of all teaching is that students take the truths of the Word of God into their hearts and minds and allow them to change them. The teacher is there to help them apply what they are taking in. "Neglecting to apply the Scriptures reduces Bible study to an academic exercise in which we are concerned only for interpretation with little or no regard for its relevance for and impact on our lives."[18]

Teaching and preaching God's Word is an awesome responsibility. Those called by God to this task will be held under a stricter judgment as to how they handled it and lived in light of it. Hendricks gives several dangers of mishandling God's Word: misreading the text, distorting the text, contradicting the text, subjectivism, relativism, and overconfidence.[19] When it comes to student ministry, the challenge of this becomes even greater with the rapidly changing culture and ever-increasing need for the truth to be heard using methods that are coherent with the culture. Those called must always resort first to their most powerful and available tool in diving into this endeavor—prayer.

NOTES

1. Kenneth Wuest, *Wuest's Word Studies from the Greek New Testament,* vol. 2 (Grand Rapids: Eerdmans, 1966), 135.
2. Marvin Vincent, *Word Studies in the New Testament,* vol. 4 (Grand Rapids: Eerdmans, 1965), 302.
3. Ken Davis, *How to Speak to Youth . . . and Keep Them Awake at the Same Time* (Grand Rapids: Zondervan, 1996), 11.
4. Ibid., 14.
5. Ibid., 63.
6. Stephen F. Olford with David L. Olford, *Anointed Expository Preaching* (Nashville: Broadman & Holman, 1992), 69.
7. George Barna, *The Second Coming of the Church* (Nashville: Word, 1998), 112.
8. Raye Zacharias, *Styles and Profiles* (Southlake, Tex.: Raye Zacharias, 1992), 21.
9. Davis, *How to Speak to Youth,* 33.
10. Howard G. Hendricks, *Color Outside the Lines* (Nashville: Word, 2000), 3.
11. Ibid., 4.
12. Marlene D. Lefever, *Creative Teaching Methods: Be an Effective Christian Teacher* (Colorado Springs: Cook Ministry Resources, 1996), 203–4.
13. Bill McNabb and Steven Mabry, *Teaching the Bible Creatively: How to Awaken Your Kids to Scripture* (Grand Rapids: Zondervan, 1990), 73.
14. Ibid., 84.
15. Calvin Miller, *Marketplace Preaching: How to Return the Sermon to Where It Belongs* (Grand Rapids: Baker, 1995), 101–5.
16. Lefever, *Creative Teaching Methods,* 293.
17. John C. Maxwell, *Developing the Leaders Around You* (Nashville: Nelson, 1995), 11.
18. Roy B. Zuck, *Basic Bible Interpretation* (Wheaton, Ill.: Victor, 1991), 279.
19. Howard G. Hendricks and William D. Hendricks, *Living by the Book* (Chicago: Moody, 1991), 202–6.

Learning and Today's Youth

HOW TEENS LEARN

The students may repeat a Bible verse by rote memory or answer a question from the Sunday school curriculum, but if there is not an inner change with an outer manifestation, no learning has taken place. I am not saying that knowledge of Scripture isn't important. The Word tells us, "Study to shew thyself approved unto God" (2 Tim. 2:15 KJV). However, we must not ignore the application of the Word for the sake of knowledge (1 John 2:6). As mentioned earlier, the evidence of effective teaching is the change in the lives of students. If life change isn't taking place, then the student isn't learning. Youth today process information differently from previous generations. They are multitasked in their ability to receive and organize information. Technology and television have played a major role in this shift. Youth have been raised on television, from *Sesame Street* to *Barney* to MTV. The visual images they view are bright, flashy, and rapid-fire. They have learned to recognize and ingest information quickly. Today's youth are not all "analytical" in style: if A, then B, then C, etc. They are able to collect information in a non-analytical fashion: A, D, C, B, etc. Because of this, we must adapt and learn new ways of presenting information about Scripture to bring the desired result.

The evidence of change is seen in many ways.

PROGRESSION

Learning may reflect itself in better motor coordination or better mental facility. The change may be the teenager's improved ability to solve the problem he is facing. The change may be new insights into life or a new interpretation of his role in life, namely, as his understanding pertains to Scripture.

EXPERIENCE

The teenager must show progress in his learning of abilities as reflected in his experience. Experience is not just an emotional feeling. Too often religious experience is interpreted to mean feeling love, hate, joy, or repentance. The term *experience* can be defined in four steps:

1. Experience begins with a stimulus from the outside: something that attracts attention and demands a response. You, as the Bible teacher, come from without and must produce a spiritual response in the lives of your students.

2. The teenager must have a sensation. Sensation simply is the bridge from the outer world to the inner man. The material and experience being presented in class must come through one of the five senses: sight, smell, hearing, taste, or touch. The senses are the windows of the soul, the media of communication by which you as a teacher may stimulate the pupil to learn. One law of teaching indicates that the greater the stimulation, the greater the sensation, and ultimately the greater the response.
3. After a sensation there must be perception. Perception is the teenager's understanding of the experience and material as well as his interpretation of the meaning. Perception is the youth's insight into relationships. The teen seeks the relationship of the stimulus to his inner understanding. Differing backgrounds in young people will produce different perceptions. True perception by the youth brings on response.
4. A response comes when the teenager acts on the stimulus. The response should achieve the aims of the lesson. It should be the desired outcome of teaching. Many times we have little response because we plan indefinitely. We do not know how we want the teens to respond to the Word of God.

True Learning

A teenager may sit in your Bible class, show progress in the use of ability as reflected in experience, and yet not have a true learning experience prompted by the spiritual and educational aims of your class. True learning must satisfy the goals of the lesson and come from the demands of the material. A teenager may sit in class and count the ceiling tiles. He can recite the number of tiles or any other thing he might count, but this experience was not prompted by the aims of the class. The aims of the Bible class must be accomplished to produce a valid learning situation.

True learning must produce a continuous experience in life (habit of the heart). The teenager may commit to memory facts, verses, and outlines, yet forget them in days. Has he really learned? Have the facts become a part of him? If true learning has taken place, the lessons become a part of him and become continuous in his experience. He may forget some of the facts, but they have added to his sum total of knowledge and will influence him in experience, decisions, and activities of the future. True learning has a permanent effect upon the individual.

PRINCIPLES OF LEARNING

When teaching teenagers, you cannot expect to ignore the laws of learning and accomplish good teaching. You must understand the laws of learning, work with them, and apply them if you are going to accomplish any results in the life of the teen. The laws of learning are more important than the application of any teaching technique in the classroom situation. It behooves the teacher to understand the nature of teens and the laws of learning as they apply to teaching teens, and therefore we will look briefly at them.

THE PRINCIPLE OF MOTIVATION

Learning is most effective when the teenager is properly motivated. The youth who wants to learn is the youth who will learn. Motivation is 90 percent of teaching. The teacher of teens may have a poor presentation and a withdrawing personality, yet if this teacher motivates the teen to want to learn, he has overcome the most difficult task of teaching. The teacher who motivates well teaches well. Motivating the teenager to work is difficult and calls for diligence by the teacher. To motivate the teenager to work, the teacher must work. There are a few practical applications that can be used in motivating teenagers. Some of the following may be applied to youth work with success:

Testimony

When someone indicates a reason that he has had success, this stimulates the teenagers to seek the same route and result. The teacher or the teens themselves can give a testimony. Use of the testimony motivates young people.

Positive Peer Pressure

"The Triple P principle" gives the idea, "Everyone is doing it; why aren't you?" The world uses peer pressure many times to oppose the principles of the church. The church and the Bible class teacher may use this to motivate the teenager. "Everyone is striving to apply Scripture; why aren't you?" "The Triple P principle" brings the pressure of teenage society to bear on the youth. Positive Peer Pressure is a method of motivating teenagers by appealing to their success. Praise motivates the youth. The general laws of teaching show that the dull student is motivated by praise, while the bright student is motivated by rebuke and challenge. No matter how weak or inefficient the teenager, give him some praise. Churches tend to overuse rebuke in motivating teenagers. We are exhorted in God's Word to judge nothing before the time. After this exhortation, God has given us the promise, "Then each one's praise will come from God" (1 Cor. 4:5). If God will find some good in every person who enters heaven, how can we who are His servants find less? This must be balanced with knowing when to call a tree by its fruit, but encouragement can work wonders.

Statistics

The use of statistics reveals to teenagers the true nature of the situation. Statistics are a great method of motivating individuals. When teenagers are told that 90 percent of young people wear this fashion, or 75 percent attend this event, this motivates them. Grades in school are statistics that motivate. Wanting a passing grade on a driver's license test moves them to learn. Statistics may be scores on college entrance exams, the number of teens involved in community service, or the number of teens going to church. Statistics give reasons for actions and impetus to follow through. Statistics force reality into the teenager's subjective thinking by putting the situation in its true perspective. One of the greatest faults of the church is the faulty use of statistics. We quote facts and numbers without seeking to validate their truthfulness. In using statistics, make sure that they are valid. Then be careful to quote statistics in light of their qualified application. When statistics are rightly used, reasons become concrete rather than theoretical.

Illustrations of Achievement

Teens are motivated to action when they hear about other teens who have had successful avenues of action. Tell often of teens who live for Christ, teens who serve Christ, teens who have successful, satisfying lives. Use current illustrations and examples to achieve this.

Negative Reinforcement

Negative reinforcement is motivation through reproof. As a teacher, you may reveal the faults or basic lack in a young person. When you lovingly point out the failures of the teen, he is motivated to work better, study harder, or strive longer. Be careful of the overuse of this motivation. Constant reproof of the teen makes him a hardened skeptic. However, the teenager who has a desire for excellence can be motivated to greater heights by a true evaluation of his lacks and faults.

Remember that we can speak the truth in love and still call a tree by its fruit. Our motivation for confronting a teen about wrong living should be rooted in love—that the youth are in a better position because I opened my mouth. However this must be done with tact and the proper goal of seeing the youth in a better position because we offered rebuke, not just rebuke for rebuke's sake. As a youth teacher you may motivate through negative means, which may include embarrassment, threats, and punishment. Note that this may bring results for a while but soon loses its effectiveness. At the same time you as a teacher may motivate through positive means, in which you involve rewards, recognition, and commendation. After all is said and done, the most effective method to motivate teenagers is through prayer. Prayer moves God to move men. Pray. Pray much. Pray much for your teen. Pray much for your teen to want to do God's will.

The Principle of Activity

Learning is most effective when the teenager has interaction with that which is to be learned. Picture the average teenager in the Sunday school. The teacher is talking. The student is sitting with both hands in his pockets. He is staring at the floor. His feet shuffle back and forth. If he had a question, he does not have the freedom to ask. The teacher believes that talking is teaching and listening is learning. In the area of activity the teacher must produce an atmosphere that is conducive to learning. The teenager will learn according to his involvement with the subject. Only as he becomes involved with the Word of God can he learn. The Bible must be examined, not explained! The Word of God must be discovered, not declared! Revelation is not only propositional; it is personal. At the same time you must realize that vigorous teaching does not produce vigorous learning. The law of activity indicates that the teenager must be active rather than passive. We learn to do by doing. Activity with the Word of God motivates to further learning.

The Principle of Readiness

Learning is most effective when the teenager has been prepared to learn. When the young person comes into the Bible class "cold" and unprepared, he cannot realize the greatest contribution of the class. He needs a background or active participation and class discussion. This background comes as the teen opens, studies, memorizes, searches, and explores the Word of God for himself. The law of readiness has been called the law of assignment. We give assignments or homework to teenagers for many reasons:

1. To prepare students for the lesson
2. To teach the teen
3. To apply the lesson to everyday life
4. To structure the experience for learning
5. To cause teens to see their own lack and hence to stimulate in them a spirit of inquiry
6. To cause students to see the relationships between facts, experiences, and life
7. To review what has been taught in former lessons

Getting teens to do assignments is one of the most difficult tasks of the teacher. The teacher who would get the teen to prepare lessons must himself be prepared. He must study far enough in advance so that he can give some preview of what is to come. He must study far enough in advance so that he can guide the teenager in reading, research, and answering questions. Ask the teenager to do extra work. Ask him to do interviews concerning the lesson at home. The teenager can gather opinions from other people concerning the questions of the lesson. Creative thought can be used.

The teacher may have a negative attitude toward the assignments. He may not understand their value and he may not want to get involved in extra work in making assignments or in listening to students' results. Also, he may not want to be exposed to the possibility of students demonstrating that they know more than the teacher. You as the teacher should believe in the value of assignments. Give assignments because you want the teenager to become more interested and satisfied in his experience of studying the Bible.

Be prepared to give assignments. Know what you are going to do and what you are going to ask. Many publications have plans for daily Bible reading, questions for discussion, and directions for research. Use them. Put some life into the assignment. Avoid routine, dullness, and busywork. Make assignments vital and interesting. You as the teacher must grasp the occasion for some interesting bit of conversation on the assignment. Indirect, spontaneous assignments by the teacher will arouse more response than any dull, monotonous statement that something should be done for next Sunday. Think through the assignment:

1. Are the questions clear and specific?
2. Are they easy enough for this class?
3. Are they challenging enough to arouse interest and curiosity?
4. Do they make sense and seem worthwhile to the student?
5. Are they too long? Too short?
6. Are they related to the aim of the lesson so that they can support the general discussion?

Expect results. Get across the attitude that you expect the student to come through with the assignment. Most teenagers will respond to the youth leader who expects something from them. There needs to be a serious note of responsibility. The teacher and the teenager must have the attitude of working together with God for His glory. The teacher has his part, and the teenager has his part. As a partner in the experience of studying the Word of God, offer help to the teenager. After the class session pause to give a few moments to discuss the assignment with teens. Give them encouragement. Visit them. Help them in any way that you can. Take a few minutes occasionally during the class period to go through the assignment. Checking up on the assignment is the most important occasion in the Bible lesson. The student who is not called on when he has his assignment ready will often become discouraged and stop studying the Word of God.

The Principle of Appreciation

Learning is most effective when the truth to be taught is learned through truth already known. When working with teenagers, take nothing for granted: where they are spiritually, what they know about the background material, or even that they have been saved. Many teenagers will give you the impression that they know it all. They do not. They put on a mask to cover up the inability to perform as adults when they desire to be accepted as adults. The teacher who takes nothing for granted and builds upon the foundation is the one who gets results. However, when the teacher has built a lesson in previous weeks, he can build on that which has been already taught. But first, review to be certain of the foundation.

Remember, the basic assumption in teaching is not how much but how well we teach. All teaching must advance in some direction. Teenagers who sit in class are either growing in faith or becoming skeptics. There is no neutral ground in the classroom. A good teacher constantly builds on past knowledge, but most important, he builds.

Knowledge does not pass from the teacher to student as bread is passed from one basket to another. Learning is a process of graded steps, and the teacher must give diligence to see that the teenager takes each step in its own logical sequence. Make sure that the learning steps are broken down into small steps so that the teen can scale them by himself. To do this the teacher must find out what the teenager already knows. Here is where the use of the question is vitally important. Make the most of the youth's knowledge and interest. Ask him questions. Encourage him to ask questions. Relate every lesson to the former lesson. Make sure by a good review that he understands before you proceed to the next point.

The good teacher proceeds from the known to the unknown. A bridge is important between the two. This bridge in the last analysis is a relationship. And learning is seeing relationships. Some relationships that can be seen are the parallels of two Bible verses, the parallel of a problem and answer in the Word of God, and the parallel of a scriptural principle to everyday life. In the final analysis, Christianity is a relationship.

An Overview of Teaching Methods

The aim of this chapter is to show you what methods of teaching Christ applied with the Twelve and then to look at how the teacher of youth today can figure out what methods work in his class. Other chapters will deal with what must be taken into consideration when choosing a method of teaching, and one chapter deals with a brief description of methods of teaching. Teaching may be in a Bible study, Sunday school class, Sunday evening, Wednesday night, or special event. How important is teaching to your ministry? The answer to that question is reflected in the attitude of Christ as recorded in the Gospels concerning this important topic.

TEACHING METHODS OF JESUS CHRIST

When we talk about teaching, teaching methods, and the application of those methods, we must look to Jesus. Jesus is the prototype of teaching that we are to follow. He is the master teacher. Many volumes have been dedicated to the teaching styles of Christ. Libraries contain hundreds of books that examine and explain how Christ trained and communicated truth to His core group and to the crowds. Our purpose is to simply list methods that Christ incorporated in His teaching and then examine and explain how these methods pertain to teens.

It is important to realize that Jesus began His ministry as a teacher, and thus He remained until His ascension into heaven. "Teacher" is one of the titles that Jesus was most frequently called while ministering on earth. As we examine any one of the Gospels, we will find that term applied to Him (see, for example, Luke 6:40; 7:40; 8:49; 9:38; 10:25; 11:45; 12:13; 18:18; 19:39; 20:21, 28, 39; 21:7; 22:11). Jesus called Himself by this name, "You call me Teacher and Lord, and you say well, for so I am" (John 13:13). The followers of Christ were called disciples or pupils, indicating that they were being instructed by a teacher, Christ. Jesus was the ultimate teacher. Even the prominent Jews who failed to recognize Him as Messiah quickly acknowledged His special abilities as a teacher (Mark 12:14; John 3:2).

John 2:23–25 gives us information concerning Christ as a teacher: "Now when He was in Jerusalem at the Passover, during the feast, many believed in His name when they saw the signs which He did. But Jesus did not commit Himself to them, because He knew all men, and had no need that anyone should testify of man, for He knew what was in man." From this passage we can observe the following: (1) Christ was focused, (2) He knew His audience, (3) He didn't need man's opinion about Him, and (4) He understood His mission and He had discernment.

Jesus is not referred to as a preacher in the Gospel accounts, even though He did preach as well as teach. "And Jesus went about all Galilee, teaching in their synagogues, preaching the gospel of the kingdom" (Matt. 4:23; see also 11:1). Four different words are used in the Gospels for the term "preaching," and all four are translated by the same English word. The word *said* used in Luke 9:60 has the meaning of "to tell toughly" and is only found in the Gospels. Preaching is translated with the sense of "telling the good news" in Matthew 11:5; Luke 1:19; 2:10; 3:18; 4:18, 43; 7:22; 8:1; 9:6; 16:16; 20:1. Another translation of the word used elsewhere means to "cry or proclaim as a herald." One exception is found in the Gospels in Mark 2:2 where the word for teaching is translated "preaching," while in other sections the word is translated as to "say" or "speak." Thus we are safe to assume that the preaching of Jesus was the beautiful and error-free communication of a teacher.

USE OF EVERYDAY ITEMS

The teaching of Jesus was always full of life and the reality of life. He stood among the people and communicated to them in the terms of their environment and thoughts, tying them to spiritual truth. For example, what prompted the figures used in Matthew 5:14; John 3:8; 4:34–35; 6:35; 7:37–38; 8:12; 15:1–7? As you read these verses, pay attention to how Jesus constantly makes use of everyday common items to draw His audience into or put upon the people some new teaching or spiritual truth.

There is a place in the church for the formal, uninterrupted presentation of spiritual truth, but that place is but small in comparison with the unconventional mode of expression that's more relevant to the audience.

ASKING AND ANSWERING QUESTIONS

A common method of Jesus that He used often is still a viable method when teaching teens. This is where the teacher asks questions to make certain that he or she is fully understood by those he or she is teaching. The students also have the opportunity to ask questions to make sure that they understand exactly what the teacher is saying. Obviously the uninterrupted discourse is easier, but it is less valuable. Most of the material is readily forgotten as average teens cannot take it all in or carry it with them. Leaders are needed who will study this method of Christ and apply it in their ministry.

As we study the early church we discover that questions were one of its methods of communicating truth. A sincere question is always welcome. These times of questioning must be incorporated into our teaching strategy. The lesson here is for each one of us to go out and use this method with teens, making our daily conversation a presentation of the wonders of Christ to teens in a way that Jesus modeled for us to follow.

According to John 12:49–50 Christ also knew God's agenda, and this agenda was His. He was not seeking to do what He wanted but what the Father wanted for Him. Christ also used a *listen first* (Father to Son) *and then speak* (Son to man) method of instruction.

SIMPLE TRUTHS

We find in John 16:12–15 that Christ models the greatest principle concerning working with teens. Christ didn't use high technology or deep theological theories in His teaching. He used parables and illustrations taken from the culture of those He was addressing. He packaged the truth so that the audience would understand the truth at hand. Once this was understood, then Christ would move to deeper truths. Christ was dependent upon the Holy Spirit as He ministered truths to those around Him.

A VARIETY OF METHODS

Christ employed various methods to help His disciples understand, as seen in Matthew 17:24–27.

> When they had come to Capernaum, those who received the temple tax came to Peter and said, "Does your Teacher not pay the temple tax?" He said, "Yes." And when he had come into the house, Jesus anticipated him, saying, "What do you think, Simon? From whom do the kings of the earth take customs or taxes, from their sons or from strangers?" Peter said to Him, "From strangers." Jesus said to him, "Then the sons are free. Nevertheless, lest we offend them, go to the sea, cast in a hook, and take the fish that comes up first. And when you have opened its mouth, you will find a piece of money; take that and give it to them for Me and you."

Here Christ uses the question-and-answer method with Peter as mentioned above. Christ asked a provocative question, forcing Peter to think through his answer. Additionally Christ used a visual aid, a teachable moment, an assignment, and personal application in helping Peter come to an understanding of the problem at hand.

Methods employed by Christ included:

1. He asked questions (John 3:1–15).
2. He recognized the personal worth of individuals (Luke 19:2–10).
3. He used word pictures from everyday life (Luke 13:19).
4. He taught by example (John 13:1–17).
5. He knew Scripture (Luke 24:25–27).
6. He showed genuine emotion (John 11:35–36).

7. He prayed for His followers (John 17).
8. He spent quality and quantity time with the Twelve (Mark 1:17–20; 6:30–31).
9. He made use of silence (Luke 23:9; John 8:3–11).
10. He gave specific instructions (Matt. 11:28–30).

Much could yet be said about the various teaching methods of Christ, but for our purposes those attributes listed above will accomplish our goal of this chapter.

BASES FOR CHOOSING TEACHING METHODS

A funny thing happens when we ask teachers to evaluate their performance and we compare it with the students' evaluation of the teaching session.

Usually there is a "gap" between the teachers' actual or perceived performance and the achievement of their goals and aims. Effective teaching calls for and in fact demands disciplined study and proper planning of each lesson. Thus thoughtful, disciplined preparation is essential for improved teaching. The better the preparation, the greater the margin for success exists. The teacher who is willing to be disciplined in planning each lesson will eventually benefit from a greater satisfaction in teaching. Diligent, thoughtful preparation of each lesson produces the most effective teaching for both the teacher and the students. Knowing one's class will help in preparation.

THE AGE OF YOUR CLASS

The age of your group is one of the most important concerns of your teaching. For our purposes we will break adolescents into three age groups: ten to twelve years, early; thirteen to seventeen years, middle; and eighteen to twenty-four years, late. Each group has its own needs.

Early Adolescents

In the early age group (ten to twelve years), you will find a tendency to do things in two separate groups, guys separate from girls.

Middle Adolescents

In the middle group (thirteen to seventeen years), you will find them becoming interested in doing things together as a group. Here you will find the teens mostly hanging out in groups as couples and as friends. You will find individuals in this age group who are interested in and those who are disinterested in the opposite sex but doing things together, if they are planned in an informal way. You will find that this age group is most critical, and that their thinking is greatly governed by the latest fashions, music, media, TV, and what they read. Cliques will become more of a problem, so you must plan your lesson to work away from these cliques and toward a Christian goal. You will find that much prayer will be needed to analyze this age group and to know how to meet their needs.

Late Adolescents

The late group (eighteen to twenty-four) consists largely of college students. They have needs completely different from that of the others. You will now need to plan programs along a more intellectual line with a logical aim behind everything that is said and done.

The Needs of Your Class

What are the needs of your group? Have you stopped long enough to consider just what would best meet the immediate needs of the teens you are ministering to? If not, stop now and do so before your organization grows less interesting or you lose another young person. Are they being taught how to be future leaders, Sunday school teachers, presidents of groups, or church leaders? Perhaps a study in leadership, unity, or dating ethics would be good material for your class's next study series.

Have you tried sitting down and making a mental or written list of the needs of your group? Keeping these needs in mind will produce a better method of presentation. Needs determine the method of approach. You will find that the needs of your group will vary with environment. Economic, social, and educational background—each of these things must be taken into consideration before choosing a method of presentation. At no time in history have the needs of adolescents been more varied or complex. Your lesson material must meet the needs of the youth under your care.

The Needs of Your Individual Students

After noting the age of your group and the needs of your group as a whole, consider the needs of the individuals within that group. Each of these individuals differs greatly from all the others. Their makeup is different. Their needs are different and complex from one teen to the next. This extends into the life of every teen in every area—physically, mentally, morally, socially, and emotionally. Have you noticed any peculiar characteristics of an individual as he appears in a group? Have you visited his home? If you haven't, do so. When you are planning a lesson, remember you are ministering to needs of individuals within a group. You must consider the individual needs of every student. You must gear your teaching to meet some need in the student's life—from those who are popular in the group to the loner in the back of the room. Your teaching must be geared to meet these needs, whatever they are. This means that a relationship must be formed so that you know what those needs are and you are in a position to help meet them.

THE ENTHUSIASM OF YOUR STUDENTS

What about the enthusiasm in your group as you prepare to lecture? Are some of the students asleep or talking so that you do not get their attention? Maybe you should try some other method of presentation. Have you ever thought of discussing this with your teens to determine which type of presentation they like best? Unless your method is interesting, you will soon lose the student's attention and even the student. Let your teens and their needs be your guide in the methods you choose. Here again you will find age group needs and individuals' needs entering into the picture as you plan what method to use. With the ever-increasing presence of technology, there is no excuse for us not to have an intelligent use of media and presentation packaging to help create an environment of enthusiasm. As you meet the needs of students in your group, a natural enthusiasm will be produced.

Determining needs of students can be accomplished in many ways. Here are a few suggestions: (1) a class survey, (2) small groups with adult leaders, and (3) relationships. As teachers we must build relationships with our students outside of the classroom if we are to be as effective as possible.

CONDITIONS OF THE CLASS

Equipment

Having the proper equipment—chalk and chalkboard, whiteboard and markers, maps, pictures, overhead, Power Point, a stereo system, and VCR equipment—is vital. The facilities at hand will largely determine what methods will be used. The more tools to choose from, the greater the end result.

Time

You must have adequate time to present the material using the method you have chosen. Something that is not finished during one class or meeting period will not hold interest when finished at a later time. You as a leader are responsible for planning or seeing that you have the time to present your material through the method chosen. Remember, going overtime is not the answer to a program that has too much content. Interest is lost when your time is up. Make sure you quit before your students do.

Place

Do you have sufficient room for your presentation? Is the seating capacity sufficient to allow room for your teens? If they are crowded together, interest will be harder to hold. Is the room adequately ventilated, lighted, and heated or cooled? All these things must be taken into consideration if you are to be an effective teacher.

The Aim of Your Class

What is the purpose of your time together? Is it just to fill up time, to entertain, to hold interest, or is it geared to meet a need in the lives of the teens? Every meeting, small or large, should have a goal. The purpose you have in mind should always be to meet the need of your group. The method and purpose should fit together perfectly.

The Spiritual Level of Your Class

If you consider your group a relatively immature one, then you have an idea as to some of the needs of the group. You may now plan a class and use methods of presenting the need for a dedicated life to Christ. Do not try to teach an immature group as you would a mature group, because you will not be meeting their immediate needs.

Then again, if your class is a spiritually mature group and is living for Christ, you have the opportunity of leading them into a deeper spiritual knowledge of God. You may also use this type of class for planned expression, projects, or creative expression. This group will probably have resourceful individuals. Planned responsibility may be used to help the youth get experience that they may use as they become the future leaders of the church. Use methods that will apply to your group in the light of whether they are carnal, new babes, dedicated or spiritual Christians.

CONCLUSION

As spiritual shepherds we would be wise to model the teaching methods of Christ with our teens. In addition we should understand the working of the Holy Spirit in the preparation and teaching process as we prepare and teach the Word of God, relating biblical truth that will meet the needs of our students and equip them for victorious Christian living.

Methods in Teaching Teens

This chapter will examine various methods to consider and employ when teaching teens. As previous chapters have laid the groundwork on how to effectively prepare lessons, this chapter will suggest various methods for the actual presentation of your lessons. An effective teacher of youth will use various methods in the quest to present meaningful, insightful, and relevant lessons.

THE LECTURE

Bill Jones had just taken over the youth Sunday school class. He had been warned that these teens are not interested in the Bible. Therefore, he determined to get "ready" for them. The apparent solution, Mr. Jones reasoned, was to show them that he meant business and is not going to take anything from these teens on the very first day of his reign and will not willingly let up on this policy or discipline. He reasoned, after all, that the Bible says, "Discipline yourselves." At the first sign of resistance, he rebuked the ringleader to sit still, obey God, and listen to the lesson. Later he reported to the parents some out-of-school behavior he had discovered in one of the boys of his group.

Mr. Jones rigidly assigned the lesson and made precise requirements of the young people who came. The amount of material to be covered necessitated a daily detailed time schedule. "This is one Sunday school class that's going to get results." In the same way Mr. Jones had disciplined himself to cover the lesson. If his students strayed from the subject matter, he called them back to the topic with the remark, "We have much to cover; there is no time to lose." He chastised them repeatedly to "redeem the time." Mr. Jones used pop quizzes as a method to motivate his students to study better. In private talks with the young people he urged them to try harder to meet the curriculum demands of the lesson.

Mr. Jones not only demanded a great deal of his students; he also expected a lot of himself. He spent long hours preparing lessons, calling absentees, and visiting sick teens. The young people of the church were aware that he was a very conscientious teacher and that he was not hostile toward them personally. It was not that Mr. Jones was not interested in the young people as human beings. He was! But as the teaching year progressed, tensions mounted among the young people in Mr. Jones's class. Some teens quit coming. Others whose parents attended Sunday school continued to come but showed apathy or rebellion. The conscientious students responded. Several young people dropped out of church altogether.

Marshall Adams's youth class meets in a large old church. Trees and shrubbery, a bit tall and overgrown, give the church an air of stability and belonging to the neighborhood. If you arrive in Marshall's room early, you will note a number of students in small groups talking informally or working on a variety of projects. One group of students is working on a debate to be presented next Sunday. Another group is going over the worship service to be presented that day. Still a third group is discussing a research project assigned by Marshall.

After the class begins, you note a warm spirit of cooperation in the class. There are some Christian magazines, some CDs, and a few videos and books available. A class of nine teens is seated around a table with open Bibles, outlines, and pencils ready. Marshall has studied well, has his lesson plan written out, and knows what methods he is going to use. Some would say that he lectures to the students. He prefers to call it a "conversational discussion" method of teaching. Marshall introduces the subject by relating it to a problem in life. Next he asks for student reactions. "Maybe we could start off with a few quick reactions. What impresses you about it? Who wants to start?" Several students start to talk and Marshall nods to a girl across the table, "Mary, you start." There is a spirit of permissiveness. When a shy sophomore responds, he does not feel that he needs to make a speech. Most of the young people feel that they can interrupt Marshall at any time in the lesson to make a point or ask a question.

One teenager said, "Class is like a bull session on the Bible." Since the students are sitting around the table, Marshall also sits. The table makes it easier to write. Often Marshall refers to the handout, and the teens fill out the questions there. There is no attendance problem in his class. Marshall's classes are considered difficult but exciting. The youth feel that he cares about both his subject and them. Often a student will suggest a question that stumps Marshall. In these cases he works with the teens to find a solution to the problem. Marshall feels that he can do a good job in making the Bible alive for his students, and he is confident that his classes are contributing to the development of their maturity by challenging them to think for themselves and stimulate their interest in the Word of God.

Bill Jones's lecturing is not wrong; it's the way he goes about it that's wrong. Both Mr. Jones and Marshall Adams lecture, but they have different attitudes toward the lecture. Today many authorities criticize the lecture, yet it is still the predominant method used in reaching and teaching teens. You will probably continue to use the lecture. We know we will. Let us do all we can to improve its use. First, we should give a definition. The lecture method might be better called "oral presentation by the teacher." Lecture is the procedure that includes all oral presentation by the teacher, whether it be by way of remarks made to clarify issues, to elaborate on teens' answers to questions, or to supplement data already at hand, or whether it be by way of an extended formal exposition or indicating how something is to be done. Oral presentation is used to a great extent at all levels of instruction.

Lecture cannot be avoided, even at the teen level. It is impossible to eliminate oral presentation even from the methods of instruction that allow for greater teen participation. Lecture must, then, be done effectively and intelligently with understanding of the fundamentals of the teaching-learning process. If you have a sense of responsibility for the quality of your work, you will wish to master the technique of effective oral presentation.

Advantages of the Lecture

1. *The lecture makes possible the effect of the spoken word.*

Spoken words are more effective means of communication, on the whole, than printed material. Inflection, emphasis, and explanation make the oral presentation an energetic and dynamic method of transferring knowledge. Teenagers are at the age when they can begin to think in concepts and are motivated through the lecture. The spoken word has a dynamic quality that draws them, causing them to follow the direction of its emphasis.

2. *The lecture makes possible the effect of the teacher's personality.*

Through lecture the total impact of the teacher's personality becomes greater. Sometimes communication is affected by the way we express ourselves more than the content of our expression. At this point attractive Christian character does much to communicate. Teenagers will be motivated by what you are, as well as by what you say. The teacher should be fully organized and properly prepared to interpret the material to the teenager. The lecture affords opportunity for the imparting of information so that the teacher can be certain of the correctness of the statement. Good organization ensures good teaching.

3. *The lecture saves time, space, and energy.*

When a teacher uses the lecture, more ground can be covered in a short period of time than by use of any other method. Some classes of teenagers are large. The lecture can be prepared and presented to a large group better than other types of teaching methods. Then, too, it is easier to lecture than to teach by the discussion or question method or any other method. Since not all teachers are well trained in the more difficult methods of teaching and many churches find it difficult to enlist and train many teachers, the lecture is more popular. However, just because it is popular and easy does not mean it is always the most effective method. Care must be used in choosing the right method of teaching teenagers.

4. *The lecture makes possible more effective use of supplementary material.*

Most other methods of teaching revolve around the lecture, such as discussion, question, drama, forum, panel, and debate. Often written material presents only one view. The lesson or curriculum presents one side of the picture, but the teacher through lecture can give a wider experience and interpretation to the text. Lecture can present a broader picture.

5. *The lecture provides a method of giving the teen proper perspective.*

Immature minds experience difficulty in making proper evaluations. Teenagers are growing into adults; however, they are still immature in their understanding. The lecture can cause them to see relationships, give them reasons, and help them discriminate between what is important and what is not important. Through the lecture the teacher can use motivation and/or indoctrination.

The lecture must be made interesting with up-to-date illustrations from real life. There must be a striving after teen participation, because teenagers are growing rapidly, and interest is the key word. Teenagers may be restless and awkward and unable to find a comfortable position in their chairs. Lectures must be well supported with good authority and allow the teenagers to think for themselves. Teenagers begin to question the validity and authority of presented ideas at school, home, and church. This is the age when they want to reason everything out and they are asking "why."

When lecturing to teenagers make sure that new concepts are always introduced. They enjoy the thrill of adventuring with their minds. Leave some time for review of each past lecture, but don't bore them with review. Teenagers are experiencing an increase in their memory span, and too much review becomes boring. They accept the challenge of new concepts. Teenagers like to think. Lectures must take on a practical nature related to the actual problems in their lives. This satisfies their desire for pragmatic knowledge. What they hear must work in everyday life. Lectures must not be too dogmatic or try to force ideas upon teenagers. They must present a reason "why." The lecture must be logical and orderly. Arguments must be clear, because teenagers have a new sense of independence and self-sufficiency. They have a great desire to think for themselves.

When to Use the Lecture with Teenagers

For Large Classes

When the class is large and teen participation must be limited, use the lecture. However, always speak to individuals, never to the group, no matter how large the group becomes.

When Teens Have a Limited Background

When teens' background and introduction to the subject are limited, use the lecture. Minimize teen participation and do not ask the teen for an opinion he has not yet formed. You will seriously hamper the effective use of the teens' participation if they have a limited background.

For Introduction of New Material

When introducing new or unfamiliar subjects, use the lecture. Here it is easier to give an introduction, survey, and summary into the entire subject. The confidence of the speaker's voice will give assurance to the teenager as he listens. The entire attitude and expression of the teacher is building up to the climax. Awakening expectancy on the part of the students will gain and keep attention.

With Limited Seating Facilities

When the classroom seating arrangements are limited and are not conducive to informal discussion, use the lecture. There may be other circumstances presented by the physical facilities of the room that require the lecture. Use common sense in choosing your teaching method.

When You Have Restricted Time

When time becomes restricted, the lecture can be easily altered. It is easy for a well-prepared teacher to expand or condense the material when lecturing. When teens are participating, it is sometimes hard to restrict their contributions. When you are discussing printed material, it is sometimes difficult to skip over material. However, when the lecture is being used, material can be deleted and the lecture can be easily summed up.

To Motivate, Provoke, and Stimulate

Use the lecture when the entire personality of the teacher is geared to provoking and stimulating thinking and imagination. Every method of motivation should be used to cause the student to think. When a teacher imparts vision, he is imparting some of himself. The lecture can best be used to impart vision. The lecture must challenge, motivate, and show the value of things, because a teenager's mental abilities are at the most productive stage. The lecture can incorporate the vast amount of knowledge and background of the teacher and make it pertinent to the teenager. The many years of judgment and experience can be brought to bear on the immediate situation, and hence motivate, stimulate, and provoke the student to thinking.

When Not to Use the Lecture

When Experience Is a Necessary Factor in Learning

Practice perfects theory, and theory perfects practice. There must be demonstration and opportunity to learn in every situation. For example, one learns to teach by teaching. The teenager learns to pray by praying, and he learns to explore the Bible by exploring.

When the Class Is Small

Small classes are well suited for other methods of teaching. Small groups do well in exploration, silent thinking, discussions, and/or questions. Use other methods with smaller classes. However, do not rule out the occasional use of the lecture method in small groups.

When Students Are Eager to Participate

You must not stifle their desire to learn by enforcing silence. When teens want to participate, you must not force them to sit and listen to a lecture. Involvement equals learning.

THE DISCUSSION METHOD IN TEACHING TEENAGERS

Discussion is talking about a subject from various angles, including discussing the pros and cons. Our goal here is to have teens think about and discuss information with each other concerning the topic at hand, regardless of how wrong they might be. We are making a distinction here between using discussion as part of a lesson and using the discussion method as the lesson. Some subjects that lend themselves to the discussion method are relationships, peer pressure, unity, gossip, and servanthood.

Teenagers love to talk. Therefore, use the discussion method often when working with teens. Discussion enlists the active cooperation of the whole class. The teen will actively participate in class if he knows that he has the opportunity to discuss, he may be called upon to give an opinion, or he is listening to a fellow teen give an opinion.

Advantages of Discussion

1. *Discussion broadens the thoughts in the class by presenting all sides of a vital question.*

Sometimes the teacher may be narrow-minded or ill prepared. Through discussions, teens who have background and viewpoints can add their opinions. Opinions added by other teenagers, with reasons, arguments, and conviction, cause them to think. Discussion produces thought.

2. *Discussion teaches tolerance and cultivates respect for the judgment of other teenagers.*

Most young people reach the teen years with a "know-it-all" attitude. It is difficult for them to realize that parents, teachers, and friends know as much as they do. In discussion, arguments from an opposing point of view are entered with reasons and stimulation. Teenagers learn to give and take in a discussion.

3. *Discussion gives teens and teachers practice in thinking clearly, honestly, and persistently.*

Churches must do more than indoctrinate. Churches must produce young people who think for themselves from a biblical foundation. Mature faith is not blind faith but rational faith. Discussion can stimulate teenagers to think clearly and persistently and hence arrive at mature faith for themselves.

The Teacher's Attitude Toward Discussion

1. *Discussion demands more ability, resources, and preparation on the part of the teacher than any other method.*

Discussion brings out the very best in some teachers; however, some teachers are lacking in their own resources and should be careful about leading a discussion.

2. *Discussions are limited to provocative problems in which there are different viewpoints within the group.*

It is difficult to have a discussion over a point in which all are of common consent. Also it is difficult to discuss a Bible passage in which there are no conflicting interpretations. The nature and aim of the class will determine whether you should indoctrinate and lecture or discuss and stimulate thinking. If you are going to lead a discussion, you must know the limitations, capacities, and interests of each member of the group. Do not press a teenager beyond his own resources. Do not call for an opinion from a teenager when he has not had a basis on which to form an opinion.

3. *Discussion requires thorough preparation in advance on the part of every member of the class.*

When leading a discussion, you must do more preparation than when leading a lecture. In lecturing, you present the material that you have on hand or have investigated and packaged. In a discussion any related subject may be brought up, and you should have some background and knowledge. If the class and the teacher do not have a thorough preparation for discussion, then it merely becomes a discussion of opinions and ignorance. Good discussion demands resources from materials, opinions, facts, and arguments. Make certain that the topic has been investigated thoroughly before discussing. In the local church, most often, resources reside in an individual. Make sure the key individual is present for a good discussion.

How to Lead a Discussion

The teacher must open by developing within his group a problem or situation through the skillful presentation of questions. Next, the problem must be defined by different members of the group stating the matter as they see it. Then all the possible ways of acting under the circumstances should be considered. Once more the leader should skillfully ask questions that will shed light on the material. Each proposal must be weighed pro and con and, if necessary, assigned to committees or individuals for further study and then reported to the next class. Alternatives should be listed on a chalkboard, and continual summarizing should be made throughout the discussion to bring out the exact status of the problem. In the summary, the teacher should clinch the argument in a few words and give impetus for the discussion to follow. After the thoughts have developed into a coherent pattern, he should define it in a conclusion. Once the best solution is decided on, the last step is to plan a definite program to use the decision in future study or activity.

Dangers and Weaknesses of Discussion

Discussion demands more ability, resources, and preparation on the part of the teacher than many other methods. Also, it is limited to provocative problems in which there are differing viewpoints within the group, but common interests. Discussion requires that the teacher know the limitations, capacities, and interests of each teen in the group. Discussion requires thorough preparation in advance on the part of every member of the class, lest it be merely a discussion of opinions and ignorance. Also, discussion necessitates making sources of material relating to the problem available to the student. Finally, discussion requires time for the teens to learn the procedure itself.

THE QUESTION-ANSWER METHOD

Fred Johnson came home from church discouraged after teaching the youth class. Things weren't going well and he was ready to quit. The eleven students weren't responsive, and Fred felt he was morally obligated to resign. His wife knew that he studied well and was devoted to seeing the group grow spiritually. She was shocked to hear Fred talking of quitting and asked him why. "I just can't seem to get through to the kids. I don't know what they are thinking in class. They don't seem to be with me, nor do they care about the lesson."

"Perhaps your answer is not to resign but to change your method of teaching. Why don't you try using a lot more questions in your teaching?"

"Use questions with them? Not me! When I'm in class and telling them what to do, I'm all right, but when I ask questions they clam up."

Fred's wife had been a schoolteacher. She replied, "Maybe I can give you some help on how to use questions. Try coming to class with a series of thirty questions on the Bible passage you're trying to teach. Continually ask questions of the teenager. If one question doesn't get a response, go on to the next question. Surely if you use the question method of approach, you can reach them and know where they are."

"I don't think so. When the students begin to discuss, they run away with the class. Instead of wanting to talk about the Bible lesson, they just want to talk about their own interests and problems."

"Maybe through the questions you can find out what they are interested in and help them."

"If I allow them to ask questions, they may put me on the spot and find out I don't know much about the Bible. I'm afraid I'll have to leave this questioning to someone else. I'm just a teacher; I tell them what to do."

Do you feel like Fred? Do you feel as though you don't know how to use the question-and-answer method of teaching? Are you afraid to make use of some questions in the classroom? Questions and answers appeal to the nature of teenagers. The adolescent age is the stress and strain period of life. Teens like to ask the question "Why?" The question-and-answer method of teaching appeals to their nature. Use it to stimulate their natural tendency to inquire into the unknown.

A seventeen-year-old girl may sit in class with a nice smile. Her face shows attention to the lesson, and her Bible is open in her lap. However, her mind may be confused. She doesn't understand why Christ would spit on the ground and apply clay to a blind man's eyes to heal him. Use a series of questions with young people to test their understanding of the facts and their ability to express insight into the Word of God. If a teenager is confused on step one, he will never reach step two. The teenage mind is like the medieval castle. The teacher must storm the walls. Use questions to arouse curiosity and stimulate their interest in class.

Jesus used questions in His dialogue with Nicodemus (John 3). We can follow His example in asking questions of the teens about the Scripture passage at hand. Teenagers enjoy the thrill of adventuring with their minds. They are experiencing an increase in their memory span, and they accept the challenge of new concepts. Ask questions to cause them to think.

Some youth workers are disturbed when their young people have questions. They should be concerned when teenagers have no questions. Growth comes through stress and pressure. Mental growth results in mental stresses. The youth faces opinions that contradict childhood beliefs. As the teenager struggles to synthesize all information coming to him into a consistent belief, he will have questions. Fight fire with fire. Question his questions.

By properly directed questions you can ascertain what your teens have already learned. Also, you can correct misconceptions and help them to see the relationship of the Word of God to their lives. Questions aid young people to organize their thinking and lead them to fruitful expression of their ideas. If your questions drive students to find answers in the Word of God, you will produce educated enthusiasts. If not, you will produce hardened skeptics.

A good question should be brief, clear, direct, challenging, and original. Ask the question of the whole class before selecting one teen to answer. If you mention a teen's name first, the rest of the class goes to sleep mentally. Give the teens time to answer. Just because the classroom is silent doesn't mean that learning is not going on. If the pupil has difficulty, rephrase the question and make it a little easier. Don't embarrass the teen. Accept any answer or any part of an answer that has value. Use any suggestions and never make the teen feel silly, whether he asks the question or answers the question. Be courteous. Question and answer is a give-and-take proposition. Avoid calling on or accepting too many answers from the same student. Teachers often go to two extremes: One teen is continually called on in class because he always has the right answer, or another is picked on because he seems to be uninterested and unwilling to participate in class.

Learning equals involvement; therefore, involve all students through the use of questions. Throughout the history of teaching, the question-and-answer method of education has been recognized for its value. Socrates made the question famous as a form of teaching, although the method of questioning was used long before his day. The question lay at the very heart of the teaching methods of Jesus Christ, as the Gospel record discloses more than a hundred questions asked by Him. Today, among the multiplicity of methods, much teaching is done by means of the question, either as the chief method or as a component part of other methods of teaching. Teenagers love questions. To them life is a question mark.

PANEL DISCUSSION

Teenagers seek authority and direction. Even though they like to discuss and take part, they also seek and need mature direction. This can be brought to them through the use of a panel discussion. A panel discussion is an informal discussion by four to eight persons with different points of view, or backgrounds of knowledge and experience, before an audience. It may involve about fifty minutes of panel discussion with a half hour allotted to audience participation. Summation by the chairman ties the ideas together. A panel encourages interaction, provides perspective through information and additional knowledge, and stimulates the audience to join in the problem-solving process.

HOW TO USE A PANEL

Participants

The members of the panel should be specialists in the area to be discussed and have experience in the art of discussion. The chairman/leader is the key to a successful panel discussion. He must regulate, focus, guide, clarify, point up key factors, and summarize the total contribution made.

Preparation

The room should be so arranged that the participants can see and talk with one another, yet be easily seen and heard by all members of the audience. The number of participants should be limited to five or six; more would make a balanced, integrated discussion difficult. Three to four are preferable. If an audience participation period follows, no more than an hour should be given to the panel. Agreement should be reached on the following points:

1. Boundaries of the discussion
2. Division of the problem into sections for discussion
3. A specific time limit for each section
4. The assignment of any special individual participant responsibilities
5. Some form of group outline or discussion plan that is simple, short, and flexible.

Procedures

1. Chairman/leader opens discussion by introduction of the subject problem and the panel members.
2. Chairman/leader secures interest of teens and prepares for the following discussion.
3. Chairman/leader explains the procedure to be followed, indicating whether or not the teens will have opportunity to participate.
4. Chairman/leader opens the discussion with a question or statement concerning the topic at hand.
5. After the panel's discussion period, discussion opens up to the teens.
6. Finally, the chairman summarizes the conclusions of the total discussion period.

Principles to Follow

Since participants in panel discussions speak to the teens as well as to each other, their language should be more precise and explicit than it would be in a private committee discussion. They must speak more deliberately and fully, avoiding verbal shortcuts and technical language. Simple and direct language is always appropriate. It must be suited to the basic aim of problem solving. The chairman/leader should lead off at the beginning and at junctures of the discussion by asking appropriate questions or making transitional statements. At every point in the advancing of group ideas, clear statements of belief accompanied by reasons should be made. Relevance to the problem is essential at every stage of the discussion.

Limitations to Panel Discussions

Beware of the tendency of some present to monopolize time. Some teenagers know it all, and they tend to have an opinion on everything that comes up. Use tact in guiding these teens out of the discussion. At the same time, use tact to bring all teenagers into the discussion. Another weakness of the panel discussion is the tendency of some present to ramble from subject to subject and make speeches instead of discussing. Well-prepared speeches may be enlightening but may not contribute to the point of the discussion. Also, in panel discussion, panel members tend to ignore the teens. They may discuss among themselves, attack one another, quibble over points, or tend to follow personal tangents. The point of a panel discussion is to communicate to the group.

THE FORUM

The forum has not been used much in the evangelical church, but it is an effective method of communication. A forum is a period of teen (or class) participation. It may follow a lecture, a panel discussion, a conference, or another form of public discussion. Usually, it is a lecture followed by a question-and-discussion period. In the classroom it would take the form of class questions and discussion.

Why Use a Forum?

1. It enables the teens to gain supplementary information from experts on points not fully developed.
2. A forum helps to give final form and organization to knowledge gained in the pre-forum period.
3. It provides an opportunity for correcting any distortion of facts or misunderstandings.
4. It provides opportunity for verbal expression by the teens as a supplement to their silent thinking, and it reviews the material covered.

How to Use the Forum Method

The forum must be guided by a chairman/leader. He may be the lecturer, the panel moderator, the conference leader, or someone designated for the task. It is important that he be skilled in the art of guiding discussion. His duties are:

1. To instruct the teens as to the mode of participation desired, i.e., informal discussion, questions and answers, comments from the floor, or a combination of these.
2. To stimulate participation by the use of leading questions, striking statements that draw comment, challenging issues previously discussed, etc.
3. To restate questions whenever there is a doubt that they have been heard or clearly understood.
4. To advise beforehand of any limitations on questioning or speaking so as to keep the discussion within reasonable bounds in regards to time and relevance.
5. To bring the forum to a satisfying conclusion by summarizing aptly and briefly while there is still interest in the subject.

The effective use of this method will depend, in a large measure, upon the teacher, lecturer, or expert who provides the preforum information. The best teacher will be free from contention and dogmatism. He will be frank and enthusiastic in advocating his position, yet cooperative in providing data and advice needed for full understanding. Further effectiveness can be attained if the audience is instructed to ask questions useful to others as well as to themselves, to phrase their questions and comments clearly, briefly, and interestingly, and to maintain good taste and temper no matter how controversial the issues.

When to Use the Forum Method

It is best to use the forum method with questions of a controversial and contemporary nature, i.e., the type that would stimulate teen participation. Its primary purpose is to stimulate thinking and provide information—not to solve problems, although it may be used to explore problems with a view to gaining a tentative solution.

THE DEBATE

The debate is a technique of communication to teenagers that has not been used much in the church. Debates are better adapted to youth groups. The minimum age for the use of the debate should be the senior high level. This group is just beginning to think in terms of issues rather than of pure emotional response. It should be a selected group because of the demand of time and effort involved in building a good case. A good maxim for debate is: "Read, read much, read very much," and "Think, think much, think very much." The place of a leader in fostering debate is that of a guide, not a coach. He should make research material available to both sides in planning for the first few debates. The building of the case, however, must be left up to the members of the teams with occasional assistance, where needed, for special problems.

The leader must strive for absolute justice on each side, making sure that no debater holds the opposite position from that which he is proposing. The students must have a real desire to find the true solution to the problem. This means that the subject should hold vital interest in their minds and be closely related to their interest span. The material should be controversial in nature and a practical problem facing the age group using the method. Furthermore, the subject must be nontechnical enough to be of interest to the team's members and the average teens, thus stimulating involvement in the issues and their implications.

The debate method should be used where there is a definite attempt to get the audience or group to see the full implications of a problem, to see the other side or both sides of a question for perspective. It should always be in the form of a resolution in the affirmative, placing the burden of proof on the affirmative. Sample propositions might be: "Resolved: Christian colleges give the finest preparation for life to the Christian student." "Resolved: All Christians should try to go to the mission field." "Resolved: A Christian should participate in labor unions."

Debate is a form of argumentation that has the following features:

1. It is the analysis of a problem with both sides defended.
2. It is a logical argument based on evidence bearing upon the subject presented by each side, out of their independent research and study.
3. It is a brief persuasive composition created with a view to winning acceptance of the listeners that its view is true.
4. In the delivery it involves all phases of the public-speaking science.

5. Debate differs from argument in that it involves a definite time limit for each speaker; it is governed by parliamentary rules; there is an equality of speakers on each side; and it is couched in resolution form.
6. The review is accomplished through rebuttal by both sides in an equal amount of time.
7. A vote decides the case, either by the audience or by a judge.

WHY USE DEBATE?

The debate brings the teenager to recognize a definite standard of achievement. This demands a thorough knowledge of the subject and develops a wholesome analytical attitude, reliability, and resourcefulness through sustained and rigorous thinking. Debate fosters genuine humility in learning and brings the debater and audience a keen awareness of the disparity between finite and infinite knowledge. Debate engenders objectivity in thinking and enables the participant to make a genuine contribution to his home, church, and community life.

COLLOQUY

The colloquy is a learning-group method usually used by groups of from twenty-five to seventy-five persons. Basically the colloquy is a pattern of purposeful, cooperative interaction between three units of participants—an audience, a panel of resource persons, and a panel of audience representatives. The interaction is controlled by a moderator. The audience representatives present a problem or initiate questions that originated in the audience. The resource persons present information designed to help answer the questions, and members of the audience participate actively whenever feasible, under the direction of the moderator. The aim of a colloquy is to secure information from experts on the problem or issue under consideration, by allowing representatives of the larger group to question the authority.

When to Use Colloquy

1. It can be used in many cases as an effective method of following up a speech, a symposium, or a panel presentation.
2. It can be used effectively by a group that has been studying some problem or need area and has accumulated a fund of questions or issues they need to clarify with trained resource persons.
3. It can be used effectively to arouse interest in a problem area and in a series of follow-up meetings.
4. It can be used to illustrate the value of two educational principles:
   a. molding a program to the problems and needs recognized by the participants
   b. using resource persons at the moment they are needed

How to Use Colloquy

The leader needs to prepare for the setting and to facilitate the experience. He is responsible for several steps.

1. He places two tables facing one another diagonally in the front of the room and places the appropriate number of chairs behind each table. Group representatives will sit at one table and resource persons at the other.
2. He selects resource persons in advance and gives them instructions about their responsibilities.

3. He introduces the problem or issue to the entire group.
4. He requests suggestions from the group members that might solve the problem, clarify the issues, or answer the question.
5. He selects three to four persons from the group to act as group representatives.
6. He acts as moderator of the colloquy as the group representatives ask questions of the resource persons.
7. He requests additional questions from the group as a whole if the time or occasion permits.
8. He summarizes the contributions of the resource persons.
9. He proposes additional study or a course of action.
10. He evaluates the learning experience.

Strengths of the Colloquy

The colloquy combines the virtues of the forum, the lecture, and the panel. Like the forum, the colloquy encourages questions from the audience; like the lecture, it seeks to bring out evidence bearing on the questions raised; from the panel it borrows a technique of drawing an audience into a discussion and a weighing of the evidence.

The colloquy not only is an efficient way of using experts and meeting the needs of the audience, but also the colloquy is a stimulating and intellectually exciting large group discussion method.

Weaknesses of the Colloquy

One main disadvantage of the colloquy is its need for trained or highly prepared personnel to man the experts' panel. These people not only need to be knowledgeable in the topic at hand, but they must also be able to respond to the needs of the group.

Because the size of the group is usually most effective with twenty-five to seventy-five, there are situations where its use would be a disadvantage. The vital part of the colloquy is not so much the questions asked by the audience representatives or the answers handed down by the authorities: The most vital contribution is the *active clarification* by the *audience* of the significance of the informational material they receive from the authorities. In an effective colloquy the audience often does as much talking as the resource experts. This is desirable, since it is the participants' job to actively discover personal meaning and obstacles to understanding.

SOME OTHER METHODS

THE DEMONSTRATION OR DRAMA METHOD

One of the favorite methods of teaching used by Christ was demonstration. When teenagers see a truth demonstrated, they remember much more than if they are told. Demonstration as a teaching method is the re-enactment of a given situation, scene, or sequence of facts before a class. The demonstration is pupil-centered and therefore gives maximum involvement to the student in learning. Also, involvement sustains the interest of the teenager, creating and holding maximum motivation. Demonstration also gives variety to the teaching process and affords opportunity for the teen to learn by example and experience.

All things considered, demonstration can become the most effective means of communication to the teenager. Who would try to teach a course in swimming by correspondence, or instruct a teenager in driving a car over the phone? Demonstration is indispensable to instruction of many subjects. Demonstration is adaptable to all age groups but works especially well with young people. It must be adapted to the particular situation and course. Teenagers involved in the demonstration should be given ample time beforehand to prepare sufficiently so that the demonstration will be effective. In some cases, especially with young people, the participants should not be allowed to converse with each other before the actual demonstration—to add a real-life flavor as well as aid in negative and positive teaching. This is most important in evangelistic procedures and counseling demonstrations. The following are some examples that would be considered for drama or demonstration.

Demonstration of Bible Truth

For example, a demonstration could be done of the reenactment of the religious and civil trials of Christ, using students to portray the individuals involved.

Evangelistic and Counseling Demonstrations

Here are two possible scenarios that can be acted out: Selected students re-enact, before the class, a meeting of two high school students trying to win a friend to Christ. The scene could be in a school lunchroom. In an alternative scenario, a pastor can deal with a teenage problem. The youth would then have a chance to view the problem from two points of view.

Church Training Programs

Many things are easier shown than described. For example, defective and effective teaching methods may be enacted before the class that is learning how to teach others. Teen visitation procedure can be effectively taught as a mock situation. Or the creative teacher may decide to have students conduct a judgment day hearing. Song leading is an action that can be taught effectively through demonstration.

Secular Subjects Demonstrated

Areas of usage are as multiple as there are subjects. Brief historical scenes and events can be enacted. Scientific demonstrations are most effective and perhaps most common. Language demonstrations, such as those used by Wycliffe Bible Translators, are also effective and valuable.

Small Group Method

The small group method of teaching is a valuable method for instructing and teaching others. This method has also been called "discussion groups" or "cell groups." When using this method of teaching, the group is divided into groups of four to ten persons to discuss or solve problems introduced by the teacher. Many times the teacher will begin with the lecture or some other form of instructing. Then at a set time, and according to the needs, the larger group is divided into discussion groups. The smaller groups usually do not leave the larger classroom or auditorium. When several groups are discussing at the same time, there is usually little distraction between the groups. When two groups are in the same room, teens hear one other distinct conversation in the room. When there are three or more groups discussing a problem, teens hear a diffused sound rather than a distinct voice. When the larger group is divided, each smaller group should be given direct and clear guidance. Perhaps each group is given the same problem; or, to cover more ground, each group is given a different set of problems. The directions to each group should be written, either on paper or on the chalkboard or overhead.

When the group first assembles, a leader should be chosen. He should then direct, not monopolize, the conversation. A member of the group should be chosen to record the thoughts and progress and ultimate conclusion of the group. Each person should be allowed to take part in the discussion. This is one of the advantages of the group method. Teenagers will enlarge their capacity according to their involvement in the learning situation. However, some teens who like to monopolize the conversation will have to be courteously "muzzled," while the bashful youth are encouraged to speak. After a suitable length of time, the teacher should call the entire class to attention. Each group should be called upon for a report of its discussion. The teacher then gives an overall summary based on each group's report. This summary is as important as the investigation and discussion by the group. Those leading the session should read the section on leading group discussion. Apply those principles in this method. There are limitations to teaching through small groups. When the teacher desires to communicate content or give inspiration, another method should be used. Small groups should be used when the teacher desires to get student expression or involvement. Also, this method should be used when exploration or problem solving is needed.

Circular Response

When circular response is used as a technique of teaching, teens are usually seated in a circle; however, circular response can be used when they sit auditorium style. A topic is announced, and each person is given an opportunity to respond. Circular response will give all your students an opportunity to make contributions on the announced topic. If possible, have the class seated in a semicircle. Then proceed around the group clockwise, giving each person opportunity to contribute. If the class is seated auditorium style, have each person in a row contribute, going from left to right, until each row has had opportunity. Ask each teen to contribute the first thing that comes to mind on the topic of the lesson. Remember, many teens are reluctant to speak before a group, so encourage them. Remind the teen that his contribution may be (1) an illustration from life, (2) a question regarding the lesson, (3) a fact from the Bible,

(4) a verse from the Scriptures pertaining to the lesson, (5) a question based on a previous contribution by another member, or (6) a personal insight regarding the lesson.

Do not make evaluative comments on the contributions of class members as the contributions are being made. The teacher who points out the more significant contributions may embarrass the shy person who has only asked a question or read a verse of Scripture. The teacher should stand by the chalkboard, overhead, or dry erase board and be prepared to write down questions that students may ask during the circular response. Again, do not try to answer the questions at this time, for this would only discourage contributions by others. Simply list the questions. After each person in the group has had opportunity to contribute, stop and discuss the questions that have been raised. Some may feel that a circular response takes away from class time, or believe that students are not learning because specific lesson content is not being presented. However, teachers should think in terms of meeting the needs of students. Perhaps the contributions of the students may not be as substantial as those of the teacher, who has studied the lesson in detail. But discussion and involvement by individual members of the class may provide just the needed motivation to make them consider their Christian faith more seriously. Involvement in the class by students is the key to personal growth.

BRAINSTORMING

Brainstorming is a technique of teaching that is also used in problem solving. A problem or question is introduced to a group of people or a class. The teacher steps out of his traditional role. He does not assume that he has the answer, nor does he try to lead the class to an answer. The topic may be written on the chalkboard or printed and distributed. Each teen is allowed to share his thoughts and solutions to the problem. In the initial stage of brainstorming, the purpose is not to analyze the ideas but to get as many thoughts as possible on the table. When the flow of ideas dries up, then the group can begin to fit the ideas together. Another approach to brainstorming is to give each student a 3 x 5 card on which you have written the topic for discussion. Have each one write down the first thing that comes to his mind concerning the topic. You can discuss these contributions later. Right now you are interested in getting students to think creatively.

After each teen has written something on his card, give them the opportunity to share their ideas with the class. The reason you have them write their ideas out is to clarify their thoughts. The ground rules for brainstorming are simple. Each person says what is on his or her card or whatever comes to his or her mind that he or she may not have written down. As the students react to what is said by others, they should not question the validity of the contributions. When such questioning and refutation begin, creativity generally stops; and the aim of brainstorming is creativity. Encourage your teens to amplify what is said by other teens. This is called the "snowball" effect as the teens continue to build on the thoughts of their peers. The contribution of one student may bring to another person's mind a further thought on the topic. This person simply tells his new or expanded thought.

PARAPHRASING

Paraphrasing is an effective teaching tool with teens. Students are guided into the learning activity of rephrasing verses of Scripture. Many classes have found that restating the truths of Scripture in modern lingo is a helpful learning procedure. When this technique is used, each Scripture verse under consideration is rewritten in the words of the teens. Care is taken to avoid using the original words of the text; yet the paraphrase must communicate the true meaning of the text. Paraphrasing yields new understanding to youth who are seriously seeking to study the Scriptures.

The teen's ability to paraphrase a passage depends upon his grasp of the initial idea in the passage. Many times the King James Version expresses thoughts in a language that is now considered archaic. However, it must be noted that any person who honestly seeks to find the true meaning of Scripture can do so. Perhaps twenty-first-century Christians need to use modern translations for better understanding, but the primary need is for the healing of their own spiritual blindness so that they can perceive God's Word. Occasional archaic language is not the main obstacle that keeps people from understanding God's Word, though modern translations do have a place in the Christian's library. Using paraphrasing as a technique of teaching is different from using a modern version. Paraphrasing is used to place emphasis on study by the teen. Modern versions are used when emphasis is to be placed on the final product. Paraphrasing is not an attempt to change the meaning of Scripture. In fact, if teens change the meaning of Scripture, they have missed the point of paraphrasing. The purpose is to express the meaning of the Scripture passage in a way that will give clarity and understanding to each teen.

Supply paper and pencils for each teen. If possible, it is best to work at one or more tables where your students can spread out their Bibles and notepaper. Teens can work as a team on a verse. They learn as they discuss the Scripture and arrive at a finished wording. Also, teens may work individually on a Scripture assignment. Class members will get more out of the Scripture passage if they are given ample opportunity to discuss their written material. Misunderstanding and lack of clarity in thinking shows up quickly in such an exercise. Have several teens' paraphrases read aloud. In paraphrasing Scriptures, a variety of tools for Bible study will be helpful. Have several copies of Bible dictionaries on hand to which students can refer. Two or three copies of a regular English dictionary will also be helpful. A thesaurus may also prove useful.

CONCLUSION

This chapter has attempted to give only a brief introduction to methods of teaching teens. Not only were some methods neglected, but the methods that were mentioned have been abbreviated because of space and purpose. The conscientious teacher should consult a book on teaching methods and principles. Since entire volumes are given over to one method of teaching, it would be impossible to be complete in this chapter. A recent book on teaching teens advertises 365 ways of communicating biblical truth. Note that many of the techniques of teaching are built around social groupings. These are especially effective with teens since teenagers seek social interaction. The lecture is still the best method to communicate biblical content, but these additional methods will support the lecture and give the teen insight, understanding, stimulation, practical application, and growth, our ultimate goal.

Programming Youth Ministry

Programming is the most overlooked and the least understood aspect of youth ministry. This chapter will establish some guidelines to employ as you seek to carry out the ministry implications of the previous chapters. Without proper planning and programming, our ministries will fail and fall short of all that God has intended for us to accomplish with those under our care. Dr. Matthew Willmington, the executive pastor at West Ridge Church in Atlanta and a former colleague of ours, provided the essential information contained within this chapter.[1]

In 1 Chronicles 28, King David is passing on his plans, and God's specific instructions, for the temple to his son Solomon, who will actually build the temple. David has collected valuable items to be used in its building, and the plans are in order. But David wishes Solomon to know that *how* the temple is built is important, so he clarifies that the plans he is giving come from God: "'All this,' said David, 'the Lord made me understand in writing, by His hand upon me, all the works of these plans'" (1 Chron. 28:19).

Imagine that we (like David) have been given plans by God to construct an incredible building. But instead of building God's temple (for He now resides within us!), we have the privilege of assisting to build God's house—a local church youth ministry. Just as constructing a beautiful building did not ensure the spiritual condition of God's people, so planning a spectacular youth ministry program does not ensure the spiritual growth of teenagers.

Nonetheless, you are being invited by God to build a healthy youth ministry program that can serve as a vehicle for teenagers to experience the life-transforming process of following Christ. Planning is a spiritual process, which requires a vision from God, a mind for strategy, a strong hand for hard work, and eyes to assess the effectiveness of the program. God is a God of order, not chaos.

Consider the following:

> May he give you the desire of your heart and make all your plans succeed. (Ps. 20:4 NIV)
>
> Plans fail for lack of counsel, but with many advisors they succeed. (Prov. 15:22 NIV)
>
> The preparations of the heart belong to man, but the answer of the tongue is from the Lord. (Prov. 16:1)
>
> Commit your works to the Lord, and your thoughts will be established. (Prov. 16:3)
>
> A man's heart plans his way, but the Lord directs his steps. (Prov. 16:9)
>
> There is no wisdom, no insight, no plan that can succeed against the LORD. (Prov. 21:30 NIV)

"For I know the plans I have for you," declares the LORD, "plans to prosper you and not to harm you, plans to give you hope and a future." (Jer. 29:11 NIV)

Let all things be done decently and in order. (1 Cor. 14:40)

YOUTH MINISTRY MISSION/OBJECTIVES IN FOCUS

Before we can embark on a mission of planning a youth ministry program, we must decide where we are going! (See chapter 11.) The following questions act as mortar between the bricks of our established ministry aims. These questions will help to define the reason(s) behind "why we do what we do." The questions are as follows:

1. What kind of student do we want to produce?
2. What kind of youth ministry can produce that kind of student?
3. What kind of ministry programming/curriculum can produce that kind of group?
4. What kind of professional and lay staff will it take to produce that kind of programming?
5. What kind of ministry leader can produce that kind of lay staff?

The answers to these questions will vary from ministry to ministry; however, the whole process of answering these questions is guided by our aims, goals, and ministry model established in chapter 11. The goal of youth ministry is . . .

To produce spiritually maturing adolescents.

PRAYER: THE CRUCIAL FORCE

Without God's guidance, our programs are useless. As Henry Blackaby comments in *Experiencing God,* God is always at work around us. Our job is to seek God, determine what He is doing in the lives of our teenagers, and plan programs accordingly. We must develop a vibrant prayer life that plugs us into God's direction, God's vision, God's burden, and God's plans. E. M. Bounds in his 1907 book *Power Through Prayer* states:

> We are constantly on a stretch, if not a strain, to devise new methods, new plans, new organizations to advance the church and secure enlargement and efficiency for the gospel. This trend of the day has a tendency to lose sight of the person or sink the person in the plan or organization. People are God's method. The church is looking for better methods; God is looking for better people.
>
> What the church needs today is not more machinery or better, not new organizations or more and novel methods, but people whom the Holy Spirit can use—people of prayer, people mighty in prayer. The Holy Spirit does not flow through methods, but through people. He does not come on machinery, but on people. He does not anoint plans, but people—people of prayer.

Proper Youth Ministry Model

Our biblical mission is to produce spiritually maturing teenagers. It may seem like that is a logical approach and we are overstating the obvious. But the truth is many churches operate under a different model, consciously or not. Usually, one of three ministry models is chosen as a basis for formulating a ministry model: (1) the curriculum, (2) the programming, or (3) the shepherding. Notice how the curriculum and programming models differ from the last, shepherding, which is based on our mission.

CHARACTERISTICS OF EACH MODEL	CURRICULUM	PROGRAMMING	SHEPHERDING
Goal of ministry model	Religious education	Healthy environment	Spiritual growth
Agent used to achieve goal	Sunday school teacher	Activity director	Pastors, workers (all considered shepherds)
Prize of reaching goals	Knowledge	Activity	Growth
Basis of evaluation toward the goal	"How much Bible do the youth know?"	"How busy are the youth at church?"	"How much are the youth like Jesus?"

YOUTH MINISTRY PROGRAMMING PRINCIPLES

It is crucial that we understand the relationship between programming and ministry. The following three principles serve as the foundation and guide to our study of programming.

1. *Programming is potentially your ministry's number one enemy.*

Many church leaders view "good programming" as equal to "good ministry." Oftentimes church leaders consider an abundance of programming to be biblically dictated. The truth is, there is almost no prescribed programming in Scripture.

2. *Powerful programs are purposeful programs.*

Programming is an extension of your philosophy and aims; simply, programming is a tool. The goal of youth ministry is "to produce spiritually maturing adolescents." As stated earlier, this includes all of the implications and considerations that flow from this statement. Thus, programs do not generate ministry. Ministry is the spiritual force and work of the Holy Spirit. Programs are the youth leader's work to harness and channel into the lives of teens the stated aims of the ministry.

Further programs do not produce disciples—God does, using our lives and the instruments (programs) we design. A true child of God will have a natural hunger (albeit sometimes hidden) for God. Our programs must channel this gravitational force toward Christ, drawing the teen through the various stages of spiritual growth.

3. *Powerful programs are professionally planned.*

Proper planning results in programs that are thoroughly proposed, organized, prepared, presented, and evaluated. Planning equals programs that are prayerfully balanced according to the levels of ministry we are trying to accomplish and the established calendar.

4. *A strong program is built for the desired product.*

As we look at our youth ministry mission statement, our various ministry levels, and spiritual characteristics that we want to produce, we must remember to always program with them in mind. Thus the following questions should be asked:

a. What programs could help produce a convert?
b. What programs could help produce a churched teen?
c. What programs could help produce a Bible-craving teen?
d. What programs could help produce a compassionate teen?
e. What programs could help produce a consecrated teen?

5. *Planning now allows shepherding later.*

Much planning equals much shepherding. Little planning equals little shepherding. If we will invest time up front in planning our programs, it will save us the last-minute work that will rob us of our time with teens while the program is in progress.

6. *A plan is only helpful if it is used.*

As you establish and bring closure to your plan, use it. Rest on the fact that you have put together, through prayer and dependence on God, a workable plan.

PROGRAMMING AND PLANNING OVERVIEW

The questions now become:

1. What are programs?
2. What are the misconceptions about programming?
3. What are the three types of programs?
4. What are the three types of planning?

Let's begin with "What are programs?"

DEFINITIONS OF PROGRAMS

First we must establish what programming is not. There are many common misconceptions of youth ministry programming. Some people see programs as merely a reward, a party, recreation, a time killer, or a baby-sitting service.

Although there may be some merit in each of the above points, they are not the primary objectives of youth ministry or its programming. Simply defined, programs fall within two categories:

1. Macroprograms—the entire ministry vehicle, everything done during the ministry year to fulfill the objectives for the youth group
2. Microprograms—one activity of the ministry vehicle that has a specific objective and is proposed, organized, prepared, and presented in a professional manner

Program Types

Youth ministry includes three programming types listed below. As you read the description of the three types of programs, try to see the place of all programs in your ministry in these three categories.

Events

Events are activities presented within a short period of time (one to forty-eight hours), such as a theme or "leisure day." Events should be established through the following means:

1. forecasting—asking, What is the state of your group today? What should be the state of your group tomorrow?
2. brainstorming—creative thinking, critical thinking
3. mapping—calendar design, budget, staffing

Microplanning (programs)

Micro-planning needs to be conducted for each event, marathon, and series. Think through the following as you move from the event/activity date to the specifics to see it through.

First you need to ask, What's the purpose? (See goals/aims listing at the end of chapter 11.) Once you know what you are doing and why, it's time to move forward:

- organize—delegate all the various aspects of the event.
- prepare
- present
- evaluate—leaders and key youth should do an evaluation. Make necessary changes for the future.

Mobile Planning (moment)

Mobile planning is conducted as needed, in reaction to immediate changes in the culture and condition of the community, church, or youth group. The only constant in ministry today is change! Youth culture changes every three to six months. Economic problems, natural disasters—anything can void your best-laid plans. Be ready to plan on the run and take advantage of every situation the Holy Spirit guides you through.

THE MACROPROGRAMMING PROCESS

How does a ministry plan a yearly youth ministry calendar?

PERSPECTIVE

As you begin to map out the programs for an entire year of youth ministry, your calendar must be born out of your philosophy, bathed in prayer, and based on the church calendar year.

Churches establish their yearly programming calendar in one of four ways. They can approach their programming year based on

1. a fiscal year (July 1–June 30)
2. the school year (Sept. 1–Aug. 31)
3. a normal calendar year (Jan. 1–Dec. 31)
4. Sunday school promotion (Oct. 1–Sept. 30)

Once the calendar dates are established, you must next facilitate a calendar planning meeting. Two important activities that you will engage in during this process are *ministry forecasting* and *brainstorming*.

Ministry Forecasting

Forecasting means attempting to determine what God is doing and where He is leading your ministry. It requires a sensitivity to the Spirit of God and an understanding of church growth principles and adolescent ministry. Ask the following questions concerning the present and future ministry conditions:

1. Climate report—the present condition

A. What is God currently doing in our community?
B. What is the spiritual condition of our community right now?
C. What is God currently doing in our church?
D. What is the current spiritual condition of our church?
E. What is God presently doing in our youth department?
F. What is the spiritual condition of our teenagers right now?
G. What are we presently doing to fulfill the church mission and to carry out the church mandates in the youth ministry?

2. Ministry forecast—the future possibilities

A. Where might God be taking our community spiritually in the next twelve months?
B. Where might God be taking our church spiritually in the next twelve months?
C. Where might God be taking our youth department spiritually in the next twelve months?
D. What programming should we consider implementing to carry out our mission and mandates during the next twelve months?

BRAINSTORMING

Brainstorming is the process of dreaming up unique ideas and then thinking them into reality. The following notes on brainstorming are based on material presented by Craig McNair Wilson at a 1995 Youth Specialties Conference session called "Disney Imaginuity."

1. *Setting the Environment*

  a. Establish groups of five or seven people (odd number prevents deadlock).
  b. Assemble off-site away from the group's normal routine and meeting place.
  c. Cultivate a casual atmosphere.
  d. Make room for participants to move around.
  e. Provide refreshments.
  f. Have plenty of supplies (a flip chart or butcher paper, markers, 3x5 cards, tape, bulletin boards).

2. *The First Session—Creative Thinking*

  a. Your goal
    (1) nonlinear, free flow of ideas
    (2) large number of ideas
    (3) wild ideas, bigger than you are comfortable with, ideas that will stretch you, illogical and curious
  b. Most important rule—"there are no bad ideas"
  c. Methods employed
    (1) Use "yes, and . . ." technique, "pulsing"—adding ideas onto someone else's idea.
    (2) Incorporate the piggybacking technique—adding ideas unrelated and/or unconnected.

(3) Use anthropomorphism—thinking of the event as a person . . . "if the Saturday night rally were a sixteen-year-old teenager, what would it look like or be like?"

d. The dangers
   (1) Condescending is equal to throwing cold water or negative comments on someone's ideas; condescending can also be done through the listing of problems with ideas presented.
   (2) Blocking is simply stopping someone's idea and not allowing time or freedom for the "yes and . . . ," piggybacking, and anthropomorphism methods.

e. The process
   (1) Choose a specific topic or event.
   (2) Generate as many ideas as possible, and write them on 3x5 cards or butcher paper. If using 3x5 cards, hang them on the wall or bulletin board so they can be readily seen. When using butcher paper either cover the table and record ideas as they come or hang on the wall and list all ideas.
   (3) The group *must* use pulsing and piggybacking.

3. *The Second Session—Critical Thinking*

   a. Narrow the selection of ideas presented, then decide on a direction.
   b. Group 3x5 cards of ideas by category. Formulate some organization to ideas presented.
   c. Now turn the ideas into a production schedule.
   d. Develop a "mythology" of the event. This is a make-believe story that explains the event in a clear and concise way.
   e. Group unused idea cards; file them away for another occasion.

MACROPLANNING THE CALENDAR IN TEN STEPS

Your youth ministry program calendar can be effectively designed during a planning session or retreat. Keys to remember: The session/retreat should be held at least three to four months before the calendar year begins. For example, meet in May to plan the August to July program calendar.

1. *Step One*—Assemble the participants. Who are the key people who need to attend the session/retreat?

   a. other staff
   b. lay staff

2. *Step Two*—Pray and conduct a ministry forecast based on the previous questions.

3. *Step Three*—Study all relevant calendars.

   a. the overall church calendar
   b. Christian school(s), both the church's and others in the community
   c. public school(s)
   d. national and community key holidays or community events
   e. each personal worker's key dates, holidays, weddings, etc.
   f. last year's youth calendar

4. *Step Four*—Record all regular, confirmed series programs.

5. *Step Five*—Conduct a brainstorm session. List dozens of potential programs that are guided by your goal—to produce spiritually maturing adolescents, through a spiritual-maturity-driven program. Resources include:

a. resource books, idea books, phone book, brochures, and community information
b. history of your ministry (teen survey)
c. evaluation of
   (1) successes
   (2) failures
   (3) new activities we should try
d. other youth works

6. *Step Six*—Compose a tentative list of programs.

   a. balanced in purpose, finances, time, etc.
   b. useful rule of thumb: establish four to six major events with ten to twelve minor events

7. *Step Seven*—Complete a calendar balance sheet. If you are unbalanced at this point, go back to Step Two. Cautions to look out for and syndromes to avoid:

   a. the spiral effect—avoid a bigger and better activities mentality
   b. numbing effect—too many big activities will numb the youth and lose their effect
   c. overburdening the youth and families with too many activities

8. *Step Eight*—Complete a proposal planning sheet for every program.

9. *Step Nine*—Confirm the calendar.

   a. Meet with the pastor, administrator, committee, or elder(s) to discuss the calendar and vision for the year. Be organized and thorough.
   b. Follow up the meeting with the lay staff.
   c. Record all events on the church calendar.

10. *Step Ten*—Complete a production schedule for every program.

11. *Step Eleven*—Publish the calendar.

   a. Announce the calendar to the core teens.
   b. Send the calendar to parents and staff on a quarterly basis.

THE MICROPROGRAMMING PROCESS

What are the steps in planning a specific program? Successful programs just don't happen—they must develop through a process. Remember Principle #3: "Powerful programs are professionally planned." So, what are the different stages in the development of a program? Let's do the process for a possible activity.

K-MART EVANGELISM

Scene One

You have been burdened by the lack of vibrant evangelism that your youth ministry is having with secular teens. You host evangelistic rallies in the church gym, but lost teens just don't come. One Friday night, you are standing in the Hardee's parking lot, drinking iced tea, and watching all the cruiser teenagers sitting on the hoods of their cars in the adjacent K-Mart parking lot. Your heart cries out to God, "How can I reach these kids?!" Suddenly, you have a vision! Bring the Gospel to teens . . . where they are. You see a summer Friday night, the K-Mart parking lot, multitudes of teens, a flatbed truck stage, a Christian band, and you presenting the Gospel message.

Scene Two

As you sit in your office, mulling over the dream God has given you, you realize there are many details and a lot of work that must happen to fulfill this dream. You take your proposal planning sheet and begin thinking your way through the process, scratching down your ideas of what needs to happen, when it needs to be done, and who needs to do the work. Permission from K-Mart, a flatbed truck, security, a Christian band, promotion, sound and lights, electricity—these are just some of the things that must be secured.

Scene Three

It's Sunday afternoon, and you are meeting with your lay staff. You hand out copies of the production schedule for the K-Mart rally. You talk it through with your staff, assign jobs, and send them out. Over the next several weeks the staff members carry out their jobs, and each staff meeting includes a time of checking the progress and making changes to the production. You focus on being thorough in the details.

Scene Four

Finally, the big day arrives. Your staff has done a great job of building this program, although a few problems have appeared within hours of the program. The forecast is calling for rain, the band's van has broken down on their way into town, and one of your stage light trees was dropped and busted by one of your ninth-grade helpers. You scramble to adjust, and the rally goes off without any major problems.

Scene Five

Sunday afternoon after the Friday night rally, you meet with the lay staff to assess the program. As you watch the video from the rally, your staff laughs, makes excited comments, voices concerns, and talks about how it could have been improved. The sound should have been louder. There weren't enough adult security personnel for the rowdy crowd. Maybe you should have stopped the concert when the thunder and lightning started. Thankfully, only two band members were fried. Should you do the rally again next year? How will it be better?

PROGRAMMING STAGES: P.O.P.E.

The K-Mart scenario gives us a picture of the stages of program development. Specifically stated, the stages look like this . . .

STAGE	ACTION	PERSPECTIVE	PRAYER FOCUS
Purpose	Dream it	Big picture view	What do you want to do?
Organize	Think it	Bird's-eye view	Show me how to do this.
Prepare	Build it	Detailed view	Help me be thorough.
Evaluate	Ponder it	Hindsight view	How did you like it?

YOUR ROLE

There will be one of these stages that you will be more motivated and talented to handle. But if you are the leader of a youth ministry, you must be involved in every stage—not for every program, but you must know how to function in each role and train your staff how to do the same.

EVALUATION OF PROGRAMS

How do I evaluate my programs? Imagine the classic scene of an exhausted family on a long, weary cross-country vacation. As the car pulls into a truck stop, the mom storms into the station. She's not talking to Dad because he wouldn't check directions, and as a result, they have been lost for four hours. Teenage son spills out of the car, screaming at the middle child, while the baby daughter proceeds to throw up (again) because she's hot, tired, and carsick. The gas station attendant informs the dad that there is no oil in the engine and that major damage has been done. You ask the dad, "So, how's the trip going?" He smiles and says, "Wonderful." You ask how can it be wonderful with all of these problems, and he answers, "What problems?"

That might make for a hilarious movie plot, but it's a lousy way to run a youth ministry! If you don't know where you've come from, how the trip is going, or where you are headed, it makes for a meaningless journey. Teenagers can sense this type of aimless activity, sometimes sooner than adults. We may think our program is wonderful, but the truth is, we just are not asking the hard questions.

The solution? Evaluation. For the sake of your ministry, you must learn how to evaluate every aspect of your program. It is not just a matter of keeping your teens, their parents, and the pastor happy with your work. God has given you the sacred responsibility of shepherding, and it demands that you are a wise steward of time and resources.

So, what is evaluation, and how do we do it?

MacroEvaluation

The first *scope* of evaluation is macroevaluation. This refers to evaluation of an entire program, as in a year of programs. It may be conducted at the end of a year, perhaps during a planning retreat. Broad evaluation such as this is called summative evaluation.

Summative evaluation lets you take the hindsight view and judge whether the program was a success, based on your stated objectives. Decisions can then be made as to whether or not the program should continue as designed. For this type of assessment, we must look back at our mission and objectives. Based on Matthew 28:19–20 and Ephesians 4:11–12, the goal of youth ministry is . . . *to produce spiritually maturing adolescents.*

1. What kind of student do we want to produce?
2. What kind of programming/curriculum can produce that kind of group?
3. What kind of lay staff can produce that kind of programming?
4. What kind of leader can produce that kind of lay staff?

A second type of evaluation is called formative evaluation. This type is conducted during a program and is used to make midcourse adjustments. It might be used in the middle of the year, asking questions such as, “How is our Sunday school running?”

MicroEvaluation

The second *scope* of evaluation is called microevaluation, and it refers to examining the quality of a specific program. For microevaluation, an immediate procedure must be established, which includes who will be evaluating, how it will be done, when it will be done, and what will be evaluated.

The procedure starts with determining the evaluation process.

1. who—workers, core teens, parents, staff
2. how—meeting form, video
3. when—not immediately, but two to three days later

Evaluation Questions

1. Philosophy

    a. Does it fulfill our group/church mission?
    b. Is it biblically based (principles)?
    c. Does it balance in our year calendar?

d. Is it age appropriate?
e. Does it fit the youth and church culture?

2. People

a. Does it have pastoral staff support?
b. Does it have parents' support?
c. Does it have lay staff support?
d. Does it have teenagers' support?

3. Tools

Do we have adequate money, equipment, materials, facilities to sustain it?

POSTEVALUATION OPTIONS

1. Maintain
2. Intervene (retool or redirect)
3. Hibernate (discontinue for now)
4. Terminate

NOTE

1. Matthew Willmington, Ed.D., taught "Programming for Youth Ministry" at Liberty University for ten years before being called to West Ridge Church. Dr. Willmington has graciously permitted a small section of notes from his class to be the basis for this chapter.

Music and the Adolescent

Nothing in youth ministry will provoke more controversy than the topic of music and the manner in which it is handled by the youth leaders. It is important to understand that since the inception of modern-day rock and roll, adolescents have been its primary target. Consider the following quote from Michael Green, the CEO and president of the Recording Academy, taken from his address at the forty-third annual Grammy Awards:

> Listen, music has always been the voice of rebellion—it's a mirror of our culture, sometimes reflecting a dark and disturbing underbelly obscured from the view of most people of privilege, a militarized zone which is chronicled by the CNN of the inner city–rap and hip-hop music. We can't

edit out the art that makes us uncomfortable. That's what our parents tried to do to Elvis, the Stones and the Beatles.[1]

By the music professionals' own admission, rock music has as its goal to assume the role of the voice of rebellion for teens. Whether the message is subtle or not, the fact remains that today's teens (as those that have gone before) understand the role of music in their lives. One musician explains, "That's one of the greatest questions I get all the time: *Do you think the kids get it?* You saw them out there. The message, the band's philosophy, isn't hidden. It's on every shirt and on every video and in every song."[2] Teens get the message of today's music regardless of how "correct" it may be or how blurred the message. Another musician says, "We'll never tell [our fans] to do drugs, burn people's houses down, kill people or worship Satan. I'm really into Jesus Christ, God, all that. I really am a big believer. I'm a Christian. I just happen to have a foul mouth, and I try to make kids laugh. But that's just me. I'm as God made me."[3]

Statistics continually point to the importance of music in the lives of teens. This chapter will focus on the impact of music on the day-to-day lives of teens and suggest some basic guidelines for establishing boundaries within your ministry concerning music.

THE POWER OF MUSIC

At the onset we must establish the power and impact that music has on our lives. We are not arguing the positive or negative aspects of lyrics, rhythm, or beat. This section will simply present the facts of the impact and influence that music has on adolescents. "Music affects the 'whole' person; making music exercises the whole brain and mind."[4] Studies have shown that "making music increases the brain's capacity and resources by increasing the strength of connections among its neurons."[5] These connections between music, motivation, learning, and memory have proven to be so strong that "many music therapies are in widespread use for a variety of behavioral and neurological problems."[6] The plain fact is that music can and does affect the life of adolescents. Its influence and power is far-reaching, whether that be positive or negative in nature. Let's think through some areas affected by music.

Motivation

At the next sporting event you attend, listen to the type of music that is piped through the public address system. Whether you're at a middle school, high school, college, or professional event, the music is planned to get you on your feet, clapping, singing, and stomping your feet. The music influences your behavior; it gets you into the game. Professional athletes play all season long for home field advantage. Why? So that they can feed off the "home court" crowd and atmosphere, largely cultivated through the motivation provided by the music played.

Learning and Memory

How many of us have put information into our minds through the use of a tune? We all have, and regardless of our stature and achievement we still do. From our earliest days we learned the ABCs through the jingle or the books of the Bible through song. Music helps us to learn and to remember.

Comfort and Inspiration

Throughout history music has been a source of inspiration and comfort, from the "Star Spangled Banner" to the moving rendition of "Candle in the Wind" performed at the funeral of Princess Diana. Songs have the ability to make us feel a sense of comfort and inspiration to conquer the struggles in life. Music can speak to us on a personal level, and lyrics to a song can fill a gap that nothing else can.

As we can see from the above, we must admit the influence that music has on our lives as well as the lives of teens. If we say on the one hand that music can affect us positively, then on the other hand we must admit that music can also affect us in a negative manner. We must not ignore the impact that music has on the development of the teens under our care. The simple truth is that music at its best and worst affects us in many ways. Keep this in mind as we look at the phenomenon of modern-day music.

IMPORTANCE OF MUSIC IN THE LIVES OF TEENS

The importance of music in the lives of teens can readily be seen through their own opinions concerning the subject. This section will list statistics concerning teens' views on music:

"More than 60% of people aged 14 to 30 would give up food before giving up music, according to a recent survey. More than 56% say they'd rather be music stars than movie stars or famous politicians."[7]

"During junior and senior high, teenagers spend almost 10,000 hours listening to music—close to all the hours they spend in class by the time they graduate from high school."[8]

"Teenagers spend 4 and 5 hours a day listening to music and watching music videos."[9]

Teens name "music listening as their preferred non-school activity."[10]

"Four out of five teenagers we surveyed said music is either 'important' or 'very important' in their lives."[11]

"Girls find more meaning in their music than guys do."[12]

As seen through the above statistics, music is of the utmost importance in lives of today's teens. For better or worse it is the source through which teens find meaning and release.

Whether that release comes in the form of "head banging" at a concert or music that is quite melancholy, music today is meeting the needs of today's teens.

Violence in Today's Music

This section will focus on the violence in today's music, but that doesn't mean that other aspects of music should be ignored (such as sex, sexuality, and sexual violence). These areas have been and will be covered in other places throughout the book.

Today's music has a more definite bent toward the violent, with its angry lyrics and driving beat. This trend has not gone unnoticed by teens and adults. The following are statistics that point out this disturbing trend.

"Forty-eight percent of Americans say that violence in popular music should be more heavily regulated and fifty-nine percent would like to restrict violence in music."[13]

"Music lyrics have also become increasingly explicit in the past two decades. Songs commonly make graphic reference to sex, drugs and violence, whereas such sensitive topics were cleverly veiled in the past."[14]

Studies and surveys have found that exposure to rap music "tends to lead to a higher degree of acceptance of the use of violence."[15]

"One study of 400 male and female students showed that the more violent music videos were, the more angry, fearful and aggressive viewers felt."[16]

"Another study reported that eliminating access to MTV decreased the number of violent acts among teenagers and young adults in a locked treatment facility."[17]

"In a 1998 study of 518 music videos from the four most popular music video networks, almost 15% contained interpersonal violence, averaging 6 violent acts per violence-containing video."[18]

Violence in today's music is a given, and the parallel between music and behavior is evident.

Music Videos

Nothing has molded adolescent culture over the past twenty years more than the music video. Music Television (MTV) has redefined the music industry through the creation of the music video and the interweaving of musical sound with video imagery. For the first time in history an adolescent could sit down in front of the television and consume images of his favorite rock star, singing and dancing to the delight of fans. Over the years since its inception, MTV has made a conscious effort to transform itself into more than just "Music videos, 24 hours a day."

> MTV has transformed itself from a kind of video jukebox into a programming service pandering to teens and their legion of base instincts. The channel is now defined more by shows like the stunt-moron showcase *Jackass,* the shockingly kinky (and even more shockingly tedious) soap opera *Undressed,* and the . . . dull bacchanalian throb of its annual (and nearly perpetual) Spring Break programming. . . . Only by a definition written under the influence of hyperactive hormones is fare like this good entertainment.[19]

Before this quote is dismissed as a "knee-jerk" reaction to MTV, consider the following: "A 1999 study revealed that music videos were more violent than feature films and television, averaging four violent scenes each."[20] An additional survey reported that 22.4 percent of MTV videos contained overt violence and 25 percent depicted weapon carrying.[21] Keep in mind also another study that "revealed that boys and girls ages 12 to 19 watch MTV for an average of 6.6 and 6.2 hours each week respectively."[22]

As the above section points out, music is important to today's teens, even as the content becomes more violent and the consumption of videos that portray this violence and sexual promiscuity become habits in the lives of teens. Remember, if music can and does affect us positively, then the opposite is also true. Teens are affected by the total package of today's music.

MINISTRY IMPLICATIONS OF MUSIC AND TODAY'S YOUTH

What are the ministry implications of the statements above? How can we minister effectively to teens based on the information given to this point? These are great questions that deserve an answer, for if we fail to adapt to the culture and minister accordingly, we have missed an opportunity to reach teens with the Gospel message and encourage their ultimate maturity in Christ. First, how should we respond? Consider the following possibilities:

Attitude Toward Culture	Likely Response to Culture
Outraged	Removal
Take pleasure in	Integrate
Concern	Engage

If we assume the attitude of outrage concerning teens and their music, our tendency is to remove ourselves from the problems and issues that are raised through music. This is the extreme response to the problem of music and teens. To back away and refuse to become involved with teens at this level is in essence to turn our backs and even assume the attitude of "stop listening to that type of music and then I can help you." This is a dangerous place to be, for very little if any ministry will be accomplished.

If we take pleasure in today's music, then we will integrate it into our lives. This is the opposite extreme. To enjoy the current music scene and all that comes with it, we in fact become "pseudo-teens" and incorporate the current styles and lingo into our lives. This extreme is no better than the above, as teens can spot a fake teen, a wannabe, a mile away. Thus here again very little or no ministry will take place.

The answer is to be concerned with what's going on with today's music and to engage it accordingly, based on Scripture and the needs of the students. To be concerned is to face the problem head-on, not agreeing with current music culture, while not turning our backs either. The key is balance, balance that comes from a nonjudgmental heart that seeks to understand why music is so important while not becoming immersed in it.

How can we remain balanced in our ministry to teens in this critical issue? Some guidelines follow, in no particular order.

Use Their Culture to Reach Their Culture

Use their music to your advantage. We are not advocating that your ministry become a nightclub for teens. However, we can use teens' opinions concerning popular music to better reach them. This can be accomplished in many ways. To begin with, you can survey your youth concerning what types of music they listen to, who their favorite artists are, and why they glean importance from their music. Once this survey is complete, a better strategy can be formulated to use popular music to your advantage.

Set the Boundaries on Music in Your Ministry

As the leader you will have to set some boundaries concerning the use of popular music among your teens—for example, no headphones, CDs, or MP3 players on youth activities. You cannot be afraid to establish these rules for your group. The key here is to communicate clearly the purpose behind your decision. They can be as simple as "we can't fellowship together if we're all wearing headphones," or "I'd like to use the time in the van or bus to expose you to some current contemporary Christian music." Your explanations do not have to be "deep"; however, they do have to be thought-out and readily explained. So take some time and think through some boundaries that need to be established in your group concerning popular music.

Research Current Trends

As the leader of teens each of us will have to become a student among students. This means that we will need to read, listen to, and watch all sources of media that are affecting today's youth culture. We must understand what we are up against if we are to combat it effectively. The better we understand the topic, the easier it is to communicate a proper biblical point of view. This of course includes today's music and the entire music scene. We will have to pick up current music magazines and read the articles on the "hottest" artist. In addition the viewing of some music videos and special events such as the Grammies, MTV music awards, and the Country Music Awards will be necessary. It is here that we can glean the greatest amount of information on today's music with the least amount of exposure. Further, the Internet is a viable source for discovering information on many of today's popular stars. Information can include brief bios, sound bites, and lyric sheets. Also use your own teens in your research.

Understand the Needs of Your Youth

As we try to come to grips with the effects of music in the lives of teens, we must understand the needs that our teens face. There is a reason that music is so important to teens today. We must get to the root of the problem. We must learn what these needs are and address them accordingly. Music as mentioned above serves to fill some form of void in the lives of our teens.

We must uncover these voids so that we may fill them with the values and principles found within the Word of God. In addition, different types of music (soft rock, metal, rap, and alternative) that teens listen to may help indicate some of these voids:

> Teenagers who prefer Hard music are more dominant in their relationships, more indifferent to others' feelings, more verbally impulsive, more disrespectful of others, and more eager to push societal boundaries. These kids are also emotionally discontented, not sure of who they are, and have difficulty relating to their families—particularly their parents.[23]

We must understand the deep-rooted needs of our teens to unmask the reason(s) behind their allegiance to popular music.

Critique the Music Culture from a Biblical Perspective

If you are currently in the habit of attacking popular music through attacking the musicians, you are losing the battle. With music being as important to teens as it is, this methodology will serve no purpose other than to alienate youth from your ministry. Phrases like "you just don't understand" or "what did they ever do to you?" will resound. We must adapt a strategy that will win the battle based on a biblical perspective. Attack the music culture from a biblical perspective; don't attack the musicians. Topics such as stewardship of money, the thought life of a believer, and "trash in, trash out" are just a few ideas. Remember, no matter how hard it is, that these musicians need the Lord. Our responsibility is to lead our teens into spiritual maturity, and this effort will be seriously hampered if we attack people who are important to teens, no matter how right or wrong they are. Use the Word.

PROVIDE MUSIC RESOURCES WITHIN YOUR MINISTRY

Start a library of contemporary Christian music as well as student reviews of popular secular music. This can be accomplished through various methods. First you may have to add money to your budget or subscribe to a music service such as "Interlinc."[24] Let these contemporary Christian CDs be readily available for your teens. If possible, match Christian artists with their secular counterparts based on sound and music style. If parents have held the line in what kind of music style is acceptable for their child, you need to respect that and limit that youth's choices. In addition have the teens compile reviews of popular secular music. Establish some sort of review system for teens to use as well as an organized system for easy retrieval. This will have greater impact with your teens as these opinions will come from their peers and not from you.

Remember our goal is to engage the current pop music culture, not to assimilate it into our lives. Our concern must drive us to comprehend as much as we possibly can so that we can be as effective as possible as we strive to minister to those entrusted to our care.

CONCLUSION

Music is a powerful source in the lives of teens. For better or worse, music affects us in many different ways. Our responsibility is to lead teens into a deeper relationship with Jesus Christ. For those who are immersed in the popular music scene, we must engage them from a heart of concern. We cannot withdraw from this issue, nor should we integrate the popular music scene into our lives. We can, however, engage music from a biblical perspective, discovering the needs of our teens, thus winning those who may have been lost.

NOTES

1. www.youthministry.com/articles/trendwatch/quotes.asp
2. Tom Morello, guitarist of the left-wing band Rage Against the Machine, *Vibe,* February 2000. The band's political causes aren't always clear to adults; however, the anger of Rage Against the Machine is crystal clear. The band burns with anger against the church, the rich, and the government with an attitude of violence and no "peaceable" solutions. The band preaches anarchy and violence as the viable solution to problems.
3. Blink 182 guitarist-singer Tom Delonge, *Teen People,* April 2000. Even though Mr. Delonge claims Christianity, the band's message is far from it. Blink 182 promotes through their music such topics as alcohol abuse, defecating in a bathtub, having sex in public, failing school, and foul talk.
4. "The Effects of Music and the Brain," http://pionet.net/~hub7/irv.htm
5. Ibid.
6. Ibid.
7. *Chicago Tribune,* 6 October 2000.
8. "Special CCM Section—The Music Test," www.groupmag.com/articles/details.asp?ID=3591
9. Peter G. Christenson and Donald F. Roberts, *It's Not Only Rock & Roll: Popular Music in the Lives of Adolescents* (Cresskill, N.J.: Hampton, 1998).
10. Ibid.
11. "Special CCM Section—The Music Test," www.groupmag.com/articles/details.asp?ID=3591
12. Ibid.
13. CNN/USA Today/Gallup Poll, 3 May 1999.
14. Christenson and Roberts, *It's Not Only Rock & Roll.*
15. J. D. Johnson, "Differential Gender Effects of Exposure to Rap Music on African American Adolescents' Acceptance of Teen Dating Violence," *Sex Roles* (1995).
16. "Music Videos That Flirt with Violence," *CQ Researcher* (26 March 1993).
17. B. M. Waite, M. Hillbrand, H. Foster, "Reduction of Aggressive Behavior After Removal of Music Television (MTV)," *Hospital and Community Psychiatry* (1992), 43, 173–75.
18. "Music Videos That Affect Adolescents' View of Violence." (press release, Academy of Pediatrics, 1998).
19. Media Critic Steve Johnson, "The New MTV: Be Very Afraid," *Chicago Tribune,* 21 March 2001.
20. Television Viewing Study by Teenage Research Unlimited, fall 1996.
21. R. DuRant et al., "Violence and Weapon Carrying in Music Videos: A Content Analysis," *Arch Pediatric Adolescent Medicine* 151 (1997).
22. "Special CCM Section—The Music Test," www.groupmag.com/articles/details.asp?ID=3591
23. Mike Snider, "Report Finds No Break in Hollywood Violence," *USA Today* (23 September 1999).
24. Interlinc is a subscription Christian music service that is made available to youth leaders only. Each quarter a package is received that contains CDs, Bible studies based on some of the songs, and music comparison charts. For more information, call (800) 725-3300.

19

Worship and the Adolescent

Today's youth ministry is consumed with the methodology of worship. What method is the best or most likely to attract today's youth? As a result many types of worship are being employed around the country in an effort to please and retain youth. These various methods include, but are not limited to, traditional forms of worship, alternative forms of worship,[1] praise music, and even dancing. However, the methodology is not the issue. The issue is, Are we truly worshiping? This chapter will attempt to answer this question and establish what worship is and isn't based on the Word of God.

FIRST THINGS FIRST

Before we can begin this chapter we must establish exactly what it is we're talking about. The attempt here is not to formulate opinions on the various styles of worship that are taking place today. Rather our goal is an examination of what worship truly is according to Scripture. We will not engage in debates over matters of preference but will rest solely on biblical principles as our guidelines. Once this is accomplished, it is our hope that you will examine worship in your group through the lens of Scripture and make the appropriate changes.

There seems to be a general misunderstanding as to what worship is in the church today. We have a tendency to view worship as simply "that time during youth group when we sing." If the type of music is pleasing to the teens, the general consensus is one of self-declaration, "I really worshiped today." We must understand and help our youth to understand that worship is far more than a fifteen- to thirty-minute thing we do on Sunday during youth group. Worship goes far beyond this frame of reference and in reality has nothing to do with our methodology. Worship may include singing, but music is not worship in and of itself.

True biblical worship consists of far more than the methodology we employ, whether that be traditional or alternative forms of worship. This must be balanced with the fact that "the church seems increasingly outmoded and irrelevant. The tragic irony is that . . . at a time when spirituality is very much on people's agenda and part of their lives . . . they are not looking to the institutional churches or the Christian faith to meet their quest for spiritual meaning and experience."[2] With music being so important in the lives of teens, we must make an effort to be as biblically relevant as possible with the types of worship we employ while maintaining the true essence of what worship is. Hence the question "What is true worship?"

WHAT WORSHIP IS

If we are to understand the act of worship, then we must come to a consensus as to the definition of the term. If we do not achieve a common definition, then we will have nothing more than a discussion that is based on subjectivity and personal preference.

A few definitions to consider: First are the biblical meanings of the term *worship*. In the Old and New Testament the term *worship* can be conveyed through various words, each with a different emphasis, helping us to understand the entire meaning of the term. Meanings include "to bow down," "to prostrate oneself out of respect," "to serve," "praise," "adoration," and *latreuo*, meaning the worshipful serving of God in heart and by life.[3] From these various words we can draw a more complete picture of what worship is, specifically that worship is a matter of the heart and an expression or outpouring of the relationship between the believer and God. This may include private worship and/or public forms of expression.

As mentioned above, in the Word of God worship consists of many things and is not limited to one area. Aspects of worship according to Scripture are:

1. *We are called to worship God.*

"Give to the Lord the glory due His name; bring an offering, and come before Him. Oh, worship the Lord in the beauty of holiness" (1 Chron. 16:29). "Oh come, let us worship and bow down; let us kneel before the Lord our Maker" (Ps. 95:6). "Then saith Jesus unto him, Get thee hence, Satan: for it is written, Thou shalt worship the Lord thy God, and him only shalt thou serve" (Matt. 4:10 KJV). Also see Revelation 14:7; 22:9.

2. *We are to worship in spirit and truth.*

"God is a Spirit: and they that worship him must worship him in spirit and in truth" (John 4:24 KJV). Worshiping in spirit is worshiping with our whole selves; worshiping in truth is worshiping truly, based on scriptural knowledge of who God is.

3. *We are to worship with the proper attitude.*

"God is greatly to be feared in the assembly of the saints, and to be held in reverence by all those around Him" (Ps. 89:7).

4. *The main place for worship is in the house of God.*

"Surely goodness and mercy shall follow me all the days of my life; and I will dwell in the house of the Lord forever" (Ps. 23:6). "One thing have I desired of the Lord, that will I seek: that I may dwell in the house of the Lord all the days of my life, to behold the beauty of the Lord, and to inquire in His temple" (Ps. 27:4).

5. *We worship through singing praise.*

"Sing praises to the Lord, who dwells in Zion!" (Ps. 9:11). See Psalms 81:1; 95:1; Isaiah 30:29; 1 Corinthians 14:15.

6. *Our worship should be continual.*

"Therefore by Him let us continually offer the sacrifice of praise to God, that is, the fruit of our lips, giving thanks to His name" (Heb. 13:15). "My tongue shall speak of Your righteousness and of Your praise all the day long" (Ps. 35:28). Worship must be a habit of the heart, not simply condensed into a certain time frame. Youth must come to understand that worship can be done all day long and that we worship each day.

7. *We worship through declaring what God has done.*

"Declare His deeds among the people" (Ps. 9:11). "Then the shepherds returned, glorifying and praising God for all the things that they had heard and seen, as it was told them" (Luke 2:20). We are to testify of all the blessings God has bestowed on us, from answered prayer to the unexpected. Furthermore, we must share our testimony with others as a form of praise and worship, telling what God has delivered us from and where His will is taking us.

8. *We worship God through the use of musical instruments.*

"Praise the Lord with harp: sing unto him with the psaltery and an instrument of ten strings" (Ps. 33:2 KJV).

9. *We worship God through obedience to the Word of God in daily situations.*

"Whoever claims to live in him must walk as Jesus did" (1 John 2:6 NIV). The Bible has several things to say about the place of obedience in the life of the believer. First, the entire heart is required: "This day the Lord your God commands you to observe these statutes and judgments; therefore you shall be careful to observe them with all your heart and with all your soul" (Deut. 26:16). Second, the cost is given: "This Book of the Law shall not depart from your mouth, but you shall meditate in it day and night, that you may observe to do according to all that is written in it. For then you will make your way prosperous, and then you will have good success" (Josh. 1:8). Third, obedience is better than sacrifice: "So Samuel said, 'Has the Lord as great delight in burnt offerings and sacrifices, as in obeying the voice of the Lord? Behold, to obey is better than sacrifice, and to heed than the fat of rams" (1 Sam. 15:22). Fourth, it proves our love of and for God and secures us in His love; "If you keep My commandments, you will abide in My love, just as I have kept My Father's commandments and abide in His love" (John 15:10). "If you love Me, keep My commandments" (John 14:15).

10. *We worship God through spiritual markers or memorials, including the keeping of ordinances.*

Throughout the Old Testament, memorials were instituted for the remembrance of the mighty things God has done. These memorials include the Passover (Ex. 12:14), the laying up of manna (Ex. 16:32), the stones of the ephod (Ex. 28:12), the censers of incense (Num. 16:46), the twelve stones from the Jordan (Josh. 4:5–7), Joshua's stone memorial (Josh. 24:27), and the Jewish holiday of Purim (Est. 9:26–32). In the church today, obedience is required through the participation of the ordinances. Baptism is observed as obedience to God: "Go ye therefore, and teach all nations, baptizing them in the name of the Father, and of the Son, and of the Holy Ghost" (Matt. 28:19 KJV). And so is communion, "This is My body which is given for you; do this in remembrance of Me" (Luke 22:19). These memorials, like the Old Testament ones, were also instituted for remembrance of the mighty things God has done. Likewise today, youth can benefit from other spiritual markers: things as simple as the journaling of Bible reading, prayer requests, and blessings. These will serve as a source of the things God has done in their lives and an inspiration for praise and worship.

11. *We worship God through prayer, adoration, confession, thanksgiving, and supplications.*

"Rejoice always, pray without ceasing, in everything give thanks; for this is the will of God in Christ Jesus for you" (1 Thess. 5:16–18). You will need to allow time for this in your program, whether that be times and days of prayer or specific and general requests taken during a youth class. If youth pray together and for each other's needs, they will form a bond, and a cord of unity will be established.

12. *We worship God through the use of our spiritual gifts.*

"And He Himself gave some to be apostles, some prophets, some evangelists, and some pastors and teachers, for the equipping of the saints for the work of ministry, for the edifying of the body of Christ" (Eph. 4:11–12). "And to one he gave five talents, to another two, and to another one, to each according to his own ability; and immediately he went on a journey" (Matt. 25:15).

13. *We worship God through the reading, studying, and teaching of the Word.*

"Therefore with joy you will draw water from the wells of salvation. And in that day you will say: 'Praise the Lord, call upon His name; declare His deeds among the peoples, make mention that His name is exalted. Sing to the Lord, for He has done excellent things; this is known in all the earth. Cry out and shout, O inhabitant of Zion, for great is the Holy One of Israel in your midst!'" (Isa. 12:3–6).

In addition to the above, the apostle Paul reminds us as to what true worship consists of: "Present your bodies a living sacrifice, holy, acceptable to God, which is your reasonable service" (Rom. 12:1). Notice here that the apostle Paul clearly states that we have a responsibility to worship God in the spiritual realm, not just through physical expression. As seen above, our worship is carried out through physical means. However, here Paul reminds us of what true spiritual worship is. The simple truth is that anyone can go through the physical movements of worship. That doesn't mean that the person is worshiping. To worship God according to this passage is to present oneself as a "living sacrifice." An oxymoron? By definition, sacrifices are dead. How can one be a living sacrifice? Believers are to submit to the will of God in our lives. A sacrifice has no rights of its own, only the will of the Father. As living sacrifices, we are to live holy and pleasing lives unto God. Some of these attributes of how one lives a holy and pleasing life are mentioned above.

Worship must be considered to be much more than the methodology we incorporate with the youth. It must go deeper, representing a heart that is full of the blessings and grace of God. Thus worship becomes the expression of gratitude in the life of the believing teen.

What Worship Isn't

Now that we have established what biblical worship is, let's look at what worship isn't.

1. *Worship is not used to increase numbers.*

Worship cannot be seen as something that we do to increase the attendance in our youth group. Worship needs to be relevant (discussed in the next section); however, "big numbers" cannot be our only motivation in seeking relevant methods for today's youth. How can the unsaved teen worship God when he is spiritually dead?

2. *Worship is not separate from obedience.*

The two go hand in hand. How can we or our teens worship the one true God apart from obedience? As we read through the points above, we must conclude that worship is a direct result of God working in our lives, whether that be salvation or victory over sin as we strive to conform to the image of Christ. Obedience enhances our worship, and the Holy Spirit working in our lives enhances our obedience.

3. *Worship should not be done with an improper attitude.*

This speaks directly to motivation: motivation not only of the leader of worship within the group but also of the worshiper. As seen above our attitude must be one of humility and gratitude as we enter into the presence of our God. God is not our buddy but the Creator and bestower of all things. Our motivation must be to worship, to bow down, before God—nothing else.

So What Do We Do?

Good question! Some would suggest that we establish worship that is "engaging." However an examination of this term raises more questions than it answers. According to Webster's New World Dictionary, to engage means to "involve or occupy" or has the idea of "meshing" things together. Worship is not something to "occupy" or simply "involve" our teens with; it is far more. We must thus incorporate worship that is "authentic," based on our standard (the Word of God), our history (as a body of believers), and our culture (the various methods we must employ). Authentic worship can be achieved in our teens through the following ways. (This list is by no means exhaustive; it appears here as a starting point for incorporation in your ministry.)

1. *Teach what authentic worship is, based on the Word of God.*

The points listed in the section "What Worship Is" are a good starting point. You will have to take the lead concerning this topic. Spend time talking, teaching, and incorporating biblical truth on this subject. Use this as an opportunity to instruct your teens as to the nature and attitude of worship.

2. *Understand the history of worship in the church.*

This will enable you to understand how the methodology of worship has changed since the inception of the church and to not degrade those who find meaning in a style of worship that is not your or your teens' preference. Don't fight over preference.

3. *Make it relevant to the culture of your church and your teen community.*

The methodology or methodologies that you employ must be relevant to today's culture. Worship styles have changed with the times, from chants to use of harpsichords to hymns and electric guitars. We are not contradicting what has been already established, for spiritual worship has everything to do with the heart of the worshiper, not the methodology. However, if your teen culture is on the "cutting edge," then your style(s) of worship must incorporate these aspects. This is not done to increase numbers but rather to speak to teens where they are. Have you ever wondered why the classical hymns don't have relevance to teens today? It's not the current culture. We must have balance; just because you have drums and a praise band doesn't mean that authentic worship is taking place. The worshipers' hearts must be involved, for when the hearts are involved the methodology is insignificant.

It is of the utmost importance that all three of the above are used in formulating authentic worship within your group. For if we teach biblical standards of worship with no methodology, then we produce "smart" youth with no substance. If we study the history of the church without Scripture, then we've completed an ancient history lesson. And employing current methodology without proper biblical standards and understanding produces teens who are simply going through the motions. None of these imbalances will result in authentic worship.

CONCLUSION

Worship must be authentic and real in the life of teens. We must help teens come to a biblical understanding of what worship is, all the while teaching them in different expressions of worship. We must strive to discover methods that will resonate with our teens. The heart and the method must come together in an illustration of our goal. We must stop fighting over expressions of worship that we disagree with and rest on the Word of God as our standard.

NOTES

1. In Jonny Baker's work *Alternative Worship and the Significance of Popular Culture,* (www.freshworship.org/zine/altworshipandmodernculture.html; accessed April 2000), he states the following: "Alternative worship is much more than a cosmetic change to the style of church. It really has a different plausibility structure with its own authenticity. . . . One way in which alternative worship is deemed to be authentic is if it resonates with the curators of the worship and with the culture outside the church." This is key in understanding and applying various forms of worship, that it resonates with the culture. What we see today is worship styles that resonated with the popular culture decades ago, thus possessing no relevance with today's youth.
2. Baker, *Alternative Worship and the Significance of Popular Culture.*
3. Lawrence Richards, *Expository Dictionary of Bible Words* (Grand Rapids: Zondervan, 1985).

The Foundation of Counseling Young People

INTRODUCTION TO YOUTH COUNSELING

Counseling has become one of the greatest ministries in the church because our society has spawned a pandemic amount of social problems and behavior. Counseling has grown in importance and will continue to grow.[1] As we discuss counseling, we are writing from the perspective of lay counseling. This is in no way to minimize the importance of professional counseling, but the conscientious youth worker who desires to remain on the cutting edge of ministerial effectiveness must, at the very minimum, get some training in this important area.

Our society's ills have made professional counseling a significant and worthwhile vocation. Yet if the church is to continue to meet the needs of its young people, counseling must include the conventional wisdom and experience of an expanded circle of laity and not rely solely on professionals. Youth workers will perform a considerable amount of counseling and must see it as a ministerial responsibility. Church teaching is effective when it is meeting needs and solving problems. Since the ministry of counseling is helping people solve their problems and meet their needs, one can see why counseling has become a great ministry in the church.

In fact, counseling has become prominent in our society. As proof, a majority of high schools in North America employ a full-time counselor. For the most part, they have influenced teenagers toward positive and attainable educational and vocational goals, along with encouraging them to make good decisions about substance abuse and promiscuous sexual behavior. As one glances through any phone book or uses an Internet search engine, results will reveal marriage counselors, investment counselors, guidance counselors, psychiatrists, psychologists, psychiatric social workers, welfare counselors, etc. Why not the church? The church has been counseling and meeting needs since its inception. Recent developments and trends of guidance and counseling have made the church take stock of its basic ministry to individuals. As our society has organized and refined its techniques of counseling, so must the church.

Our basic approach to counseling is biblically centered. There are no new discoveries pertaining to the field of counseling. The Word of God must be applied to modern counseling techniques.

> Someone has counted more than two hundred and fifty approaches to counseling. Each of these schools of thought claims to be successful in understanding human problems. All have developed a model of how people are supposed to function, what goes wrong, and how to intervene when problems become unmanageable.

> The influence of these varied theories on Christian counseling has created a debate in the church. People are divided over whether we need more than the Bible, prayer, and faith in Christ to deal with our problems. Many disagree about the meaning of "the sufficiency of Christ." Do His provisions and mercies include medication, support groups, and an understanding of family history, temperaments, and deeply buried motives?
>
> What we do know is that wise people look for help when facing the problems of life. The book of Proverbs encourages us to look for good counselors, while being just as careful to avoid the bad ones. Proverbs 11:14 says, "Where there is no counsel, the people fall; but in the multitude of counselors there is safety." Proverbs 12:15 says, "The way of a fool is right in his own eyes, but he who heeds counsel is wise." And Proverbs 20:5 adds, "Counsel [purposes, motives, and plans] in the heart of man is like deep water, but a man of understanding will draw it out."
>
> Proverbs also makes it clear that good counsel can come from many sources, some as close as a friend. Proverbs 27:9 says, "Ointment and perfume delight the heart, and the sweetness of a man's friend gives delight by hearty counsel."[2]

What is also true, however, is that counsel can be as dangerous as it is helpful. Psalm 1:1 says, "Blessed is the man who walks not in the counsel of the ungodly." There have always been counselors who have told people what they wanted to hear rather than what they needed to hear.

Where the latest techniques of counseling are in opposition to the Word of God, the techniques must be sacrificed. Where the Word of God is silent, principles governed by reason are applied in harmony with the principles of God's Word.

When a Bible-centered approach to counseling has been used, the extremes of a strict Freudian approach to counseling will be avoided. The opposite extreme of mere "advice giving" has also been avoided. We will call this biblically based approach the inductive approach to counseling.

As stated, this section is geared toward the lay youth counselor. Thus the question becomes, When and from whom should young people seek counseling? "From childhood through late adulthood, there are certain times when we may need help addressing problems and issues that cause us emotional distress or make us feel overwhelmed. When you are experiencing these types of difficulties, you may benefit from the assistance of an experienced, trained professional. Professional counselors offer the caring, expert assistance that we often need during these stressful times. A counselor can help you identify your problems and assist you in finding the best ways to cope with the situation by changing behaviors that contribute to the problem or by finding constructive ways to deal with a situation that is beyond your personal control. Professional counselors offer help in addressing many situations that cause emotional stress, including, but not limited to:

- anxiety, depression, and other mental and emotional problems and disorders
- family and relationship issues
- substance abuse and other addictions
- sexual abuse and domestic violence
- eating disorders
- career change and job stress
- social and emotional difficulties related to disability and illness
- adapting to life transitions
- the death of a loved one
- uncontrollable spending"[3]

Dr. Gail Robinson, past president of the American Counseling Association, offers a more succinct reason why people should seek counseling: "Good indicators of when you should seek counseling are when you're having difficulties at work, your ability to concentrate is diminished or when your level of pain becomes uncomfortable." Dr. Gail Robinson adds, "However, you don't want to wait until the pain becomes unbearable or you're at the end of your rope."[4]

Yet many Sunday school teachers, youth sponsors, camp counselors, and parents counsel teenagers. Many of them are doing an acceptable job. However, if given better techniques, they can do a more effective job. The aim of this section is to produce a Bible-centered concept of counseling that will give skills, understandings, and techniques to lay workers in the church so that they may help average teenagers solve average problems.

Who Can Counsel?

The Christian church exists partly to help individuals. We should take advantage of every opportunity to minister to teens. The entire organization of the twenty-first-century church—the physical plant, nurseries, classrooms, technology, music program, and well-trained ministers—exists for the purpose of ministry. Those who work in the church as Sunday school teachers, youth workers, directors of Christian education, and parents can give help to the teenagers in this area. Many people who need help, including the teenager, turn very naturally to the church. The already overworked pastor cannot meet every demand that comes to him. Many in the church have the potential of being counselors.

The ministry of counseling is open to any Christian in the church. One of the tests that you should ask yourself before beginning counseling is, "How constructive is my counseling?" If God has used you to help other people, you can be a counselor. Counseling does not necessarily take a great amount of knowledge about techniques. Perhaps you have the gift of counseling and the principles presented in this section will help you become a more effective counselor. If you can help yourself spiritually, you can help others. Helping yourself may be simply analyzing problems in your life and finding solutions. A primary criterion for being an effective counselor is personal adjustment to the will of God.

What Is Counseling?

Counseling is not limited to professional full-time workers. Mature adults in the local church can help young people face and solve their problems. The dictionary defines the word *counsel* as "opinion, advice, direction, instruction, or recommendation given especially as a result of consultation." Counseling, then, is guiding a person to a better understanding of his potentialities and problems. One teacher has defined counseling as "the use of techniques to help a person solve a conflict or better his life adjustment." There is a technical sense in which counseling is given by the person professionally trained to give therapy. But the definition of this section centers around helping average young people with average problems. Most of the problems facing teenagers can be solved with help from the counselors already ministering in their church. When those problems become more complex and consequential, referral to those in the profession will then become a critical part of the counseling solution (the issue of whether the counselor is a Christian should be addressed).

In addition, "counseling services can be effective in helping children improve behavioral self-control (decrease tantrums and defiant behaviors), improve self-confidence and self-image, decrease depression and increase happiness, and improve parent-child and peer relationships."[5]

What, then, is counseling? Simply stated, it is helping another person analyze and solve his problems. Counseling is nothing new. As a science (in which laws, principles, and techniques are studied and presented), counseling may be a relatively new field. But as an art, counseling is an ancient practice. Whenever a father has helped his son with a personal problem, counseling has taken place. Whenever a teacher has helped a novice learn a skill, there has been counseling.

COMMON ATTITUDES TOWARD COUNSELING

You will meet many kinds of people in your counseling ministry. First are those teenagers, like the ostrich with its head in the sand, who deny that they have problems, yet their lives are unhappy and unproductive for God. These young people are basically unsatisfied and their lives are purposeless. Even though these young people do not enjoy a life of happiness, they refuse to admit they have a problem.

Also in your counseling ministry you will meet young people who realize they have problems. Some of these people take the "fire escape route." They seek to run from their problems without really facing them. However, running from a problem never solves it. If a young person runs from his problem, eventually he will find that the problem has increased in proportions. Each time we meet the same unsolved problem it has a sinister face. It is truly childish to run from problems (even though we do not belittle young people for being childish). The mature approach is to face the problem, learn from the experience, and make a satisfactory adjustment.

One thing that complicates this is that a teenager is still under the authority of parents. What if the parent is a big part of the problem? How does a counselor back up parental authority in this or other instances? Generally speaking, the wise counselor should "err" by "siding" with parents. He should never encourage a teenager to go against his/her parents, unless it is something that is illegal or immoral or physically harmful. If it is illegal or immoral or physically harmful, the counselor must gather all the facts, which may include face-to-face confrontation with the parents.

Other teenagers who have problems won't seek a solution. These young people follow the "grin and bear it" route. Many young people today feel that they are doing God a service by disciplining themselves and becoming martyrs. These young people feel that if they are living a happy, satisfied, well-adjusted life, something is wrong. This may be called "spiritual fatalism." There is no merit in living a miserable life. Christians are told to rejoice and live happy and contented lives. "You will show me the path of life; in Your presence is fullness of joy; at Your right hand are pleasures forevermore" (Ps. 16:11). "I have come that they may have life, and that they might have it more abundantly" (John 10:10).

Then there are Christian teenagers who feel that they can go directly to the Lord and the Bible to solve their own problems. The impression is given that youth counselors are unnecessary. It is true that God speaks through prayer and the Word of God. However, the Bible also tells us that we should go to others for counsel. "Where there is no counsel, the people fall; but in the multitude of counselors there is safety" (Prov. 11:14). Christ exercised the office of Counselor. The Scriptures are adequate, but they need interpretation. The blind reading of the Scriptures without understanding will not bring satisfaction, nor will it solve a problem. Sometimes the ministry of a youth counselor is to get the teenager to understand the problem and then lead him into a correct understanding of the Word of God.

FOUNDATION STONES OF COUNSELING

The general aims of counseling are as broad as the aims of the Christian church. These goals are (1) to bring teenagers to know Christ and the fellowship of the Christian church; (2) to help them acknowledge and repent of sin and to accept God's freely offered salvation in Jesus Christ; (3) to help them live a victorious Christian life; (4) to lead them to serve Christ. Through counseling you can help Christian teenagers live in faith and confidence instead of doubt and anxiety, in peace instead of discord.

In another sense, however, counseling has specific purposes. Counseling consists of many implicit and self-contained goals. These short-term goals are like the rungs on a ladder that, when taken in order, will lead to the general aims of the Word of God. Broadly speaking, counseling is the attempt of the counselor to help teenagers help themselves through gaining an understanding of their inner conflicts. You must help the teenager see himself as he really is—as God sees him. Sometimes counseling is referred to as emotional reeducation. The book *Handbook on Counseling Youth* identifies the three objects of youth counseling as spiritual wholeness, emotional wholeness, and relational wholeness.[6]

> Often normal adolescent development brings about restlessness, conflict, personality or behavioral change. This often produces greater family turmoil and upset. Effective counseling provides support for the young person as he/she experiences growth and resolves internal and interpersonal conflicts. Counseling can also help make this transition less stressful for the entire family through bringing about more positive interactions.[7]

In addition to counseling's helping the youth with an immediate problem, counseling should enable them to help themselves with other problems. As a youth counselor you will have to guard against being blinded by the immediate situation and losing sight of the future. For if the method of solving the problem will not at the same time prepare the youth to face the future and the next problem, you may have left him no farther along on life's road than where you found him.

There are four key considerations to Christian counseling.

Counseling Is a Ministry to the Individual

The Lord had genuine compassion for the needs of people. Many such incidents are recorded in the Gospels, including

Jesus' concern for Nicodemus, the Samaritan woman, the woman with the issue of blood, and Peter. The Lord was vitally concerned with the needs of each of these counselees. Much is said concerning the preaching and teaching ministry of the Lord. However, His greatest sermons were preached to individuals. These sermons were communicated in counseling situations in which the Lord led the person to whom He was talking to a better understanding of God the Father in heaven and his relationship to Him.

Counseling is a ministry of meeting needs. When you regard ministering in terms of meeting needs, you readily see how it applies to the counseling situation. Essentially, a counselee comes to you because there is a need in his life. So when we think of counseling, we must think in terms of meeting individual needs.

Counseling Is a Relationship Between Two People

The teenager who has a problem and is seeking help is the counselee. The one to whom he goes for help is the counselor. The counselee comes to the counselor and together they seek for the answer. This is the counseling situation. The counselee must have confidence in the counselor to receive help. The youth counselor must be thoroughly interested in the counselee and make him aware that he will do all he can to be of help. From this mutual interest arises a mutual relationship between the two. This relationship has often developed into lifelong friendship.

Counseling Is a Process of Education

Counseling is, in every sense of the word, education.

Christian education is the process of transmitting the truth of God to teens in such a way as to bring wholehearted response and obedience to the nature and will of God. The aims of Christian education are like the aims of counseling. They consist of bringing students to Christ, bringing them up in Christ, and sending them forth in Christ. Maturity is the goal of both education and counseling.

Christian teaching is guiding students to solve life problems. Counseling is guiding young people's experience through questioning, dialogue, and presenting the Word of God. This kind of teaching and counseling demands a counselor who is an example of the Christian life and a mature leader. He should use many techniques such as telling, showing, questioning, helping students to discuss, exploring, research, etc., in order to provide opportunities for teenagers to live out God's Word. Christian teaching is successful only when constructive change has taken place in students' lives. In the same way counseling is successful only as it meets needs and changes the lives of teenagers. This change may be internal, with a long-range plan of action. The change may be external and result in immediate adjustment. Christian teaching must be structured according to the problem-solving process. In the same way effective counseling is structured toward solving the problems of teenagers. As teenagers gain insights and solve their own problems, they mature in life. Using words that are unknown to the young person must be avoided both in the teaching and counseling situation.

The Word of God is a living Book that was written for people, including young people, who want to live. Teenagers must have an opportunity in teaching and counseling to see living truth and to make that truth an inner conviction. Christian teaching begins where the students are—mentally, culturally, socially, emotionally, and spiritually—and takes them where they should be. Christian counseling has the same purpose and goal. Teenagers will develop as they see the relationship between the directives of God, their current need, and their environment. This relationship must constantly reflect emphases consistent with the whole Word of God. Therefore, you must continually evaluate the students' current stage of development.

Christian teaching and counseling are based on experience.

This experience is Bible-based, life-related, and Christ-centered. All learning, whether in the classroom or counseling session, takes place through experience. Experience is necessary in order to confirm the truth of God's Word and provide contemporary interpretation to life's problems. True Christian experience involves both scriptural content and living responsibility. Christian experience is unique in that the Holy Spirit works upon and within the teenager to illumine the written Word of God. Scriptural authority sets standards and provides divine power that makes genuine discipleship and discipline possible for teens. Through personal experience teachers and counselors help their students form adequate concepts of life, adjustment, and maturity. Young people who have developed a scriptural concept of life can live to the glory of God.

Counseling Involves Interaction

Knowledge, facts, and understanding cannot be passed from mind to mind like apples from one basket to another. They must in every case be recognized, rethought, and assimilated by the receiving mind. It may be unfortunate, but is nevertheless true, that a teenager may listen to a lecture from an adult without "hearing" anything. Picture the youth listening to his parent. He is looking at the ground and digging in his pockets. Is he learning? Has the parent communicated? Is the teen listening? Does meaning pass from one to another? To do so, what must be present? The answer is interaction. Interaction is activity and response on the part of the youth counselor and the teen. The teenager must reproduce (in his own mind) the truth to be learned, then express it in his own words. Counseling, then, is not giving something to a listless, inactive student; it is exciting the teenager to definite, purposeful self-activity. Thus, the true counseling situation must be a reciprocal action called interaction. Interaction in counseling is absolutely necessary if any help is to be given.

VARIOUS TYPES OF COUNSELING

There are many types of counseling. The youth leader should not be content to use only one medium in dealing with teens. He must be acquainted with these various approaches to counseling if he is to adequately meet the needs of his youth.

PREVENTIVE VERSUS REHABILITATIVE COUNSELING

Counseling can take place before or after the problem arises. If the counselor knows that the young person is facing a problem, it is his responsibility to seek out the young person, counsel with him, show him principles from the Word of God, and attempt to lead him to adjustment before the problem actually arises. A good counselor will detect danger signals from dating and social relationships. Watch for the loner in a crowd who has been socially isolated by the dominant peer group because of self-inflicted or socially unacceptable behavior. There are times when the problem has happened and only a cure can help. It is best to prevent but better to cure than to give no help at all. The adage "It is cheaper to build a fence at the top of the cliff than a hospital at the bottom" is certainly true here. As youth workers, we need to be ready for both scenarios.

FORMAL VERSUS INFORMAL COUNSELING

Formal counseling takes place when a youth counselor has scheduled office hours for counseling and does it by appointment. Usually the counselee initiates the session and asks for the appointment. This type of counselor needs to be careful about being too formal. Sometimes the desk itself becomes a barrier to effective communication. The position of the counselor on one side of the desk and the youth on the other side is a disadvantage. Sometimes the most effective counseling is done not in the office but on the athletic field, by a lake, or on a bus seat during a long road trip.

The formal situation can help in many situations, but it has its barriers. Informal counseling includes nonscheduled conversations that go on at the fast-food restaurant, in the park, or on the ride home after a youth activity. This is sometimes called casual counseling. The barriers are down. A question is approached, and you are asked for an opinion. Many times the question is not the deep problem but only a surface question. The counselor must take advantage of this situation and determine what answer is to be given. A wise youth counselor will make an informal situation lead into a friendship and perhaps into a future time of counseling the teenager.

Single Interview Versus a Series of Interviews

In the single interview the young person may drop in and ask you about some help on the young people's program. The teenager may ask you to help him decide an answer to a problem that is facing him. The counselor should look at single interview sessions with real anticipation and realize he is there to help the teenager all he can. In a series of counseling sessions the youth counselor should realize that as the teenager returns, the youth is being educated. Perhaps the teenager needs to be helped gradually. As the young person's capacity grows, he can be fed more, until he comes to a time of complete adjustment. Generally, counseling sessions with teenagers are few in number since teens are, for the most part, quick to make adjustments. Their resilience keeps them from becoming long-term and frequent counselees.

Personal Versus Group Counseling

The kind of counseling discussed in these chapters is primarily personal counseling. The ministry of the public speaker with the group has been emphasized throughout the years. The Christian counselor should work closely with youth leadership committees and their youth activities. When the youth leader solves problems on the group level, he is counseling. The obvious advantage is that he is dealing with a whole group instead of a number of individuals, saving a massive amount of time and energy. However, there are many disadvantages. Interaction is poor. The young person will not confide in the leader in a group situation. In group counseling, problems are solved but there is little personalized help. Preaching and teaching may be forms of group counseling. This is especially true when the session is structured in a problem-solving approach.

In group counseling you should have the same goal as you would in individual counseling—to help individuals face and solve their problems. Also under the category of group counseling you may have a family conference when you deal with a family problem. Premarital counseling falls under this title.

Face-to-Face Counseling Versus Distance Counseling

Face-to-face counseling is the best type. You are dealing with an individual young person. There is no danger of warping or misrepresenting the truth. Genuine communication is possible and can be experienced both by the counselor and the counselee so that clear understanding will result.

Distance counseling is sometimes the only route. Correspondence is helpful, but it can be only relative. In writing, don't make bold statements. Be careful of trying to diagnose too much through letters and e-mail. Do that counseling that has to be done through correspondence, but keep it limited. Counseling by telephone can be used, but only when time, proximity, and convenience are significant and limiting factors.

CONCLUSION

We can conclude that counseling is an important ministry. As defined in this chapter, counseling is not the professional approach of the psychiatrist or psychologist. Church youth counseling does not have as its aim special therapy. Counseling is helping average young people with average problems.

Many leaders in the church have been counseling teenagers. If they are given some technical help, these youth counselors can do a more effective job. Counseling is a ministry and as such it meets needs. Counseling is much like teaching. Teenagers are guided toward solutions to their problems. Counseling is a relationship of interaction in which both counselor and counselee seek the solution from the Word of God.

NOTES

1. Check the latest issue of *Christian Counseling Today* magazine and count the number of Christian colleges, universities, and graduate schools that are advertising some type of counseling degree or certificate.
2. Tim Jackson, *When Help Is Needed: A Biblical View of Counseling,* Discovery Series (Grand Rapids: Radio Bible Class, 1993), 3.
3. http://navigation.helper.realnames.com/framer/1/0/default.asp?realname=American+Counseling+Association&url=http%3A%2F%2Fwww%2Ecounseling%2Eorg%2F&frameid=1&providerid=0&uid=30214325 (accessed 10 October 2001).
4. Ibid.
5. http://www.nire.org/chilco64.htm (accessed 10 October 2001).
6. Josh McDowell and Bob Hostetler, *Josh McDowell's Handbook on Counseling Youth* (Dallas: Word, 1996), 12.
7. http://www.powerscounseling.com/html/adolescent.html (accessed 10 October 2001).

Principles of Counseling Young People

Someone has said, "Find me two people and I will show you two different philosophies of life." This statement has more truth than meets the eye. Because of different environments and people's choices and beliefs, everyone views life differently. So is the case in counseling. There are many philosophies of counseling. If you were to view two counseling situations, you would perhaps notice different techniques being used. In one session you could find a permissive atmosphere of interaction with freedom of expression by the teenager. The next session might resemble a lecture. The teenager is being told what he must do. Both approaches may be effective. Different philosophies of counseling dictate different techniques of counseling. The use of the question may be a technique of producing motivation in one session, while the question in the next session may be a diagnostic instrument.

NONDIRECTIVE COUNSELING

The nondirective counselor believes that the pupil has within himself resources for solving his own problems. He believes that through counseling he can help the teenager remove the emotional blocks that prevent him from solving his own problem. The counselor also affirms that since the teenager has such a strong drive to become well adjusted in every area of life, he will strive to become independent and to accomplish for himself the changes that are necessary to achieve full maturity. Carl Rogers has set out the nondirective form of counseling in characteristic steps. They are as follows:

1. The individual comes for help.
2. The helping situation is usually defined.
3. The counselor encourages free expression of feelings in regard to the problem.
4. The counselor accepts, recognizes, and clarifies these negative feelings.
5. When the individual's negative feelings have been quite fully expressed, they are followed by the faint and tentative expressions of the positive impulses that make for growth.
6. The counselor accepts and recognizes the positive feelings that are expressed in the same manner in which he has accepted and recognized the negative feelings.
7. This insight, this understanding of the self and acceptance of the self, is the next important aspect of the whole process.

8. Intermingled in this process of insight (there is no rigid order) is a process of clarification of possible decisions, possible courses of action.
9. Then comes the initiation of minute, but highly significant, positive actions.
10. There is a development of further insight and more complete and accurate self-understanding as the individual gains courage to see more deeply into his own actions.
11. There is increasingly integrated positive action on the part of the client.
12. There is a feeling of decreasing need for help and a recognition on the part of the client that the relationship must end.[1]

This philosophy of counseling is called the "Talk Therapy" method of counseling. Therefore, the teenager is not only permitted but also encouraged to focus attention on the issues that are important to him. There is no direction given by the counselor. The teenager is permitted to talk at will about what is interesting to him. The conversation jumps from sports, to school, to social activities of the church. Many times at the end of such a counseling session the counselor may feel that nothing has been accomplished, yet at the same time the teenager may have been helped a great deal.

When a student seeks the nondirective counselor's help, he soon discovers that the counselor will accept him for what he is and will believe in his ability to solve his problems in his own way. The teenager believes by previous experience that counselors are ones to "give advice." He now finds that he is talking with a person who is trying to understand him, trying to follow what he is saying and feeling, trying to help him understand himself. He finds that this counselor neither gives advice nor attempts to manipulate him into making a decision that the counselor believes is best. Many times the teenager will restate or attempt to clarify something that the counselor does not understand. The teenager can make a contradictory or inconsistent statement without being challenged. He also may reveal something of a terrible nature without the counselor's being shocked. The teenager should feel that the counselor understands why he sees things differently at different times.

There are times when the teenager may become aggressive and want to attack the counselor verbally. He tells the counselor what he thinks of life, the church, and the youth volunteers. In return he does not receive a scolding, but the counselor accepts these aggressive feelings and helps the student express them. If the teenager is truthful in admissions of feelings of aggression, the counselor can expect the teenager to be truthful in other admissions. When the young person finds expression difficult, the counselor helps him tell why he is finding it difficult.

Some of the questions that the counselor might use are: "Is this what you are trying to say?" "Am I following you?" "Do you feel this?" or "Is this what you mean?" These types of responses by the counselor will help to pull the answer out of the teenager. A good response may be, "Then you are bothered over what your parents think about you?" or "You are wondering whether you have what it takes to go to a Christian or secular university?" or "You would very much like to know how those in your youth group feel about you?" In assisting the student to express his feelings, the counselor helps the pupil realize that he may discuss whatever bothers him.

The nondirective counselor gives full attention to the counselee during such a session. He puts aside all his own needs and enters into the world of the student. Indeed, he tries to be "another self." Only then can he comprehend the teenage view of life and the problems that the teen faces. As a result he does not give advice or force information on the pupil.

The nondirective counselor's task is to free the student from emotional blocks or inhibitions that impede his use of his own potentialities. By creating a situation in which there are no tensions, the counselor helps to build maturity in the teenager. The teenager approaches maturity as he unfolds his own life, seeks his own problem, finds his own way to the Lord, and ultimately stands on his own two spiritual feet. Hence his growth is accelerated toward adulthood. Occasionally the teenager wants advice and resents not getting it. At such times he may feel that he is alone with his problem just when he wants someone to lean upon. There are times in which the teenager should feel that there is someone on whom to lean (which is the biblical idea: that the older teach the younger). At this time the counselor will want to take a directive approach. More will be said about this in subsequent paragraphs. On these occasions the counselor and the teenager should talk about the facts on which the student wants advice, why he wants the advice, and the effect that giving advice may have on him.

DIRECTIVE COUNSELING

In directive counseling relationships, the counselor has a much larger emphasis. Emphasis is given to the diagnosis of the problem, questioning whether the student has within himself the power first of all. Whereas the nondirective counselor is primarily interested in helping the teenager learn to cope with himself, the directive counselor appears to be primarily interested in helping the pupil solve the immediate problem. The directive counselor is also interested in helping the pupil achieve a better overall adjustment. This adjustment is made by solving problems one at a time. Large problems must be broken down into small segments.

In seeking answers, the counselor relates the problem back to the young person's background and experience. This solution is then discussed with the teenager. As he finds an answer, it is applied, and as a result the youth is helped. The directive counselor believes that the persistent unsolved problems account for the student's present behavior. As a student solves immediate problems, he will gradually acquire better adjustment. Also, it is believed that the student's satisfaction that comes from solving the immediate problem will increase the teenager's confidence in himself and in his counselor. As this confidence grows, the teenager will attack his less obvious problems with increasing success to see and then to solve his problems. Information is given to the teenager only when it is meaningful to him and he realizes that he needs it. The Word of God is used as a direction sign pointing young people to the true answer.

It is at these times that we cannot become overconscientious as to the feelings of the teenager. The counselor must speak, determine the direction, and cause the teenager to surrender and accept the will of God. Directive counselors believe that counselors may give advice. They also feel that it is their duty to question the student's inappropriate decisions and to take the initiative in helping him re-examine the implications involved in questionable choices. Nevertheless, it should be noticed that the student should select the alternatives. This is done with the counselor's help.

Before the interview the directive counselor studies the story of the counselee's life and pertinent details. He reviews counseling notes and looks for possible solutions to the problem that the student faces at the moment. The better he knows the student, the more helpful he can be in interpreting for the student the forces that are creating his problem. Before the counseling situation the counselor plans ways to help the teenager see the relationship between his immediate problem and any other problem that the counselor may have discovered. At the beginning of the interview the counselee and the counselor get acquainted. The directive counselor may discuss a variety of topics. Sometimes this counselor does not begin by talking about the problem at all. The student is made to enjoy this interview. Sometimes the counselee doubts if all of the "small talk" is helping him. Nevertheless, the teenager will find that the counselor is usually very friendly. He has confidence that the counselor must know much about people and how to help him solve his problem.

During this counseling situation the counselor asks questions to bring out points that the student usually forgets to mention. Nothing can be overlooked. The counselor must secure the complete picture before he can provide his best help. The teenager usually realizes that he must be cooperative and does not have much difficulty accepting this fact. The young person must provide the counselor with all of the information that the counselor requests. The counselor usually asks questions concerning his happiest moments of life and his feelings of rebellion toward God; the awkward moments in the youth group; questions concerning his home, members of his family, and how he feels about his friends; the things he likes, the things he does not like; and how he stands with God at the present. This conversation usually runs along so smoothly at times the pupil hardly realizes that he is answering very personal questions. When the teenager has gained confidence in the counselor's ability and discretion, he does not worry about providing the counselor with the information requested. Usually the counselor does the worrying for the teenager. Usually the young person feels good about knowing his counselor is making it possible to know himself better, and the counselor is going to do his best in preventing him from making any other mistakes, while being under his counseling care.

Eventually, however, the teenager must make some decisions. If he cannot identify any acceptable alternatives, he can always count on the counselor to identify the solution to his problem. Though the counselor believes that the student should make the decision, he also feels that it is appropriate for him to supply the information that the two of them need for defining alternative solutions. If the teenager chooses an alternative with which the counselor disagrees and one he believes to be an unwise decision, the counselor raises questions to cause the pupil to reevaluate the choice.

Most directive counselors take very complete notes either at the time of the interview or immediately after the interview. The counselor who does not take notes during the interview usually believes that the note-taking may interfere with the building and maintaining of good rapport, and thus he prefers to run the risk of losing pertinent facts. Because the directive counselor assumes the responsibility for diagnosis, he must create a friendly climate in which the pupil will tell his own story and reveal his own feelings and those values that he most cherishes in life. The release of the student's feelings is very important. The nondirective counselor tries to help the student clarify his feelings by expressing them. The directive counselor tries to free the student of emotional tensions so the student can attack his problem from his own point of view.

INDUCTIVE COUNSELING

Inductive counseling is taken from the phrase "inductive Bible study," where the Bible is approached objectively to allow its message to speak for itself. Inductive Bible study applies the scientific method of inquiry, which is also called inductive logic, to the Word of God. Since the Bible has the answer to life, the Scripture must be applied objectively to the problem. Inductive counseling applies the same methodology to the teenager. The counselor applies inductive reason to determine the problem, as it exists, not as his prejudice directs.

Inductive counselors select the best technique from both the directive and nondirective methods of counseling. Some tend to be nondirective, but others tend to be directive, depending on their basic attitude toward pupils and the amount of responsibility that they assume. Since we have already considered the relationship of nondirective and directive counselors, we will not repeat them in discussing the relationships of the inductive counselor; instead we shall consider only the unique features of inductive counseling.

One point of view held by the inductive counselor is that while he can choose his techniques from both nondirective and directive counseling, he cannot adapt his techniques to the particular pupil and his problem because his basic value and especially his attitude toward his pupils will determine the way in which he works with them. The inductive counselor believes that he should select the appropriate technique on the basis of the student's needs and problems. He believes that it is inappropriate to make certain diagnostic judgments beforehand.

Some inductive counselors function in a nondirective capacity while they are classifying a student's problem and then function as a directive counselor in the solution of the student's problem. The inductive counselor has a goal and a solution. However, it is not his desire to force this solution on the teenager but to cause the teenager to see the solution for himself. It is the attempt of the inductive counselor to introduce into the life and thinking of the teenager the facts, the information, the problem, the relationship, and the Word of God. The teenager, having all of these facts, makes his own decision, and is ultimately led to maturity.

In nondirective counseling there appears to be no standard or criterion. It seems to be an aimless wandering, searching, following the leading of the counselee. In directive counseling there is a goal, an aim, and the counselor leads the teenager by the hand to the solution of his problem. This solution may be correct and the problem may be solved, but this is a short-term solution with no overall solution to life's problem. The directive counselor tends to be problem-centered rather than student-centered. The ultimate life of the teenager is not usually changed in this manner.

In inductive counseling there is a goal, a criterion, and a standard. The goal is perfect maturity in Jesus Christ. The criterion is the Word of God. The duty of the counselor is to guide the pupil and his problem to the Word of God. Then, an open-faced relationship between the student and the Word of God will be established and maintained for the present as well as future help of the student. Inductive counseling is sometimes called "eclectic counseling." In the *Journal of Clinical Psychology*, psychologist Frederick Thorne's concepts have been adapted, giving a general approach to counseling:

1. In general, nondirective methods should be used whenever possible.
2. Directive methods should be used only when special conditions merit and then with caution.
3. Nondirective techniques should generally be used at the beginning stages of counseling when the counselee is telling his story and also to permit emotional release.
4. The simplest techniques are the best, and the counselor should never become involved in complicated techniques until the simple methods have been tried and found unsuitable.
5. It is desirable to let the counselee have an opportunity to resolve his problems nondirectively. If a counselee is not making progress when nondirective methods are being used, it may be an indication that more directive methods should be utilized.
6. Directive methods are usually indicated when the counselee is surrounded by circumstances that must be changed or the cooperation of other people sought.[2]

Inductive counseling uses a two-way relationship and communication. This is the basic concept of counseling. Counseling is a process rather than a lecture or an advice-giving session. It is a process in which there is a mutual quest for the solution of the problem. The teenager's problem is often too deep to be solved in one easy advisory session. So it becomes a process as the counselor and the teenager search for the answer. Notice the difference between directive and inductive counseling. The following explains the directive method from the perspective of a counselor with a biblical perspective.

1. The teenager brings his problem to the counselor. The discussion of this problem may be formal or informal, but the young person indicates he needs help. The first line of communication is from the counselee to the counselor.
2. The counselor considers the problem and goes to the Word of God for the answer. This is the second line of communication. This assumes the counselor has access to and understands the Word of God. In the Word of God the counselor finds certain directives from God. The counselor must understand the problem and the relationship of the problem and God's will.
3. The counselor finds the answers in the Word of God. Now the Bible must communicate to him. Principles of life must leap from printed page into everyday meaning.
4. The last form of communication is from the counselor to the teenager. The communication of these answers from the counselor to the teenager may be in the form of a conversation as they talk out the problem, or it may be in the form of a lecture. Even though the biblical insights are the counselor's, and the solution to the problem may be temporary, the young person has found the answer to his problem. It is now his prerogative either to accept the advice and follow the solution or to ignore the advice and go his own way.

The major weakness is that the teenager has found the answer for his own problem but has not learned the secret of finding his own answer to future problems. The next time a problem may arise, the counselor may not be available. The young person, having no source of advice, may flounder. As a result he may fail in his Christian life. If the teenager had access into the Word of God (and the wise counselor who takes the teenager to Scripture has, at minimum, provided a model) and discovers his own answer, the next time there is a problem he might have a means of solution. This solution is an access to God, filling out the third leg of the triangle.

Giving advice fills only two legs of the triangle. The law of mathematics indicates this triangle is incomplete, so our young people who are raised on advice are not mature. Giving advice when exercised by itself is against the concept of spiritual maturity as taught in the Word of God. Giving advice such as we have seen above in directive counseling could be called a type of spiritual "apron strings." As the young child is tied to his mother's apron strings, so the teenager is tied to the counselor. He never thinks for himself, makes decisions for himself, or grows to be an independent person walking before God. In the same way the teenager becomes dependent upon the counselor for advice in life and never establishes his own roots. In this process the teenager comes with his problem to the counselor.

Inductive counseling will follow the first three steps as seen above:

1. The counselee will come to the counselor for help.
2. The counselor will have access to the Word of God as the source for the problem.
3. There is a communication from the Word of God to the counselor. This communication involves understanding and meaning on the part of the counselor. He gives meaning to the words of the Scripture and understands the relationship between God's principles and everyday life.

However, the inductive counselor's method of communication is different. This time he doesn't give the answer "ready mixed" to the teenager and send him on his way. Instead he guides the teenager into the Word of God. The counselor is the agent guiding the teenager to the solution. By guiding him into the Word of God, he helps him to find the answer.

The Bible must be understood and must have meaning to the teenager, as it does to the counselor. The teenager must see the Word of God as a living Book, with principles for living teenagers. God has a will for teenagers in the twenty-first century, and the teenager must see the meaning of the Bible as well as understand the relationship to his life. The Bible must be discovered rather than declared. The Bible must be examined rather than explained. Therefore, the role of the counselor is that of a guide.

As the counselor and counselee get into the Word of God, they find that God speaks to the counselee. Only as the young person understands the meaning of God's Word can eternal perspective be given to the problem. In this way the counselee has established the third leg of the triangle and God speaks to him. While the young person strives for independence, he is still dependent upon God. The teenager will thus become dependent upon the Lord and His Word rather than upon the counselor and will eventually develop true spiritual maturity.

The critics of inductive counseling contend that the switching of the role of the counselor confuses the student and interferes with his experiencing a successful counseling session. Instead of changing roles, the counselor should clearly define himself from each point of view. Then he should select only those techniques from both directive and nondirective methods that will allow him to practice within his principal frame of reference. Thus the counselor can maintain one relationship with the student rather than changing roles from a "fellow searcher" to one who "gives advice." From what has been written it should not be implied that directive or nondirective counselors fail and that only inductive counselors are successful.

Counselors must always maintain an effort to communicate their attitudes toward the teenager.

The inductive counselor does not force his diagnosis into the student's thinking. Instead, he uses his understanding of the problem and the student to have rapport with the young person and to help the student answer his own questions. The counselor lets the student lead the way. He knows where they are going, and he constantly checks to determine whether he is following what the student is saying. He tries to make sure that he is seeing the situation as the student does. At the same time he is leading the teenager to understand himself as he really is. The inductive counselor reflects the pupil's feelings back to him in order to force the student to look at himself.

The inductive counselor makes sure that their communication channels are always functioning properly. He believes that when the student expresses himself so that his words are meaningful, the student probably is improving his understanding of himself. The inductive counselor knows that the ultimate aim of the teenager is full maturity in Jesus Christ as seen in Ephesians 4:12–15. Therefore, he has a goal, while at the same time he realizes that every teenager is different. The gifts of God to every person are different; the calling of God to every individual is different; and the capacity, the background, and the environment of every individual are different. The young person must be allowed to unfold from within his or her own limited spheres of capacity into the man or woman that God would have him or her to become.

Inductive counseling involves the uniting of two apparently contradictory approaches to counseling. The methods, results, and attitudes of nondirective counseling are assumed, while the direction, authority, and criteria of the directive method are embraced.

CONCLUSION

There is no single "best" method of counseling. At times the directive method of counseling is all the counselor can use. This may be the result of circumstances, time, or personality. Other times nondirective counseling is the only method possible. Problems are complex and personalities are interrelated. Times are demanding and problems have varied implications. The method that will become most effective in solving immediate problems and producing long-lasting results is the inductive method. Whenever possible the counselor should attempt to employ this approach, guiding the teenager to the solution of his problem. Even though the inductive method is recommended, the counselor will have to determine the best method to use. His judgment should be made after a careful consideration of all aspects of the situation, personalities, backgrounds, and factors. In the last analysis, the best method is that which produces the adjustment and maturity of the teenager.

NOTES

1. Carl R. Rogers, *Counseling and Psychotherapy* (Boston: Houghton Mifflin, 1942), 30–44.
2. Frederick C. Thorne, "Principles of Personality Counseling," (*Journal of Clinical Psychology*, 1945): 88–89.

Structuring the Actual Counseling Session

The counseling approach will be considered in this chapter. What shall be the modus operandi? How will we proceed to help our youth with their problems? There are certain basic attitudes the counselor should have in his mind before the counseling situation ever comes into existence. This is true whether the counselor will use the nondirective, directive, or inductive type of counseling situation.

There are universal laws and methods of attacking a problem that should be followed in every situation. There are times when informal guidance will have to be the rule of the day. This method of informal counseling may be used any time and at any place by the counselor. Perhaps the teacher or youth pastor will be having lunch with a young person or discussing sports after a game.

During this informal discussion the young person may approach him with a problem. At this time a formal counseling situation cannot be structured, but the counselor will learn to give what help he can at the time and meet the immediate need without going into the involved session.

In this chapter we will look at the steps that make up the typical counseling session or season.

REFERRAL

It should be the duty of the counselor to draw out the young person and let him express his problem. Then the counselor's advice should be given. It should not be a self-talk, therapeutic type of counseling situation. The successful youth worker will do 90 percent of his counseling in this informal method.

The counseling situation under consideration in this chapter is the formal one in which the young person comes to you with his problem. This counseling session is worthy of a definite appointment. The young person who brings his problems to the counselor is expecting help. At this time you should have those basic rules in mind with which you will attack the problems that are brought to you. Here you must structure the actual counseling situation. In counseling, details are very important. To be an effective counselor you must be conscious of every detail. For example, teenagers will come to you with problems of how to choose the right college, how to know the will of God concerning marriage, how to get along better with teachers in school, or how to have a better personality. By knowing more about proper techniques you are provided with increased effectiveness in all of the guidance services for which you are responsible.

On the other hand, you should not think that you are expected to give therapy. Therapy requires a complex understanding that should be reserved for the specialist. In most churches those who give counsel are not trained to go beyond helping "normal" students with their disturbing problems. Therapy involves serious personality disorders and should be reserved for the counseling psychiatrist or psychologist. However, the average Christian counselor is a needed individual; he must understand and give understanding to those who come to him for help. There are several reasons young people come to you:

1. Young people usually turn to someone they know.
2. Young people take their problems to someone they like.
3. Young people take their problems to someone they respect.
4. Young people go to someone who has indicated availability for counseling.
5. Young people turn to someone who is mature.
6. Young people turn to someone they feel is competent.
7. Young people turn to someone who has spiritual resources.

TYPES OF REFERRALS

Self-Referral

Self-referral is when the teenager seeks the service of a counselor. Perhaps he has heard through other young people that a certain individual in the church understands young people and gives good advice. When this young person comes and asks for some time to meet with the counselor and talk with him, this is commonly called self-referral.

Referred by Someone Else

Sometimes a teacher, youth worker, or other person in the church or community refers a young person to you for help. It may be that the teenager would rather not come, but he is coming to please the one who is sending him. Perhaps the teenager comes with confidence in you. Those who come because someone else referred them may not have the same rapport as those who come because of "self-referral."

Personally Called In

Many times you will find that you must call the teenager into your office. At this stage, perhaps you have seen some problem or apparent disorder in the life of the young person and you want to help him. You usually begin by "small talk." Use real discernment in such a case. Some young people have tremendous and deep problems. They are looking for someone to help them. And yet because of reluctance on their part, they will not seek out the counselor. When you come to them and offer them help, usually they are very thankful and in return respond.

However, some young people are rebellious toward older adults' prying into their lives and hence consider the counseling situation as nothing more than an inquisition or the third degree. Use common sense and discernment in dealing with the "call them in" approach. One of the most common questions facing new counselors is, "When are you justified in taking the initiative in counseling?" It may be that the initial question is too simple. Instead, you may ask, "What do you mean by initiative?" The conclusion is that the psychological task implies that you may approach the subject by raising the question or going to call on someone. In short, you may take a geographic or factual approach but not the psychological initiative.

Attempt to establish a good relationship with the young people to whom you minister so that they will trust you and readily come to you for help. Also, attempt to create an accepting attitude among the young people for counseling. Instilling this attitude in the young people will make for better acceptance of help by students—both spiritually, socially, and intellectually.

Types of Referrals to Discourage

There are three types of referrals for the church at large to avoid when it comes to referral for counseling:

Referrals with the Implication of a Threat

Sometimes an unwise adult may tell a teenager, "If you don't go and talk to the youth pastor, I'll tell your parents." This type of threat may cause the young person to go, but the counselor's hands are tied and there can be no real counseling relationship established.

Trying to Convince the Teenager That Counseling Is the Thing to Do

The attitude is sometimes given by an unwise small group leader, "I'll send you to the youth pastor and he will convince you this thing is right." The attitude is that the counselor will talk them into doing that which they should do.

Referring Teenagers to the Youth Pastor or Counselor Without Prior Permission

When you do not know the teenager is coming, and he is sent without knowing why he is coming, this can hurt any relationship that you might have. The teenager unexpectedly knocks at the youth pastor's office door or shows up at the counselor's home and says, "I was sent by my small group leader." The youth pastor or counselor, not knowing the background, immediately says, "Oh, I didn't realize." The rapport that might be established is thereby broken and any help that the young person might have received is lost. The teenager may see this as a breach of confidence. At the very least, he may be bewildered.

When Referral to Another Person Is Necessary

There are many occasions when the average Sunday school teacher acting in the role of counselor should refer the teenager to a more specialized counselor—a pastor, youth worker, or someone who can give some exact information. This is not interpreted as need for psychological therapy but help for normal teenagers with normal problems. Some of these are as follows:

1. An unusual amount of aggressive behavior is shown by the teenager.
2. The student is maintaining a record of underachievement and disinterest in the youth group's small group meetings.
3. The student is undecided as to his future vocation or plan of life, or he constantly changes his life's goal from one type of vocation to another.
4. Students or teenagers do not participate in the normal activities of the church group.
5. A teenager's aspiration is not in accordance with his ability. Either the aspirations are beyond his ability or his aspirations are below his God-given gifts.
6. The teenager needs special types of information that the counselor cannot give.
7. The Sunday school teacher recognizes that the problem is beyond his or her limitations.

It should be noted that the acceptance of a referral by the counselor is an obligation to report back to the person making the referral. This is not intended to give details but to inform the person making the referral that contact has been made and counseling sessions are taking place. The action taken or accomplishments made should be reported to the one giving the referral, so that together they may continue to help the individual. The establishment of good communication makes for better teamwork for the church to accomplish the goals to which God has called it.

RELAXATION

Once the student has come to see you, the first step in counseling is relaxation. The youth who comes to you must be put at ease. A young person may come all keyed up and be very uncommunicative. Other teens will come to you and enter into small talk. Some do not feel at home in the presence of a counselor. The counselor may not have built this barrier, but he must tear it down if he is to be successful. The counselor must get the teenager to have confidence in him.

First, make the young person feel at home in your presence. He must feel that you are really interested in him and want to help him. Relaxation often comes when the young person has the inner confidence that you understand his problems. If the young person realizes that you have a heart for God and a heart for young people, he is more likely to open up. There are many embarrassing moments in life, but one of the most humiliating comes to the counselor when he is caught short because he has failed to give the young person his undivided attention. His mind wanders and a few minutes later he is guessing what the young person has or has not said. You must forget what is on your own mind and enter into the experience of the young person. To do this you must listen well and put the young person at ease.

BEGINNING THE INTERVIEW

When you have the chance to study the teenager's folder or the cumulative data gathered on the student, you will find it easier to understand the student and to see his situation as he does. However, sometimes the teenager is faced with an emergency and therefore cannot wait to talk with you at a later time. In such cases you should talk with the student, even though you have not had an opportunity to understand his background. You should listen and encourage the pupil to talk about those things that bother him.

When the teenager comes to you because he himself recognizes that he needs help, he is actually motivated to do something about those problems that are bothering him. Usually he will assume more responsibility for solving his problems than those students who are not sure why they are seeing a counselor. Even when a teenager comes to the counselor on his own accord, it will not always be immediately clear to the counselor why the pupil wants help. With whom has the teenager already discussed these problems? Why did he come to you? Did he come because some friends told him you had helped them? What does the teenager expect of you?

The First Few Minutes

When the teenager first approaches you as counselor, it is your job to make him feel welcome and to help him get comfortably seated or to be in a comfortable position in which you can talk. There are no set ways to accomplish these aims because counselors differ and teenagers differ. Some counselors find it natural to open the conversation, "Hi, Josh, pull up a chair" and proceed with the conversation. Other counselors would be out of role if they did not use a formal approach.

To make the teenager feel truly trusted and welcome is the duty of each counselor, and the method must be your natural approach. Since the teenager comes to talk to the counselor about something, he will usually start talking after greetings are exchanged. Of course, he may not start talking about what is bothering him most. Many times teenagers will bring up something of an alternative pattern rather than the real problem. A teen may try you out first, before discussing his most important problem with you. If he comes to feel that he can trust you and you are trying to understand him, he will sense that it is all right for him to talk about anything that is important to him. Should the young person not start talking, you may help him start: "What is on your mind today?" or "What is it you wanted to see me about?" With such a remark you indicate that the teenager knows better than you what should be discussed in the session.

Naturally it makes a difference how you say what you say, even though you may use the right words. Your tone of voice may reflect an attitude. One young person may feel threatened by the tone, or a different young person may feel that he must fight what he believes to be a harsh comment. Neither situation has helped create a friendly and permissive attitude in which the young person feels that he can talk about his problem.

Some counselors feel that they must use "small talk" at the beginning of the interview with the young person or build up a good rapport in an informal counseling situation. This may lead the pupil out into the open, but at the same time it may lead a young person away from the problem, which he has just barely developed the courage to face. Beware of making it too easy for the young person to talk about something other than his problems. When the young person comes for help, you should help him talk about his problems rather than encourage conversation about social activities, school life, or church life in general. Under no circumstances should the counselor encourage gossip. If the young person cannot face his problem, assist him by use of the question in talking out why he cannot face his own problem.

Admission to the Teenager

The teenager usually admits that he has a problem and wants to do something about it. This is usually very difficult, but it is the first step toward solving a problem. You must then define your helping role to the youth. Let him know what you intend to do. Convey to the teenager that it is his responsibility to work with you so you both can solve his problem. There are a few basic points of clarification.

1. *The counselor must admit that he does not know all the answers.*

Here you must not play God. Be very slow to give an answer, especially until you know both sides of the issue. Sometimes the teenager may be very frank and very honest; however, you have only one side of the picture. To give an answer immediately would only be encouraging immaturity, because you do not know both sides of the picture. As you admit that you do not have all of the answers, you break down a counselor superiority attitude. The breaking down of this attitude helps get the counseling off to a Christ-centered start, rather than a counselor-centered or counselee-centered start. Point out to the counselee that only the Lord has the solution to all problems. Then the counselee and the counselor can begin working on the problem together.

2. *The counselor and the teenager must know that they will work on problems together.*

Your role is that of a guide and a participant. You are not to solve problems. You are not to give all answers. You are not to give your own opinion. Together you will work out the details, define the problem, and determine the alternatives, but the counselee applies the solution.

3. *The teenager must be told that it is only normal to have problems.*

Many teenagers feel that something is wrong if they are having problems. Modern advertisement and publicity from the television, magazines, and other media of communication have portrayed a problemless way of life. This is not possible. The teenager must be told that it is only normal to have problems. As long as he is in the flesh, while ignoring the Spirit of God and attempting to live the will of God, he is attempting to do the impossible. He will also have problems as long as he seeks God's will—for the flesh, the devil, and the power of the world are against him. But there is victory in Jesus Christ; this is the hope of the Christian counselor.

RAPPORT

You must have rapport with teens to help them. The dictionary says rapport means "a relation characterized by harmony, conformity, accord or affinity." It is an intimate harmonious relation as applied to people having close understanding. Rapport is gained in much the same way that you get youth to relax. However, there is a difference between rapport and relaxation. Through relaxation the youth merely relaxes and tells his story, but in rapport you must think along with the young person as he is telling his problem. You must forget what is on your own mind and enter into his experience. To do this, you must listen well. You must have warmth in understanding but control in your emotions. Be patient with the young person and help him talk, and be careful not to embarrass him if he cries or just cannot seem to say what he wants to.

When a student comes to you with a problem about opposite-sex relationships and realizes that you are not a judge but that you understand, this is rapport. If you come to an immediate solution or call this emotional confusion unimportant, you have lost contact and destroyed rapport. Never minimize or trivialize their problems. This would be death to any rapport you might have or are trying to development. You gain rapport by getting the young person to relax. This is a subjective experience to the young person. Rapport is a reciprocal reaction; both the counselor and counselee feel this. Relaxation is a method of gaining rapport. Often young people hesitate to divulge their basic problem when they first talk with the counselor. They begin with one problem or a surface struggle when actually they came to talk about something quite different. The wise counselor is conscious of this tendency and willing to wait for the real problem to arise to the surface. It is unwise for any counselor to jump to conclusions.

Creating a Permissive Atmosphere

What you do outside your office does much to direct your counseling and effectiveness inside your office. Your reputation is very important. What you do in social activities, in after-church get-togethers, makes a difference. Your impressions as a teacher count; spending extra time helping the students with their work attracts a student's attention. Wherever the young person meets you or works with you, he should find the personal qualities that indicate a mature Christian attitude toward life. Your everyday life should lead the young person to believe in you and accept you as a person able to give him help. The building of a good counseling relationship is interfered with when you fail to sense the importance of the student's problems. A remark like "Oh, don't let this bother you" or "You'll forget all about her in a couple of days" insults the student's good judgment and makes him feel that you don't understand him. When you try to reassure the student with such a comment, instead of causing him to see beyond the problem, you are trivializing a problem. The young person says to himself, "This guy doesn't understand me; he doesn't know how it hurts to have a girl break up with you."

Responding to Feelings

The feelings of the young person are of utmost importance in the counseling situation. All of us have said at one time or another, "I know what I should do, but I don't feel like doing it," or "I know I should do this, but I want to do something else." We must help the young person understand his feelings. Many times he has feelings within himself that he doesn't understand, and to these he cannot respond.

At the same time you should neither agree nor disagree with the attitude or feelings expressed by the young person. When the young person says, "My father is the biggest hypocrite in our church," he should not expect you to say, "Right—I think so too." He should, however, expect the counselor to accept these views. When the young girl says, "Our small group leader is the poorest teacher that I have ever heard," you should not condone or condemn the statement but should accept it. Concentrate on how the teenager feels and help the young person to discover that he can talk freely. This is not the place to give a lecture on respect for parents or respect for the teacher. Until the problem is properly diagnosed, a lecture should be withheld. The young person may express his feelings and ultimately help himself, not only to accept himself, but his father or his teacher as well. The release of the feelings is important in the counseling situation, but this in itself is not enough. The teenager must be led to understand why he feels as he does and learn what he can do to achieve the positive adjustment and happiness that he seeks.

PAUSES

There are times when the teenager wants to talk about something but he finds it difficult to express himself. He may approach a problem, or he may speak about a related problem and then abandon it for some reason or another. There are uncomfortable pauses as he struggles to tell about his inner feelings. Pauses are awkward in social conversation and they are also difficult in counseling. Badly handled problems are frustrating, both to the young person and to the counselor. If the young person does not understand the significance of the pause, he may be distracted from the problem with which he is struggling and lose his whole train of thought.

When the young person is struggling with the problem, be watchful not to break into the pupil's personal struggle, even though there is a pause. It may be that the young person is making satisfactory progress by himself. Interrupting the pupil's thinking when he is making satisfactory progress from his point of view may lead the pupil away from his important issue at hand. If you are distracted or bothered about the period of silence, your uneasiness may distract the pupil's thinking about the issue facing him. Pauses of only fifteen or twenty seconds may seem to be long and prove embarrassing because you do not know what to do. Rather than break these pauses with probing questions, try to make the youth realize that it is all right to take time to think about these things and that some topics are difficult to discuss. Pauses are not disturbing when the counselor and the young person know that it is normal for them to occur.

Making Notes

Some writers in the field of counseling believe that taking notes during the actual interview interferes with the building of a good counseling relationship. Other writers feel that taking notes during an interview helps to obtain an accurate report. The taking of notes should be examined in light of the attitude of the counselor to this problem. Some counselors feel that they cannot follow the problem without expressing themselves on paper. Other counselors feel guilty about taking notes; they recognize that they need the information but do not feel that they can justify their notes to the pupil. If making notes interferes with your ability to follow the conversation or detracts from rapport with the young person, then notes should not be taken. If you do not feel right about what you are doing, the young person will detect these feelings. The young person may not know what you are concerned about, but he will sense it; consequently, it becomes difficult for him to tell his story. Counseling should be a heart-to-heart relationship. The counselor and the young person should explore the truth of God's Word together. If necessary, when the counseling session is over, jot down key thoughts, problems, or solutions that came about from the counseling session.

ANSWERING THE STUDENT'S QUESTION

When the young person asks a question, look beyond the question to determine whether the pupil is expressing feelings of inadequacy or simply requesting facts. It may be that the question is showing a feeling of great inadequacy (e.g., "What do you think I should do about my younger brother?" "How old should a person be to single date?" "Suppose you knew someone is doing drugs . . . what would you do?"). Sometimes the facts that are desired are sought only to fortify a decision that the young person has already made. The trained counselor will learn to look beyond the questions to the reason that motivates such questions. This is the skill of observing what is not said. At times, an initial question may be a precursor to more significant and deeper questions.

REVELATION

The principle of revelation indicates that the counselor should take all the information obtained and analyze it to come up with the problem that is really bothering the youth. Revelation does not deal with the solution to the problem but the clear understanding of the problem. Guide the counselee to tell his whole story. Before you can help the counselee you must know the need. Before the doctor treats his patient he must first diagnose the case. A problem well defined is a problem half solved.

Helping the Student Talk

Helping the student talk is sometimes difficult. There are emotional blocks and the teenager cannot verbalize his problem. These blocks may arise out of conflict within the student, or they may arise out of conflict between the student and the counselor. Sometimes the young person is approaching a problem that is personal and he is not quite sure that he can trust the counselor. Assure the young person that you will keep his trust in that which he tells you, and then the teenager will have more freedom to express himself. It may be something that he has never discussed with anyone before. The teenager may not be sure that he can tell his problem to anyone, or that he wants to do so.

The use of the question should come naturally. However, be careful of using too many stereotyped questions. Be careful of using a question with the pause that implies guilt. Use the question that comes naturally. The use of the question is an art, something that comes from within and is expressed, rather than a science, that which follows rules and orders. You should be alert continually to the possibility that you may be talking too much. Some counselors immediately upon hearing of a problem say, "I went through that" or "I'm in that situation now." The teenager is not primarily interested in the feeling of the counselor; he is interested in his own problems. Therefore, resist the temptation to tell your own feelings. The feelings of the teenager are what is important at this time.

The following questions will help the counselor evaluate himself:

1. Did I help the teenager say what he wanted to say?
2. Was I trying to follow the young person?
3. Was I trying to get him to talk about those things that I wanted him to talk about?

4. How often did I interrupt?
5. Did I give him a chance to say what he wanted to say when I interrupted him?
6. Did he try to interrupt me and fail?
7. What was he trying to say?
8. Did he ever try to say it again?
9. Did I really understand what he said?
10. What did I do to help him clarify how he felt?

Creative Listening

Creative listening is a wise procedure that you should learn. Counseling is not mere advice giving. It is more than employing information or answering questions. To tell another person what to do is to assume that you know all the answers and that you are willing to assume the responsibilities for the direction given. This is a special skill of prescribing, which cannot be taken lightly, knowing that there is the potential of being wrong. Yet you must practice being a sympathetic, understanding listener. By listening, you gain insight and make progress toward a successful solution of the problem facing the young person. How can you know what the problem is unless you hear it expressed? How can you know what is in the young person's mind unless you hear him communicate it? How can you uncover the real emotional difficulties and the basic disturbances unless skillful questioning and creative listening take place?

As the skillful listener you should not talk about your own experiences and convictions. Rather you should speak only to maintain a friendly atmosphere and to draw the young person out. This requires self-restraint, patience, mental flexibility, and discipline. In an unhurried interview the young person will express himself. The young person will not reveal his innermost feelings unless you are an attentive person who seems to understand. You must express confidence in the young person so that the young person may in return express confidence in you.

In a permissive, relaxed atmosphere the young person will open up and will reveal his heart. The simple talking out of a problem may be a major step in helping the young person. The counselor has not given any direction. What has happened? The counselor has become a sounding board. Problems are subjective. As the teenager has the problems within himself, he cannot see the situation objectively. To put it in an old adage, "He can't see the forest for the trees." As the teenager talks the problem out, he is hanging his questions on the clothesline, then he steps back and looks at the problem. As he sees the problem, many times he knows what the solution is.

Summarization of the Problem

When you feel you understand the problem, determine if the youth understands it. Questions, restatement of facts, and introduction of other material should be used to make sure the youth understands the problem. Once you feel the teenager understands, then a clear statement of the problem should be made. Take the counselee back to the beginning for a review. This is not a time of rehashing but of hitting salient points, separating the wheat from the chaff. The problem must be once again brought to the point of view of the teenager. Try to establish progress during the summarization. This is not just feedback—look for insight, look for the solution, and try to better understand the problem. This is an excellent chance to objectify or review the case as he once again sees the problem out before him. He is helping himself to understand himself. You must do more than take all the information obtained and analyze the problem within your own mind. You must share with the young person the problem and together determine the courses of action. What alternatives are there? Guard against helping the young person too much.

Naturally, it is easy to presume we are showing love by doing as much as we can for young people. Is this truly an act of kindness when we tie the apron strings to ourselves? Actually we may be weakening the young person by not encouraging self-reliance and independent growth, not to mention reliance on God. If at all possible, do not show the possible solutions to the young person. If the young person can see the solutions for himself and then choose the solution that is best, he will grow to Christian maturity. During this summarization period, possible areas for future exploration might be suggested. You might pave the way for growth while saying, "Have you thought of . . .?" or "You might have . . ." Never close the door of help to the teenager.

RESULTS

After all is said and done, the true test of counseling is results. Have you helped the teenager? Results are not always the solution he wants or you want. Results may not always be the choice of an action; sometimes the teen must refrain from action. Results may not always be seen, but nevertheless they are there. The climax of the counseling situation is crucial. All the progress up to this point may be lost if the counselor does not display wisdom. There are no dogmatic rules to obtain results. What may work in one situation will fail in the next. Use your inner feeling of rapport rather than following a prescribed pattern. Even though you cannot always follow a rigid mold, there are some suggestions to follow. These general principles are applicable in most situations. They are not chronological.

DETERMINE THE ALTERNATIVES

The young person should understand the problem before a solution is attempted. There are no easy solutions to life's problems. You should realize that there are many possible solutions.

Problems are complex and solutions are complex. The first solution in the teenager's mind is not necessarily the best or right solution. The counselor and the youth should attempt to explore all possible solutions before making any decisions. When listing all the possible solutions, both the counselor and the youth should suggest all that come to mind. It may be best at this point for the possible solutions to be written either by the young person or the counselor. The listing of the solutions will help to objectify the situation in the youth's mind. The simple writing out of a possible solution to the problem will indicate to the young person the validity of the solution, and he might keep the list for examination at a later time. These courses of action should be listed together with the implications for each solution.

The young person should know what are the alternatives facing him. As he sees the alternatives, it should be brought continually to his attention that it is his decision to make. The decision is not yet the issue. The understanding of the alternatives is the present problem. There are three pitfalls to note for the counselor who pushes his solution to the problem on the youth.

1. If the result or decision is not as anticipated, the young person will not come back. You should recognize that you don't know the will of God for his life, other than clear biblical instruction. Therefore, it is best that you do not push the decision on him at this time. If the decision is the youth's and the results are not as expected, you will have left the door open for him to come back with a future problem.
2. The teenager decides against the recommended cure. If he decides against what you think is best, he feels that you are against him, so he will not return to you. Be aware of pushing your decision on the teenager.

3. If the teenager gets results, he becomes increasingly dependent upon you. You may have helped his immediate problem but started a long-range pattern of life. When he has a problem, he comes to you and expects you to solve it for him.

SCRIPTURAL INSIGHT PHASE

The most certain and helpful phase of counseling is found here. This is where you present Christ and the revelation of His Word. You must remove those things that are blocking adjustment so that the soul may heal. Doctors remove the blocks and God does the physical healing. At this stage the teenager is to the point where he comes to accept himself and his position in life. Interject Scripture at points of insight. This interjection of Scripture brings divine perspective to the human problem. The greatest use of the Bible comes in this phase of counseling, but it should not be excluded at other phases. Just as soil must be prepared before the planting of the seed, so the heart should be tilled before the sowing of the Word of God.

The Word of God is not a substitute for counseling; it is a supplement to counseling. It is not the amount of reading of Scripture but the meaningful reading of Scripture that must be emphasized. The teenager must understand what is being read. Readiness is important. The timing of the introduction of the Word of God is very crucial. It may determine the entire outcome of the counseling situation. Do not give the teenager too much Bible so that he cannot understand it. A principle of life is to introduce revelation in proportion to the teenager's receptivity. Take the teenager through the actual process of discovering for himself the answer in the Word of God. This is done by adhering to the following principles:

1. Do not read the Scripture to the teenager. The youth should read the Scripture for himself. The counselor is a

resource individual. He ought to know the Word of God and the teenager. Then the counselor should get the youth into the Word of God and the Word of God into the youth. This is called double transference.

2. Ask the teenager for the meaning. Don't assume that the teenager understands what he has read. Assumption here might be a false step. If the teenager does not understand the Word of God, he cannot apply it to his heart. Therefore, if he does not understand the meaning, go to step 3.
3. Make sure the teenager can determine the relationship between the passage and his problem. Raise questions that will point out insights and relationships. If the teenager continues in his inability to see the relationships, guide him into an understanding by every means of education available. It is now that the counselor assumes the role of a teacher. Avoid engaging in preaching and exposition. Forget "If I were you." The Word of God is alive; use it that way. A teenager is looking to you for a problem to be solved, not a sermon to be preached.

Confession of Sins to God

The confession of sin is the admission of failure in a responsibility. Confession must be self-motivated; it must come from the heart. Confession must be a personal admission of failure and a self-confessed guilt. This is the first step in deliverance from sin. As long as sin is secret, it must be repressed and guarded. Such repression of sin increases tension and anxiety. This results in a disturbed personality. There is no cure for guilt apart from a verbalized self-admission. The teenager must say, "I am wrong." The psychologist sometimes calls this an inner catharsis.

This purging and releasing of guilt tensions from the heart

of the teenager results in happiness. Only the person who knows the forgiveness of God that comes through the cleansing of the blood of Jesus Christ can have true happiness. "If we confess our sins, He is faithful and just to forgive us our sins and to cleanse us from all unrighteousness" (1 John 1:9). To reveal the secrets of the heart and confess sin leads to peace of soul. As the young person confesses his sin, talks it over with you, and observes the situation, he enters into the way of release. The Roman Catholic Church has made the confession of sin a required practice. The priest who receives the confession has been delegated the authority to allay the parishioner's conscience and to absolve his guilt. Protestant churches have not given this sense of release to their members. Pastors assume no authority to forgive sins. This authority is instead found in the Word of God. The Protestant principle is that each man has direct access to God for the forgiveness of sins (1 Tim. 2:5).

Making Decisions

Young people grow with each correct decision they make. Direct the young person toward the climax of the counseling situation in which he will make a decision. Remember that great decisions are not made halfheartedly. Many small decisions made correctly enable the youth to make great decisions for God. Young people seek help because they are faced with problems that appear too difficult for them to solve alone. Sometimes they need to recognize the tensions that prevent them from using their own resources to solve their own problems and to make their own decisions. At other times young people need facts about themselves and the conditions of their surroundings that can be used to achieve the necessary basis for a choice. Decisions come hard. Although you help the pupil achieve all of these goals, in the final analysis the young person is responsible for defining the alternatives and making the decision that he feels is best for him.

Young people learn to make independent decisions gradually, and they need the help of the human teacher as well as the divine teacher in this capacity. Young people learn to make decisions through solving problems that are important to them. When the young person comes to you seeking help, use every means at your disposal to guide him through the solving of his problem to a decision that he must make. A young person may stop coming to you for help before reaching the decision. Be able to accept such behavior. It is unwise to press a young person into a decision before he is ready to make such a choice. Nevertheless, there are times when, because of the obligations of eternity and the commands of God's Word, you should use every pressure at your disposal to cause the young person to choose the path of righteousness and the will of God. Young people should be warned concerning the serious consequences of making decisions that are wrong. The ideal is when the young person recognizes the problem, examines the alternatives, and decides the will of God for his life. This is best, but this is not always the case in a counseling situation.

RESPONSIBILITY

After the young person has made his decision, the problem is not yet solved. The problem will be solved as it is worked out in the life. It is best for you to pray with the counselee. After this, map out a plan of attack for the problem; a daily plan of Bible reading, Scripture memorizing, suggested books to read, and quiet time can be planned. Help the young person select activities that will help him become strong in his decision. There may be opportunities to witness and fellowship with other believers. The young person must be aware that just because he has told you his problem it is not automatically solved. The responsibility of change is upon the young person. The only problems that are really solved are the ones we solve ourselves. Remember that your goal is for the counselee to become autonomous. Some counselors have a strange feeling of disappointment in discovering that the youth is able to solve his own problems, but that is success.

FOLLOW-UP

You still have a role to play in prayer and interest for the youth. From time to time ask the youth, "How's it going?" When the young person realizes that someone else knows of the problem and is interested in the progress, this added incentive helps the progress of adjustment. It is good for the youth to realize someone is anxious for him to overcome his problem. Even though the responsibility belongs to the youth, you must assume some responsibility, for you have had an investment in the direction and solution of the problem. The responsibility of applying the solution to the problem belongs to the young person, but the responsibility of teenagers belongs to you.

CONFIDENCE

The counselor must have a heart like a graveyard. Many problems will be buried there. Resist the temptation to tell another person the problems of a young person. If the teens find out that the counselor spills the beans, they will stop coming to the counselor. Once a counselor loses respect from the teens, it will be almost impossible to win it back. Betraying confidence is nothing more than gossip. Be careful of sharing juicy bits of information about your youth as prayer requests. This spiritual cover-up is deadly. If you don't have the confidence of your youth, you might as well close up shop.

CONCLUSION

Every counseling situation will take a different shape. Problems are different, people are different, circumstances are varied, and solutions are complex. The general approach suggested in this chapter can be used in an ideal situation, but there are no ideal situations. Even though this structured approach cannot be employed fully in each situation, the general guidelines and attitudes of approach can be used in every situation.

In some counseling situations the problem is evident and realization can be skipped. In the next situation the counselor and counselee will have to give extra attention to relaxation and rapport. A further counseling situation will find results receiving all the attention. In any situation the goal of counseling is adjustment and maturity. The application of the several principles in "Structuring the Actual Counseling Situation" will accomplish these goals. However, the goal—not the technique—must be kept in sight. Be counselee-centered, not technique-centered. The wise counselor will choose those techniques in the required order to lead teenagers to a solution of their problems and a proper adjustment in life.

Conclusion

As we conclude this book, we have been reminded of the significance and urgency of youth ministry. September 11, 2001, redefined what is evil. The heinous terrorist acts became this young generation's defining moment and had permanent imprinting upon our minds, with the clarity of a Pearl Harbor or President Kennedy's assassination. We'll all remember where we were when we heard of the attacks.

Our wives had called several times to inform us of what was taking place. We were in our youth ministry classes. When we finally got hold of a television, students crowded around to stare in disbelief. We canceled the rest of that day's classes so students could pray, call home, or just talk. We were standing in front of students who might have to fight this war, and this frightened us. Were we dealing with what was important?

Two weeks after 9/11 we did a simple exercise, more for the purpose of venting. Everyone keeps saying how the world has changed since 9/11, so we decided to ask our students a simple question: How? How has their world changed? As we compiled almost forty pages of responses, we began to see a pattern. These mostly eighteen- to twenty-year-olds were coming to some conclusions that were insightful and mature. Some responses were: *Life is short; Family is most important; The distinction of the trivial and the important; Helping and serving others is a noble thing to do; Pride in being an American; Redefining of what it means to be a hero; Personal pursuits and interests, along with realization that self-gratification can be delayed for the sake of others,* to name a few.

After doing this exercise, we realized that 9/11 had done something to our students. It was the very thing that we oppose in our classes . . . growing up too quickly and the premature granting of adult responsibilities upon our young people. Our school does not allow eighteen-year-olds to live off campus, but we will allow our students to be called up from the reserves to fight in a war. Our students were learning lessons about life that take us adults years to get, if we ever get them at all!

Something else happened. Our students began to take more seriously the vocation of youth ministry. Not that they weren't taking it seriously before, but now it seemed that time was not on their side. Once the door of high school or college graduation begins to close, the opportunity for faith in Christ diminishes dramatically. Why? Life happens. The opportunity of adolescence cannot and must not be missed.

We are aware that many times youth ministry is misunderstood and, whether we like to admit it or not, it does look like we're having a lot of fun. We would be the first to say, "We hope so." But we would also say that it goes with the territory. Now the bar has been raised. The significance of vocational youth ministry will continue to grow, along with the message of hope we bring.

Youth workers are in a key position of influence. We may influence where a teenager will attend school, what career he or she will choose, whom he or she will marry, where the teen will spend or give money, and most important, what kind of relationship (if any) with Christ the youth will have. We cannot take this role lightly. By reading this book, you have determined not to take your role lightly. We hope and pray that this book will go well beyond an academic exercise. Teenagers are depending on you. Some teenagers may not hear this message of hope in Christ if it were not for you. We want you to be challenged and we want you to be encouraged to participate in youth ministry like never before.

Moody Press, a ministry of Moody Bible Institute,
is designed for education, evangelization, and edification.
If we may assist you in knowing more about Christ
and the Christian life, please write us without obligation:
Moody Press, c/o MLM, Chicago, Illinois 60610.